Housing the Powers

Housing the Powers

*Medieval Debates about
Dependence on God*

by
MARILYN McCORD ADAMS
with
CECILIA TRIFOGLI
and
ROBERT MERRIHEW ADAMS

Great Clarendon Street, Oxford, OX2 6DP,
United Kingdom

Oxford University Press is a department of the University of Oxford.
It furthers the University's objective of excellence in research, scholarship,
and education by publishing worldwide. Oxford is a registered trade mark of
Oxford University Press in the UK and in certain other countries

© Marilyn McCord Adams 2022; Chapter 4: Marilyn McCord Adams
and Cecilia Trifogli 2022

The moral rights of the author have been asserted

First Edition published in 2022

Impression: 1

All rights reserved. No part of this publication may be reproduced, stored in
a retrieval system, or transmitted, in any form or by any means, without the
prior permission in writing of Oxford University Press, or as expressly permitted
by law, by licence or under terms agreed with the appropriate reprographics
rights organization. Enquiries concerning reproduction outside the scope of the
above should be sent to the Rights Department, Oxford University Press, at the
address above

You must not circulate this work in any other form
and you must impose this same condition on any acquirer

Published in the United States of America by Oxford University Press
198 Madison Avenue, New York, NY 10016, United States of America

British Library Cataloguing in Publication Data

Data available

Library of Congress Control Number: 2021948408

ISBN 978-0-19-286254-9

DOI: 10.1093/oso/9780192862549.001.0001

Printed and bound in Great Britain by
Clays Ltd, Elcograf S.p.A.

Links to third party websites are provided by Oxford in good faith and
for information only. Oxford disclaims any responsibility for the materials
contained in any third party website referenced in this work.

Contents

Introduction and Cast of Characters   vii
Acknowledgments   xi

1. Medieval Architecture of Matter, Form, and Powers   1
2. Housing the Powers: Self-Actuation and Cosmic Design   19
3. Debates about Potentialities and their Relations to Being   45
4. Outsourcing the Subject: Whose Thought Is It?   83
   By Marilyn McCord Adams and Cecilia Trifogli
5. Outsourcing the Object: Divine Illumination I—Early Franciscans and Henry of Ghent   109
6. Outsourcing the Object: Divine Illumination II—Henry of Ghent and Scotus   130
7. Scotus and His Predecessors on the Metaphysics of Habits   162
8. Genuine Agency, Somehow Shared? The Holy Spirit and Other Gifts   178

Bibliography   217
Index   225

Introduction and Cast of Characters
by Robert Merrihew Adams

This is a book about medieval philosophical and theological views regarding the constitution of powers governing human psychological processes. Its central topic is views about the "housing" of those powers. Where and how, in God's universe, are they controlled and exercised? Which of them are ours to exercise and control, and which are controlled and exercised only by God and/or by superhuman creatures or emanations of God? At the time of her relatively sudden death from pancreatic cancer in 2017, my wife Marilyn McCord Adams had been working for about a decade on what she hoped would become a book on medieval views about "housing the powers," in that sense. The main focus of the project was on the treatment of that topic in Western Christian theology and philosophy from the mid-13th to the mid-14th century, with some commentary on 12th-century roots of the discussion. She wrote or drafted a number of papers on different aspects of the topic, for presentation to various scholarly audiences. She had not yet put them together as a book as she hoped to do. However, there is a group of them that do indeed add up to a book about "housing the powers," complementing each other's explorations, though generally without explicit cross-references. None of the papers is about just one philosopher; all of them present at least two philosophers, and usually more, discussing each other's views. And most of the medieval philosophers discussed appear in more than one of the papers, but in different combinations, in ways that are illuminating. The papers or chapters fall topically into two groups.

Chapters 1 to 3

Medieval Aristotelianism placed the fundamental powers of created things in the context of a metaphysics of *substance* that was also metaphysics of *matter* and *form*. Chapter 1 explores that context, with reference mainly to works of Bonaventure, Thomas Aquinas, Duns Scotus, and William Ockham. In a final section it compares their approaches with those of some present-day philosophers.

Chapter 2 discusses ways in which "medieval Aristotelian science treats perceived always-or-for-the-most-part functional regularities among macro-objects here below as explananda that require grounding in causal powers."[1] Though views of other medieval philosophers are discussed briefly, most of the chapter is devoted to clear elucidation of arguments first between Godfrey of Fontaines and Henry of Ghent, and then between Henry and John Duns Scotus. Scotus is shown to have advanced the discussion in a fundamental way by distinguishing clearly between *potentia* as potentiality or possibility, in contrast with actuality, and *potentia* as causal power.

Chapter 3 presents and analyzes a much wider variety of medieval views and arguments about the metaphysical relations of souls to their powers. Authors discussed include Thomas Aquinas, Giles of Rome, Henry of Ghent, Duns Scotus, William Ockham, and Adam Wodeham.

Chapters 4 to 8

The other five chapters share a focus on a specific family of medieval hypotheses about powers related to human souls. Marilyn called them hypotheses about "outsourcing" roles or functions involved in the functioning and government of human psychological processes.

Chapter 4 (which Marilyn co-authored with Cecilia Trifogli) is about outsourcing the *subject*—in particular, outsourcing the role of being the subject of abstract or intellectual cognition. As Marilyn and Cecilia put it, "Aristotelian reasoning told [13th- and 14th-century Christian philosophers] that the subject of *sensation* had to be or involve an organic body, while interpretations of Aristotelian cognitive psychology passed down through the Arab commentators implied that the subject of *understanding* had to be immaterial."[2] Could it therefore be, as Averroists argued, that if you and I, and perhaps hundreds of mathematicians, think exactly the same abstract thought, there is only one intellect thinking that thought—and indeed only one intellect (a neo-platonic emanation of God) thinking every human thought? That would be outsourcing the role of being a *subject* of understanding—that is, an outsourcing of intellectual knowledge that we may share with God and the angels, not of sense-perceptual knowledge, such as "That's food!" which we share with other animals.

---

[1] Chapter 2, p. 1.   [2] Chapter 4, p. 1.

Chapters 5 and 6 deal with ideas about outsourcing the *object*, rather than the subject, of understanding or cognition. They begin in Chapter 5 with the Augustinian Platonist thought that in order to "have certain knowledge of creatable quiddities,... our minds must make contact with those objects where they exist immutably: in Divine exemplars."[3] Thus they deal with debates about ways in which our having sound concepts of created things does or does not depend on our sharing God's concepts of them.

Chapters 7 and 8 also deal with views about outsourcing objects, rather than subjects—but objects of willing and action rather than of understanding and cognition. Chapters 3 and 8 have more medieval philosopher theologians in prominent roles than any of the other chapters; they each have seven, with partial overlap between the two groups. Chapter 8 covers a longer period, reaching back into the middle of the 12th century to discuss the extremely formative work of Peter Lombard at the end of his career.

Orders in which the Chapters Might Be Read

Any advice as to orders in which a collection of papers (or stories) might best be read should be prefaced by an emphatic acknowledgment that once a book has been published, it belongs to its readers more fundamentally than to its authors and editors. But a few suggestions that no one has to follow might be helpful.

My most confident advice about orders in which this book could be read is that if you are going to read Chapters 4, 5, and 6, you should read them in that order. Chapter 4 was written as a fully independent paper, but the material in Chapter 5 was written to be read after Chapter 4, and the material in Chapter 6 was written to be read after the material in Chapter 5. And I believe that the ideas flow more clearly and naturally in that order.

The other chapters of the book are not connected in that way. Most if not all of them were written with a hope that the material in them might be integrated into a single book-length essay. But that did not happen. And so, to the question in what order they should be read, or even which of them should be read, the only general answer that can be given is that it depends on what interests, and to some extent what knowledge, you bring to the reading. I have put Chapters 1 and 2 in that order and position in the book

---

[3] Chapter 5, p. 1.

because they explain ideas that are presupposed in all the other chapters. They can be treated as preparation for the other chapters in the book. Chapter 3 is as demanding as any chapter in the book, but does not discuss outsourcing. It provides a fairly comprehensive sketch of the views and concerns of the philosophers among whom outsourcing was being discussed.

About the Footnotes and Bibliography

The book has many footnotes, and non-specialist readers will have little reason to pay much attention to most of them. In order, therefore, to keep the footnotes from cluttering the pages with repetition of information that is common to many of them, much of that sort of information is to be found only in the Primary Sources section of the Bibliography at the end of the book, with brief keys to that information in the footnotes. And the Bibliography begins with some paragraphs explaining the structure and symbolism of the footnotes and its relation to the Bibliography.

Cast of Characters

Avicenna [Ibn-Sina] (ca. 970–1037)
Peter Lombard (1096–1160)
Averroes [Ibn-Rushd] (1126–98)
Henry of Ghent (1217–1293)
Bonaventure (1220–74)
Thomas Aquinas (1225–74)
Matthew of Aquasparta (by 1240–1302)
Giles of Rome (1240s–1316)
Peter John Olivi (1248–98)
Godfrey of Fontaines (before 1250–after 1304)
Guido Terrini (1260s–1342)
John Duns Scotus (1266–1308)
Thomas Wylton (active 1288–1322)
William Ockham (ca. 1285–1347)
Adam Wodeham (1298–1358)

Acknowledgments

I am grateful to Cecilia Trifogli and Giorgio Pini, both of whom have read drafts of all the chapters of this book, and offered helpful comments on them. I am also grateful to Cecilia for her role as co-author of Chapter 4 (without which this book would not exist). The comments of two anonymous referees for the Clarendon Press led to a number of improvements, for which I am grateful, as I am to Peter Momtchiloff and his staff at the Clarendon Press, for guiding this project to completion. I am particularly indebted to Peter for his encouragement of the project.

In 2015 Marilyn presented orally a version of Chapter 2 to a philosophical audience at the University of Leuven, and an abbreviated version of Chapter 6 to a conference on medieval philosophy at the University of Montreal, with Giorgio Pini as commentator on her paper. She received helpful comments in both cases.

Chapter 4 is a lightly revised version of "Whose Thought Is It? The Soul and the Subject of Action in Some Thirteenth and Fourteenth Century Aristotelians," by Marilyn McCord Adams and Cecilia Trifogli, which was published in *Philosophy and Phenomenological Research*, vol. LXXXV, no. 3, in November, 2012. We are grateful to Wiley Periodicals, Inc., for permission to republish it.

Chapter 8 is a lightly revised version of "Genuine Agency Somehow Shared? The Holy Spirit and Other Gifts," by Marilyn McCord Adams, which was published in *Oxford Studies in Medieval Philosophy*, vol. 1, 2013. We are grateful to the Oxford University Press for permission to republish it.

Chapter 7 is a lightly revised version of "Scotus on the Metaphysics of Habits," by Marilyn McCord Adams, which was published in *Proceedings of the American Catholic Philosophical Association*, vol. 88, 2014. We are indebted to The Philosophy Documentation Center for permission to reprint it.

1
Medieval Architecture of Matter, Form, and Powers

1. Substance as Fundamental

In the *Categories*, Aristotle lays out a metaphysics that makes primary substance fundamental in the sense that primary substances exist *per se*. Whatever else there may be is parasitic on primary substance. It is either *said of* primary substance (as "secondary substances" or natural kinds and/or their defining and naturally consequent properties are) or *exists in* a substance as accidents (i.e., accidental properties) do. Because *Categories*-metaphysics represents primary substances as subject to accidents, it best fits the sublunary world in which we live and move and have our being, as opposed to transcendent simple beings (e.g., heavenly unmoved movers). Without belaboring the point, *Categories*-metaphysics lays it down **that substance does not come in degrees: that is, secondary substances or natural kinds do not have fuzzy** boundaries. Moreover, *Categories*-metaphysics declares for *restricted composition*: primary substances cannot be composed of other primary substances. If they could, the constituent substances would exist *per se* and so would be naturally prior to the constituted substance, while the constituted substance would exist through them and so would not be *per se* after all.

2. The Aristotelian "Population" Hypothesis

Categories-analysis proceeds at a fairly high level of abstraction. It does not claim definitively to pronounce which are the substances and what the natural kinds are. This is something for science to discover. Rather *Categories*-analysis is about what it is to be a primary substance versus what it is to be a secondary substance versus what it is to be this or that kind of accident. *Categories*-analysis aims to identify the *propria* of the categories, those features that pertain to all and only things of that ontological kind.

Aristotle himself, however, was a part-time scientist, and his investigations led him to a distinctive "Population" Hypothesis: that plants and animals are the paradigm substances here below. This "Population" Hypothesis combines with his restricted composition assumption—that primary substances cannot be constituted from primary substances, cannot have primary substances as proper parts—to yield a rejection of ancient atomism, which (on Aristotle's reading) identified atoms as primary substances of which macro-objects are made. Aristotle's hylomorphism is invented to replace reductive materialism and material-constitution accounts of biological macro-objects. He is not interested in property dualisms that ascribe vital and psychological properties to what is at bottom elemental material stuff. Aristotle's empirical investigations lead him to posit plant and animal kinds as real natural kinds. Aristotle has no sympathy with theories that deny any reduction of specialized sciences (e.g., biology and psychology) to more fundamental physical sciences, all the while holding to material constitution at bottom. For Aristotle, the special sciences are *real* sciences because they study *real* natural kinds.

3. Substances as Functional Integrities

Aristotelian sciences infer the natures of things from observed functions. Observed always-or-for-the-most-part *functional regularities* are to be explained by positing *an essential power* to underwrite them. Observed always-or-for-the-most-part *concomitant functions* (various functions that always-or-for-the-most-part travel together) are to be explained in terms of *a substantial form that roots the respective essential powers*. The Aristotelian default is that *functional powers and their root substantial form are to be located in the functioning thing whose essential powers they are and whose natural kind is defined by the substantial form in question*. The intuition underlying this methodological default is what I will call the "Full Factory Equipment" assumption: that because to be is either to function or at least to be able to function, *substances essentially include all of the dynamic and static structures they need to be in a state of first potentiality with respect to their characteristic (always-or-for-the-most-part) functions.*[1]

---

[1] First potentiality is contrasted with states of partially actualized potentiality. For a fuller discussion of potentiality and actualization in the case of the human intellect, see Aquinas, *Summa Theologica* I, q.76, article (henceforward, a.)1 conclusion [hereafter c].

Moreover, concomitant functions are *ordered* in the sense that some are necessary for others. Aquinas takes this *teleologically*: the last perfecting form or functional state is *the final cause* of other dynamic or static structures: most obviously, sensation is the end of sense organs; vital functions of digestive and reproductive organs. The organs are *for the sake of* the functions.[2] Scotus and Ockham eschew natural teleology and instead take the last perfecting form or final state to be a *resultant*: sense organs are a condition of the possibility of sensation which results when living organs with sensory powers are placed in appropriate circumstances. The difference is that for Aquinas the functional state *explains* and so final-causes the structures and powers, while for Scotus and Ockham the perfecting form or functional state is materially and efficiently caused by the underlying structures (together with external causes). Either way, all of the powers and structures are needed for a complete functional package.

There is a further thesis: the many and various functional powers belonging to a substance are not only concomitant but also all *hierarchically integrated*, so that the higher essentially presupposes and builds on the lower. Once again, sensory powers presuppose sense organs; sensation presupposes vital functions which presuppose vital powers and vital organs, etc. Aristotle famously declares that the soul and body were made for one another, or—more precisely—the body for the sake of the soul. The soul cannot animate just any body, but only one that has the static structures that are apt for the exercise of its dynamic powers.

4. Wholes, Parts, and Reification

Categories-metaphysics premises that a primary substance is a being *per se*. To be is either to be a primary substance or to be said of a primary substance or to exist in a primary substance. But Aristotle lays it down that *unum convertitur cum ente*. Whatever is somehow a being is some kind of unity, and vice versa. If primary substance is a being *per se*, it is also one *per se*.

Experience shows, however, that plants and animals are susceptible of generation and corruption; they come into being and pass away. Aristotelian *Physics* understands change in terms of reshaping stuff and/or moving it

---

[2] Aquinas, *Summa Theologica* I, q.76, a.5 c, q.84, a.4 c, and q.89, a.1 c.

around. In Aristotelian language, it involves matter, form, and privation. There is substrate stuff which is first deprived of but in potency to receive a given form and then acquires that form, losing the form that it actually had before.

If plants and animals are primary substances, it follows that some primary substances are somehow composite, including both prime matter and substantial form. The substantial form of soul first shapes up the matter to produce a primary substance of a determinate natural kind. When the plant or animal dies, the substrate ceases to be a constituent of a complete thing of that kind and becomes the substrate of a dead body. *The formal functional principle is reified*, and the matter can be subject first to one and then to another.

Following what Aristotle often says, Aquinas tries to preserve *the fundamentality of primary substance* by insisting that—where composites are concerned—*the whole primary substance is naturally prior to its parts*—or, more precisely, *naturally prior to its constitutive principles*—because Aquinas does not speak of prime matter and substantial form as "parts." In *De Ente et Essentia*, he can still maintain that here below, primary substance is the only being *per se*, while accidents are beings only analogously in relation to something else—viz., the substances in which they exist. In *De Ente et Essentia*, in his *Metaphysics*-commentary and elsewhere, Aquinas identifies substantial form as that through which a primary substance receives its *esse* (actual existence) and that prime matter is of itself pure potentiality with no actuality of its own. The unity of primary substance is preserved because there is only one *esse* (actual existence) and only one constituent principle (a single substantial form) through which it gets its *esse*. There is not enough *to* prime matter for prime matter and substantial form to count as two separate parts; that would somehow compromise the paradigmatic and *per se* unity of the substance.[3] Moreover, what is true of the whole in relation to its metaphysical constituents is true in relation to its integral parts. Because the whole is naturally prior to its constituents/parts, Aquinas joins Aristotle in endorsing the homonymity of the living and the severed hand. The hand is a genuine hand only when it is an integral and functional part of the living thing. The separated hunk of flesh, though briefly still shaped like a hand, cannot function as a hand and so is not the same thing.

Scotus and Ockham have other Aristotelian reasons for parting company with Aquinas' analysis. Scotus argues that *because material causes are*

---

[3] Aquinas, *Summa Theologica* I, q.76, a.3 c and a.4 c.

naturally prior to the composites they produce, prime matter must be actually something in and of itself, even if it includes the passive power to receive further actuality or perfections. Ockham agrees with this conclusion. Moreover, Scotus and Ockham reason: because prime matter can exist without any of the substantial forms that inhere in it, *prime matter and substantial form must be really distinct things (res)*.[4] In addition, living substances must include *a plurality of substantial forms, which are really distinct from one another*. It will be impossible to explain how the immediately dead corpse has accidents of the same species as the living body, unless—*pace* Aristotle and Aquinas—the living and the dead body are one and the same.[5] But that means *the substantial form(s) that structure(s) the prime matter into a body must be distinct from the soul form*. Scotus in fact posits *distinct substantial forms for the distinct bodily organs* and sees the distinct bodily organs as really distinct parts unified by essential (efficient- or final-causal) orders to its soul and soul functions. Ockham argues that duplicate pro- (con-)appetitive acts and contrary (both pro- and con-)appetitive acts with respect to the same object—say a sensory urge for (against) and an act of will for (against) another chocolate or spoonful of cod liver oil—cannot exist in the same subject. Neither can a free appetitive act and a natural appetitive act for the same object exist in the same subject at the same time. He concludes that *the sensory soul form must be really distinct from the intellectual soul form*.[6]

The resulting picture is that primary substances of biological natural kinds are constituted as *per se* one by really distinct things *(res)*, which are naturally prior to the whole primary substances of which they are parts. It is still the case that all created things *(res)* are either primary substances or naturally apt to be constituents of primary substances or naturally apt to exist in primary substances. But because *it is metaphysically possible (and hence achievable by Divine power) that each thing exist on its own without the others, it follows that living primary substances are not ontologically fundamental after all*. The really distinct *res* of which they are constituted are.

While Scotus and Ockham agree about reifying prime matter and substantial forms, they disagree about *whether the composite is something over and above its constituents*. Scotus argues that it is (because prime matter and substantial form(s) produce the composite, and products are really distinct

---

[4] Scotus, *Op. Ox.* II, d.12, q.1, n.11 and q.2, nn. 3–6 (Wad VI.2.671 and 682–3). Ockham, *Quaest. in IV Sent.*, q.13 (*OTh* VII.275).

[5] Ockham, *Quodlibeta* II, q.11 (*OTh* IX.162–3).

[6] Ockham, *Quaest. in IV Sent.* q.9 (*OTh* VII.161–3); *Quodlibeta* II, q.10 (*OTh* IX.157); *Quaest. in II Sent.*, q.20 (*OTh* V.445).

from their causes),[7] while Ockham denies it.[8] Notice, however, that both positions compromise the fundamentality of primary substance, which they take to be composed of really distinct things that are what they are naturally prior to composing the whole. Notice, too, that the fundamentality of substance is an issue logically independent of hylomorphic composition. Aristotle never mentions the hylomorphic composition of substance in the *Categories*. It is driven by what Aquinas calls "the Argument from Physics" and belabored in his *Metaphysics*. And for Aristotle, the fundamentality of substance does not, by itself, entail hylomorphism.

In fact, Scotus and Ockham take *both* the hylomorphic composition and the *per se* unity of sublunary substance for granted but give up on their being ontologically fundamental. For they adhere to the notion that primary substance is not constituted by any being naturally prior to it, and that whatever is not a primary substance *is* somehow parasitic on primary substance. For Scotus and Ockham, neither hylomorphic composition nor the *per se* unity of substance entail the fundamentality of substance. What empirical observation together with Aristotelian metaphysics (in particular, the claim that duplicates and contraries can't inhere in the same subject simultaneously) and physics otherwise convince them of is that sublunary substances must be composed of really distinct things. Their conclusion—that a thing that is *per se* one can be composed of really distinct things—would be surprising—some commentators find it an incredible metaphysical confusion—if it were not for the fact that the meaning of "one *per se*" has shifted. What they mean by "*per se* unity" no longer refers to fundamental entities, but to entities that are complete functional packages that fall under one of the least species in the genus of substance.

In a remarkable book *St. Thomas and the Problem of the Soul in the Thirteenth Century*, Anton Pegis grasped the distinction between two distinctive developments of hylomorphism. For Aquinas, what substantial form does for a substance is to be that through which it gets its *esse* (its actual existence) and through which it is constituted as a substance of a certain species. One and only one *esse*, one and only one channel through which actuality is poured, one and only one substantial form and prime

---

[7] Scotus, *Lectura* III, d.2, q.2, n.80 (Vat XX.102–3); *QM* VIII, q.4, n.41 (*OPh* IV.501). For a penetrating analysis of Scotus' position, see Ward, *John Duns Scotus on Parts, Wholes, and Hylomorphism*.

[8] Ockham, *Quaest.*, q.6, a.2 (*OTh* VIII.207–19).

matter of itself *potentia tantum*—that is what preserves the *per se* unity of the substance.

By contrast, for Alexander of Hales, Bonaventure, and subsequent Franciscans including Scotus and Ockham, primary substances are complete functional packages that get built up in layers. Each lower layer has a natural aptitude to be further perfected by additional substantial form(s). Substantial forms and prime matter each have natural aptitudes to unite with the others to constitute an individual composite complete enough to fall under one of the least species (the ones that cannot be divided further into species, but only into individuals) in the category of substance. It is the natural aptitudes to unite to form a complete substance individual that guarantee the *per se* unity of the substance. And the composite will be complete only if and when it includes the dynamic and static structures that are needed for it to meet the "Full Factory Equipment" requirement (once again, for it to be in first potentiality with respect to all of its concomitant functions). The dominant substantial form caps it off and places the composite in its species. Lower layers absent the dominant substantial form (e.g., corpses) are incomplete substances, which are, in themselves, unstable because no longer empowered to engage in vital functions.

5. Functional Opacity?

5.1 Layers of Inferences

Aristotelian methodology moves from function to substance nature, but there are at least three levels: *regular* (always-or-for-the-most-part) functioning; *concomitant* functions (functions that always-or-for-the-most-part travel together); and *hierarchically ordered* functions. Regular functioning licenses an inference to an essential power. Concomitant functions license an inference to a substantial form that roots the various powers and explains why the functional powers travel together. (Aquinas says that the substantial form "emanates" and so is somehow an efficient cause of the powers.) Hierarchical ordering adds a further explanation of why these powers travel together: the lower enables the higher, while the highest locates the primary substance in its substance kind. (For Aquinas, the hierarchical ordering adds a teleological or final-causal explanation.)

Aquinas' argument that the soul is the form of the body explicitly appeals to *concomitant* functions—"the same man senses as understands"—but actually presupposes *hierarchical ordering*. For Aquinas, it is not just that understanding and sensation are both essential functions of human beings, but that understanding by abstraction from phantasms is essential to human beings. The mere concomitant connection—"the same man senses as understands"—will not force the instruments of understanding (organs of sense and imagination) to be internal as opposed to external instruments. Rather it is the fact that the essential function of the intellectual soul is to understand by abstraction from phantasms, together with the Full Factory Equipment thesis, that support Aquinas' conclusion.[9]

5.2 Christian Complications

For Christian Aristotelians, Aristotelian method as applied to human beings is complicated, first by the doctrinal claim that human souls survive death and so can exist separately from the body. If to be is to be able to function, then the intellectual soul has to be able to do something even when it is separate from the body. What intellectual souls do is think and will. But they cannot will without thinking. Therefore, if they can exist separately from the body, they must be able to think separately from the body. It follows that it cannot be essential to human intellectual souls to think only by abstraction from sense images in its own internal instrument of imagination. Aquinas himself posits another way of understanding that is metaphysically possible for human intellectual souls: like the angels, to think by means of infused intelligible species. But Aquinas equivocates as to whether this second mode of understanding is natural to us, because he recognizes that hierarchical ordering of human intellectualizing to human imagination and sensation as crucial to explaining why the human soul is embodied at all.[10]

5.2.1 Scotistic Innovations
Scotus begins with the human destiny for beatific vision, which involves an intuitive cognition of the Divine essence. Aquinas reasoned that since all of our *ante-mortem* concepts come by abstraction from phantasms, the adequate and proper object of the human intellect is the quiddities of material things.[11] He concludes that since immaterial and material beings have no

---

[9] Aquinas, *Summa Theologica* I, q.75, a.6 ad 3; q.76, a.1 c; q.89, a.1 c and ad 3 and a.2 ad 1.
[10] Aquinas, *Summa Theologica* I, q.89, a.1 c and a.2 c and ad 1um.
[11] Aquinas, *Summa Theologica* I, q.12, a.4 ad 4; q.84, a.8 c; q.85, a.1 c.

ontological constituents in common, our essential cognitive psychology allows us only analogical concepts of immaterial things.[12] Scotus admits that this is the conclusion that unaided natural reason, indeed Aristotle himself, might draw on the basis of observed regularities.[13] But once we take into account a datum Aristotle did not have—that in the life to come, the blessed will see God—Aquinas' analysis has to be rejected.

Scotus' reason is that *the adequate object of a power is essential to a power; it is what makes that power the very power that it is.* The adequate object of a power subsumes everything that falls under the power.[14] To calculate the adequate object of a power, it will not be enough to take into account what happens always or for the most part in human cradle-to-grave careers. We have to reckon with what is going to be apprehended by those powers in the life to come. If we are ever able to have an intuitive cognition of something immaterial, immaterial things must fall under the adequate object of our essential intellectual power and the adequate object of our intellect cannot be the quiddities of material things.[15] Aquinas' suggestion—that after death God supernaturally augments by widening the scope of our intellectual power to include immaterial things[16]—is a non-starter for Scotus, because, once again, the adequate object of a power is *essential* to a power and cannot be altered even by Divine power.[17] Scotus concludes that the adequate object of human intellectual power is being.[18]

Scotus further concludes that even where material things are concerned, *the dependence of human intellectualizing on sense and imagination is not essential, but a result of God's free and contingent policies for this present state.* True, in this present state, intellectual acts of understanding material quiddities are more perfect when the relevantly sorted phantasms are present in the imagination. But this is because God has freely and contingently ordered the powers to function in tandem in this present state.[19] Scotus speculates: God might have negative or positive reasons. Negatively, God might make human intellectualizing dependent on sensation and imagination as a

---

[12] Aquinas, *Summa Theologica* I, q.13, a.5 c and ad 1; q.88, a.2 ad 1 and a.3 c.
[13] Scotus, *Quodlibeta*, q.14, n.12 (Wad XII.373); *Ordinatio*, Prologus [hereafter Prol.] p.1, q.u, nn.28–9, 33, and 61 (Vat I.17–18, 20 and 37); *Ordinatio* I, d.3, p.1, q.3, n.115 (Vat III.71–2).
[14] Scotus, *Ordinatio*, Prol., p.1, q.u, n.1 (Vat I.1–2).
[15] Scotus, *Ordinatio* I, d.3, p.1, q.3, n.117 (Vat III.72–3).
[16] Aquinas, In IV *Sent.*, d.49, q.2, a.6 c and a.7 c.
[17] Scotus, *Ordinatio* I, d.3, p.1, q.3, nn.113–14 (Vat III.70–1).
[18] Scotus, *Ordinatio* III, d.3, p.1, q.3, nn.118 and 137 (Vat III.73, 85–6).
[19] Scotus, *Op. Ox.* IV, d.45, q.1, nn.6–7 and 9 (Wad X.163–4).

punishment for the fall. Positively, God might just want to coordinate intellectual functioning with bodily functioning for a time and a season.[20]

Scotus' analysis complicates Aristotelian method: "always-or-for-the-most-part" does not always signal essential. Scotus still moves from regular functioning to posit an essential power, and from concomitant functions to rooting in a substantial form. For Scotus, there is one and only one human soul form that contains formal functional principles for sensation and imagination as well as for intellectualizing. But Scotus' analysis recognizes two explanations for hierarchical integration: free and contingent Divine policies, and essential hierarchical ordering. Scotus' explanation of the hierarchical ordering of sensory and intellectual functions in human beings in terms of free and contingent Divine policies, means that *any hierarchical ordering between them is not essential.*

This result does not bother Scotus the way it should Aquinas, because Scotus does not try to prove that the soul is the form of the body from essential functions. Scotus simply takes for granted that the intellectual soul is the form of the body and then worries how to prove that it is immaterial (which he tries to do from the fact that the intellect apprehends immaterial contents).[21]

Nevertheless, should it not bother Scotus another way? If the second move is to root concomitant functional powers in a substantial form as a way of explaining why they travel together, we might wonder *why Scotus does not posit two really distinct soul forms, insofar as human intellectual functioning is not essentially, but only contingently ordered to sensory functioning? Why should all of these contingently related functions be rooted in one and the same soul form?*[22] Scotus' reply may be that explanations come to an end. It is just a primitive fact that a single soul form contains formal functional principles for sensation as well as intellectualizing, even if the subject of sensations is the living and empowered sense organ, while the subject of understanding and willing is the intellectual soul on its own.[23]

---

[20] Scotus, *Ordinatio* I, q.u, n.37 (Vat I.21); *Ordinatio* I, d.3, p.1, q.3, n.187 (Vat III.113–14); *Op. Ox.* IV, d.45, q.1, n.7 (Wad X.163).

[21] Scotus, *Op. Ox.* IV, d.43, q.2, nn.7, 9 and 11–12 (Wad X.23–6).

[22] In fact, Scotus posits one and only one soul form, the intellectual soul, which contains formal functional principles, not only for intellectualizing, but for sensing, and for vital functions. The intellectual, sensory, and vegetative principles are really the same, but distinct formally; see *Op. Ox.* II, d.1, q.5, n.5 (Wad VI.1.113).

[23] Scotus, *Op. Ox.* II, d.1, q.5, n.4 (Wad VI.1.112); *Op. Ox.* IV, d.44, q.1, n.4 (Wad X.98).

5.2.2 Ockhamist Variations

With Ockham, the complications are different. Ockham also infers from regular function to power, and from essential power to substantial form. Since "the same man senses as understands," human beings possess both sensory and intellectual powers. And since these are essential human functions, these powers must be rooted in substantial form(s). But Ockham argues from simultaneous contrary and duplicate appetites, and from freely elicited and naturally produced appetites with respect to the same object, for the conclusion that the soul form that roots sensory function is really distinct from the soul form that roots intellectual function.[24]

Although Ockham rejects traditional Aristotelian cognitive psychology which has the intellect abstracting contents from the phantasms via illumination by the agent intellect, Ockham reasons from experience that *de facto* sensory intuitive cognitions are efficient partial causes of intellectual intuitive cognitions[25] of the same object under the same aspect.[26] He also maintains that sensory intuitive cognitions are efficient partial causes of the first intellectual abstractive cognitions, and are remote causes (i.e., causes of the causes) of intellectual cognitions of abstractions—which makes acts essentially empowered by and inherent in one soul form efficient partial causes of acts essentially empowered by and inherent in another really distinct soul form.

Nevertheless, Ockham doesn't recognize such cognitive psychology—according to which sensory acts are efficient partial causes of intellectual acts—as evidently essential to human intellectual functioning. At least once, he follows Scotus in speculating that such *ante-mortem* efficient-causal dependence of intellectual functioning on sensory functioning is perhaps a consequence of the fall.[27] The separate soul is like the angels, able to have intellectual intuitive cognitions of things without any prior sensing.[28] Since intellectual intuitive and abstractive cognitions are *of the same object under the same aspect* as the sensory ones,[29] and the former are really distinct from the latter, the former could exist without the latter and be produced (as Scotus envisioned) directly by the material objects themselves. For Ockham,

---

[24] Ockham, *Quaest. in IV Sent.*, q.9 (*OTh* VII.161–2).
[25] Ockham, *Scriptum in Primum Sententiarum*, Prol., q.1, a.1 (*OTh* I.27); a.6; (*OTh* I.67); *Quaest. in II Sent.*, q.12–13 (*OTh* V.302–3).
[26] Ockham, *Scriptum in Primum Sententiarum*, Prol., q.1, a.6 (*OTh* I.64–5); q.8; (*OTh* I.208–9); d.3, q.5; (*OTh* II.149); d.3, q.6; (*OTh* II.496–7).
[27] Ockham, *Quaest. in IV Sent.*, q.14 (*OTh* VII.316).
[28] Ockham, *Quaest. in IV Sent.*, q.14 (*OTh* VII.316).
[29] Ockham, *Scriptum in Primum Sententiarum*, Prol., q.1, a.6 (*OTh* I.64–5); q.8 (*OTh* I.208–9); d.3, q.5 (*OTh* II.149); d.3, q.6 (*OTh* II.496–7).

even the efficient partial causality that there is *de facto* (between acts inhering in really distinct forms) would not enable one to prove that the intellectual soul is in the body as a form rather than as a mover.[30]

Thus, Ockham, like Scotus, denies any essential hierarchical integration of intellectual and sensory function and so any essential hierarchical integration of intellectual with bodily function. Moreover, he ontologically grounds the relevant powers in really distinct substantial forms. If we ask, then, why sensory and intellectual functions do—always or for the most part—travel together, and so why sensory and intellectual soul forms have a natural aptitude to unite with the relevant sort of body all to make up a complete being, Ockham may have to hold that it is a datum that human beings are complete substance individuals, and a datum that the same man senses as understands, and so a datum that the substantial form grounding the one will have a natural aptitude to unite with the substantial form joined to the other.[31]

Overall, then, Scotus and Ockham alike deny that primary substances are ontologically fundamental, insofar as all living primary substances are constituted by really distinct things with natural aptitudes to unite to make a substance that is one *per se*, a complete functional package. This means that the "ontologically fundamental" criterion drops out as a way of identifying primary substances. The criterion that takes its place is "functional package complete enough to fall under one of the least species identified by Aristotelian science." But, of course, it is down to science to identify what the natural kinds actually are, and that is done by inferences from functional regularity, concomitant functions, and hierarchically ordered functions. Where intellectual functioning is concerned, Aquinas affirms but both Scotus and Ockham deny that the hierarchical ordering between intellect and sense is essential. The tamer question to Scotus was why they should be rooted in the same substantial form. The more radical question to both is, why they should be included in the same functional package, why they should think that any Aristotelian least species includes both. Put otherwise, essential hierarchical ordering would explain why both should be included in the same hylomorphic composite, whether grounded in numerically the same form (as with Scotus) or in distinct forms (as with Ockham). Once again, this would be a

---

[30] Ockham, *Quodlibeta* I, q.10 (*OTh* IX.63–5).
[31] Ockham, *Scriptum in Primum Sententiarum*, Prol., q.1, a.6 (*OTh* I.64–5); q.8 (*OTh* I.208–9); d.3, q.6 (*OTh* II.496–7).

natural conclusion from the data of our cradle-to-grave careers. But when we take in the data of revelation, we find that the hierarchical ordering is not essential, and—with Ockham—that the distinct functions are not even metaphysically grounded in the same soul form. So now we have both of them affirming that the grounders of these functions are included in the same complete functional package, but we are left wondering why. We have lost the essential hierarchy that made this plain. It begins to look as if for Scotus and Ockham *per se* unity is logically independent not only of ontological fundamentality but also of essential hierarchical functional ordering. Concomitant functioning gives us the complete package. And we are left to wonder why they are essentially concomitant even though not hierarchically ordered.

5.2.3 Bonaventure's Emphasis

So far, we have been looking at *essential* hierarchical ordering. But Bonaventure's discussion features hierarchical ordering that is *moral* and *soteriological*. Bonaventure follows Alexander of Hales in representing the human soul as a metaphysical straddler.[32] On the one hand, insofar as it can exist without the body and has a function that the body does not share and is related to the body as its mover, the soul is itself in Bonaventure's view an individual substance, a *hoc aliquid*, really distinct from the body.[33] After all, Aristotle argued that mover and moved are really distinct. On the other, the intellectual soul is related to the body as a perfection to the perfectible.[34] Body and soul each have natural aptitudes to combine with each other to form a complete functional package, and so to share certain functions, not only vital functions and sensation, but more importantly including moral action and merit-earning. He goes so far as to say that the soul cannot earn merit without the body.[35] Bonaventure insists that the intellectual soul does not want to be separated from the body, its companion in virtue or vice,[36]

---

[32] For a thorough discussion of Bonaventure's distinctive position, see Osborne Jr., "*Unibilitas*: The Key to Bonaventure's Understanding of Human Nature."

[33] Bonaventure, *Sent.* II, d.8, p.1, a.1, q.1 c and ad 4 (Quaracchi II.213); *Sent.* II, d.17, a.1, q.2 (Quaracchi II.415). Bonaventure's view was contrary to the view of Aquinas, which was developed somewhat later, although he and Bonaventure were contemporaries, and both died in 1275.

[34] Bonaventure, *Sent.* II, d.8, p.1, a.3, q.2 (Quaracchi II.221–2).

[35] Bonaventure, *Sent.* II, d.19, a.1, q.1 ad 6 (Quaracchi II.460–1). See also *Sent.* II, d.17, a.1, q.3 (Quaracchi II.417–18, 420).

[36] Bonaventure, *Sent.* II, d.18, a.2, q.2, c (Quaracchi II.449); *Sent.* IV, d.44, p.2, a.3, q.2 (Quaracchi IV.934); *Sent.* IV, d.49, p.2, a.1, q.1 (Quaracchi IV.1012).

and will be raised with numerically the same body so that on Judgment Day they can be evaluated, rewarded or punished, for what they did together.[37] While Aquinas and Scotus[38] do hold that external acts (e.g., pulling the trigger as opposed to willing to pull the trigger) are separately susceptible of moral evaluation, Ockham rejects this, insisting that the will alone is the proper subject of moral and soteriological evaluation.[39] External acts are called virtuous or vicious, meritorious or mortally sinful only by courtesy and derivatively, insofar as they have virtuous or vicious, meritorious or mortally sinful acts of will as partial efficient causes. Scotus also seems to say that the will is the locus of merit-earning[40] and to de-emphasize how this is shared with the body. Once again, as with Scotus and Ockham, the rationale for hierarchical organization of intellectual function with sensory and bodily function is washed out.

6. Some Comparisons and Contrasts with Contemporary Debates

It is not easy to place medieval hylomorphisms in relation to contemporary ontological disputes, because the two discussions have such different defaults and presumptions.

6.1 Part-Whole

For example, contemporary discussions of parts and wholes tend to privilege so-called classical mereology with its hypothesis of unrestricted composition. Nay-sayers respond by working over-time to make a case that composition is sometimes restricted by structuring principles, and then quarrelling over whether such structuring principles are to be reified. Some contend that if a structuring principle is required to unite an aggregate, and structuring principles are reified, infinite regress threatens.[41] Others insist

---

[37] Bonaventure, *Sent.* II, d.17, a.2, q.1 ad 3 (Quaracchi II.420); *Sent.* IV, d.43, a.1, q.4 (Quaracchi IV.888); *Sent.* IV, d.43, q.1, q.5 (Quaracchi IV.894); *Sent.* IV, d.44, p.1, a.2, q.1 (Quaracchi IV.910).
[38] Scotus, *Quodlibet*, q.18, nn.6–16 (Wad XII.479–86).
[39] Ockham, *De Connexione Virtutum*, q.7, a.1 and a.4 (*OTh* VIII.327–30 and 381).
[40] Scotus, *Ordinatio*, Prol., p.1, q.u, n.55 (Vat I.33).
[41] For example, see Johnston, "Hylomorphism."

that the regress can be stopped because the structuring principle differs in kind from the other ordered items.[42]

By contrast, medieval hylomorphists were not fascinated by the logic of aggregates. Following Aristotle, they recognized aggregation as the weakest type of unity, and their examples are taken mostly from heaps of material things, where spatial contiguity is the aggregating principle. Whatever can be heaped up together can form an aggregate, so there is at least liberality of composition because there is no requirement that merely aggregated things constitute a functional, much less a complete functional package.

Medieval hylomorphists were much more interested in the strongest kind of unity, the unity of primary substance. Here they insist on *restricted composition*: not just any really distinct things can combine to make a substance individual complete enough to fall under one of the Aristotelian least species. The (dominant) substantial form completes the thing, makes it to be the very thing it is, and subsumes it under one of the Aristotelian least species. The substantial forms are dynamic and static structuring principles and they are reified. Not all ordering principles are reified, however. For example, the natural aptitudes of substantial form(s) and prime matter to unite to make a complete individual substance are not further reified. Likewise, Scotus himself appeals to the "no infinite regress" argument as a reason for denying that there is an overarching form that unites the various organs into a single body. Rather, Scotus says the organs, each with their own substantial forms, enjoy a *unity of order*, arguably essential efficient- or final-causal orders that are not reified.

Likewise, where *accidental unities* are concerned (e.g., white Socrates), medieval hylomorphists insist on restricted composition, because—among other things—the natural kind sets a limit on the range of accidents that the primary substance is in potency with respect to and so to the kind of accidents that can exist in it. Angels cannot be green, and rocks cannot be subject to acts of sensation or intellectual thoughts.

6.2 Emergence and Supervenience

Biological substances emerge through a process of growth from a seed. Where the Franciscan sees the complete primary substance as built up layer

---

[42] For a notable development of this position, see Koslicki, *The Structure of Objects*.

by layer as perfection is added to a perfectible substrate or composite, Aquinas views embryonic development as a series of substantial changes. Seizing on Aquinas' discussion of embryonic development, Brian Leftow[43] hastens to present Aquinas as an emergentist. When material stuff is configured a certain way, vital properties emerge. When plant-like vital stuff is reconfigured a certain way, animal properties emerge. When animal-like stuff is reconfigured a certain way, the human soul or capacity for intellectual activities emerge. Leftow declares that the higher level properties "supervene" on the lower level properties: by definition, no change in the higher level properties without a change in the lower level properties.

Medieval hylomorphists do not deny that there is a causal process in which lower level stuff gets reconfigured, and upon this reconfiguring a higher level property emerges. But they reify the higher level property. Moreover, as Leftow acknowledges, unlike CD Broad they do not imagine that the subject of the higher level property is the lower level stuff (e.g., it is not the case that material stuff is the subject of mental properties, as in a property-dualist form of materialism). Rather, they maintain that the higher level property reconstitutes the composite as a thing of a different natural kind, and it is that newly (fully) constituted composite—ultimately, the primary substance—that is the subject of the properties (the bull—not atoms arranged bullwise—is black and white and weighs 2 ton and sees red).

Medieval hylomorphists would not endorse supervenience (no higher level change without a lower level change) for all intellectual functioning. This would be especially clear for Scotus and Ockham where cases of willing are concerned. And even if *ante-mortem* changes in the sensory powers are correlated with intellectual cognition, Scotus and Ockham deny that this is essential. Willing and understanding are activities of which the intellectual soul is the primary subject—activities that it can and will have even when separated from the body.

Ockham does admit that changes in sensory powers (which are identical with the sensory soul, which is the immediate subject of sensory acts) are accompanied by naturally simultaneous changes in the sense organ. But he is led to this by arguments from experience, about how our ability to see is altered by certain kinds of stimuli, not by any desire to reduce acts of sensation to material modifications of the sense organs. Ockham remains firm that the sensory soul is really distinct from the organic body. Correlations

---

[43] Leftow, "Souls Dipped in Dust."

notwithstanding, the sensory soul is the immediate subject of the higher level property, while the sense organ is the immediate subject of the lower level property. No reduction of the psychological or vital to the merely material is envisaged.

6.3 Why Not Materialist Reduction or Material Constitution?

Medieval Aristotelians are working in an intellectual environment that takes the Great Chain of Being for granted. Everyone agreed that the clearest cases of being and intelligibility are immaterial: for Aristotelians, the Unmoved Mover, the Separate Substances, or Angels; for Plato before them, the Platonic forms (which by the later dialogues are purely mathematical). Plato himself had concluded that first-class being and intelligibility are not to be found in the sublunary material world. It is only a moving likeness of eternity. The likenesses of the ideas reflected in the receptacle are imperfect and distorted by recalcitrant matter, so that the best thing a scientist can do is tell "a likely story."

Aristotle's bold "Population" Hypothesis was a counter-move to insist that first-class being and intelligibility (science, or knowledge properly speaking) are to be found in the sublunary world in biological substances, because there are biological and psychological regularities that cannot be accounted for by low-level regularities governing the elements and material compounds. Aristotle is insisting that some of the intelligibility that Plato thought had to be transcendent is firmly planted in the material world—not in such a way that material stuff becomes the subject or fundamental constitutors of the subject of higher level properties, but in such a way that the higher level properties enter the material world to transform material stuff into things of fundamentally different kinds from the elements and their compounds. Where lower level properties are correlated with higher level properties, this triggers no reductive instinct but rather is treated as evidence of hierarchical integration.

Many contemporary philosophers start from the opposite intuition. For them, the physical sciences are the paragons of intelligibility. The desire that the physical sciences should be a theory of everything drives materialist-reduction or material-constitution programs. For them, alleged facts of supervenience underwrite a reduction of higher level properties to lower level properties—or the contention that material stuff is the ultimate subject of two types of properties (some sort of property dualism)—or at least the conclusion that the subject of the higher level properties is at bottom constituted by material stuff. Even where higher level sciences are recognized as not reducible to the physical sciences, they are not real sciences in Aristotle's sense because they do not correspond to real natural kinds. Even now, some philosophers are beginning to wonder whether this isn't too high a price to pay, whether it isn't a mistake to grant the physical sciences such hegemony.

2
Housing the Powers
Self-Actuation and Cosmic Design

Medieval Aristotelian science treats perceived always-or-for-the-most-part functional regularities among macro-objects here below as explananda that require grounding in causal powers. This chapter will trace and discuss ways in which that played out, focusing mainly on the works of Godfrey of Fontaines, Henry of Ghent, and John Duns Scotus.

The Aristotelian defaults are to house functional powers in the macro-objects that exhibit the regularities and to lodge explanatory powers in transcendent objects only when that fails. Because some causal powers seem mutually repugnant, Aristotelian science offers us a sublunary universe populated with interacting substances of different natural kinds. Godfrey of Fontaines mounts bold arguments that if self-actuation were allowed anywhere, there could be no principled reason for not finding it everywhere. Henry of Ghent and Duns Scotus counter Godfrey's contentions with instructive distinctions. But Scotus' own understanding of cosmic ordering raises questions about what reasons there are for preferring Aristotelian interacting substances to self-actuating Leibnizian monads that have no windows.

1. Sketching an "Aristotelian" Cosmos

Aristotelian explanatory programs begin with perceived always-or-for-the-most-part regularities among macro-objects. They lay it down that always-or-for-the-most-part regularities require to be explained in terms of formal functional principles, in terms of active and passive functional powers. But where are such powers to be housed? The Aristotelian default is to locate the powers that underwrite the regularities among macro-objects here below as much as possible in the very macro-objects that exhibit the regularities, and to lodge explanatory powers in transcendent objects only when that fails.

Patterned regularities encourage the conclusion that combinations of active and passive causal powers travel in packages, and this fact, too, calls for an explanation in terms of formal functional principles that constitute a natural kind.

Thus, Aquinas[1] and Giles of Rome[2] discover an explanatory structure within the individual substance itself. The substantial form is the root of the functional powers, insofar as it explains why the substance has them. Powers distinctive of the natural kind are really distinct from the substance nature but naturally consequent upon it. Heat (which is calefactive power) "flows from" the substantial form of fire; vital, sensory, intellectual, and will powers "emanate" from the soul. Aquinas speaks of the substantial form and/or the substance constituted by it as being "somehow active" in emanating those powers.[3] But the powers inhere in the substance as in a subject, and any subject that has a form must also include a formal passive principle by virtue of which it can receive such accidents. Thus, for Aquinas and Giles, each individual substance is both somehow active in producing and also passive in receiving its natural powers.

Not only powers, but all of the "inseparable" accidents that are proper to substances of a natural kind emanate from its substantial form. Scotus mentions how quantity (which is itself inactive)[4] is naturally consequent upon the substantial form of all bodies.[5] Not all of a substance's accidents "flow from" its substantial form, however. Some are produced in it by the active powers of external causes. Pale Socrates bronzes under the sustained causal impact of the sun's rays. The stove's fire heats cold water in the kettle. Even where so-called "separable" accidents are concerned, however, the passive power to receive determinants of a given determinable (e.g., of corporeal surfaces to be colored) is naturally consequent upon the substantial form.

Medieval Aristotelians also work with a distinction between immanent and transcendent actions. Many actions of corporeal substances are *transcendent* in the sense that the passive potency that gets actualized when the substance acts is not in the agent but in the patient. Other things being equal, when fire heats wood, there is no new act in the fire; rather the wood's potency for being hot is actualized by the fire's production of heat in wood. By contrast, the essential functions of spiritual beings—e.g., understanding

---

[1] Aquinas, *Summa Theologica* I, q.77, aa.1–8.
[2] Giles of Rome, *Quodlibeta* III, q.11, pp. 334–5.
[3] Aquinas, *Summa Theologica* I, q.77, article (henceforward, a.)6 c and ad 2um.
[4] Scotus, *QM* IX, q.6, n.11, q.7, n.14, and q. 14, n.34 (*OPH* IV.579, 586, and 635).
[5] Scotus, *QM* IX, q.7, nn.16–17 and q.14, n.36 (*OPH* IV.587–8 and 636).

and willing—are immanent actions. When Socrates understands that he has been sentenced to death but could escape, Socrates' intellect is reduced from potency to act (or, as Aristotle sometimes says, from being in first act—possessing cognitive power—to being in second act—exercising the power) with respect to that act of understanding. When Socrates chooses to drink the hemlock, his will is reduced from potency to act (from first act to second act) with respect to that volition. These acts are *immanent* because the potency-actualization "remains within" Socrates' soul and/or soul-powers; in themselves, the acts do not "go outside" to actualize the potencies of anything else.

Here below, then, an Aristotelian cosmos is populated by individual substances of many kinds that are causally interactive with one another. The whole sublunary realm is surrounded by concentric heavenly spheres whose proper function is eternal motion, circular and oblique. Sublunary substances such as human beings and cows have no active powers causally to affect heavenly bodies, but heavenly bodies and their motions do affect things here below. Their oblique motion results in the differential heating of the earth, which is a condition of the possibility of generation and corruption. In general, *stellae ex machina* are used to house miscellaneous causal powers that are needed to explain sublunary regularities and cannot be fitted into the sublunary substances themselves.

2. Godfrey of Fontaines' Challenge

Like other medieval Aristotelians, Godfrey of Fontaines accepts much of this picture. Like Aquinas and Giles of Rome, Godfrey holds that sublunary substances come in natural kinds that are characterized by the distinctive functions and so by distinctive active and passive causal powers that are proper to them. Like Aquinas and Giles, Godfrey understands such proper powers to be accidents really distinct from and inhering in the individual substances, which must include a formal passive principle to receive them. Like Aquinas and Giles, Godfrey maintains that immanent acts are accidents whose proximate subject is the power whose exercise they are, and concludes that the powers include formal passive principles to receive such acts. Thus, according to Aquinas, Giles, and Godfrey, intellect and will are powers proper to the human soul and so are accidents really distinct from and inhering in the human soul, which includes a formal passive principle to receive them. Acts of understanding and volition are accidents that inhere in the intellect and the will, which have formal passive principles to be subjects of those acts.

Nevertheless, Godfrey thinks that the notion that individual substances are in any way active causes of their own accidents constitutes a betrayal of Aristotelian metaphysics. What includes a formal passive principle with respect to F cannot also include a formal active principle with respect to F.[6] Godfrey takes this result to be grounded on the most fundamental of metaphysical principles, and lays out his case in three arguments.

2.1 The Contrariety Argument

[1] Contraries cannot pertain to the same subject simultaneously.

[2] Potency and act (potentially-F and actually-F) are contraries.

[3] Therefore, potency and act (potentially-F and actually-F) cannot pertain to one and the same subject simultaneously. (1,2)

[4] Prior to receiving F-ness, the subject of F-ness is in potency with respect to receiving F-ness (is potentially-F).

[5] A cause cannot give what it doesn't have.

[6] Therefore, the formal active principle of producing F-ness is in something that is actually-F. (5)

[7] If the subject-receiver of F-ness included a formal active principle for producing F-ness, it would be both potentially-F and actually-F simultaneously. (4, 6)

[8] Therefore, the subject-receiver of F-ness does not include a formal active principle for producing F-ness.[7] (1,7)

2.2 The Other-Directedness of Powers Argument

[9] Active powers are powers to act on something other than the subject that is/has them: i.e., "X is active with respect to F-ness" = df. "X is/has a

---

[6] Godfrey of Fontaines, *Quodl.* VIII, q.2 (*PB* IV, 18). See also his *Disp. Quest.* 9, 10, and 12. For extensive discussion of Godfrey's position, see also Wippel's works listed in this book's Bibliography under 'Secondary Sources'.

[7] Godfrey of Fontaines, *Quodl.* VIII, q.2 (*PB* IV.19–20); *Disp. Quaest.* 12, p. 367.

formal active principle of producing F-ness in Y, where Y is not identical with X."

[10]   Passive powers are powers to be acted upon by something other than the subject that has them: i.e., "X is passive with respect to receiving F-ness" = df. "X is/has a formal passive principle of receiving F-ness from Y, where Y is not identical with X."

[11]   Therefore, nothing acts on itself.[8] (9,10)

2.3 The Part-Whole Argument

[12]   If X is a composite that is one *per se* (e.g., a composite substance such as Socrates) or one *per accidens* (e.g., a composite of substance and accident such as white Socrates), X does not generate itself as a whole or according to its parts.

[13]   The subject of accidents together with those accidents is one *per accidens*.

[14]   Therefore, the subject of accidents cannot contain a formal active principle for the production of those accidents.[9] (12, 13)

Godfrey declares that since the metaphysical principles to which he appeals are general and necessary, the conclusions are general and unexceptionable. They apply to all created substances and their inseparable and separable accidents. In no case does the proximate subject of an accident include within itself a formal active principle to produce that accident. Self-actuation is a metaphysical impossibility!

Godfrey has the courage of his convictions. His own view is that what produces an individual substance is the efficient cause not only of its substance nature but also of any proper and inseparable accidents that are consequent upon that nature. Likewise, their present and presented objects are the active causes of acts of intellect and will.[10]

Certainly, Godfrey's arguments serve to focus the attention, not least because their general conclusion seems to threaten another metaphysical doctrine of considerable ethical and religious importance. If will-power

---

[8] Godfrey of Fontaines, *Quodl.* VIII, q.2 (*PB* IV.19); *Disp. Quaest.* 12, p. 366.
[9] Godfrey of Fontaines, *Disp. Quaest.* 12, p. 366.
[10] Godfrey of Fontaines, *Quodl.* VIII, q.2 (*PB* IV.29–30).

includes no active power to produce but merely passive power to receive volitions, what becomes of the will's freedom? Of course, Godfrey was alert to this consequence. His principal target was not Aquinas' vague remark that substances and/or substantial forms are somehow active in producing proper accidents, but Henry of Ghent's doctrine that—so far from being purely passive—the will is a purely active power. The necessity of reconciling pure passivity with freedom in the will is no small price for Godfrey to pay for making such strident claims.

Moreover, if the Contrariety Argument has some *prima facie* bite, the Other-Directedness and Part-Whole Arguments seem openly contentious, even question-begging. Those who believe that the will is self-actuating will simply deny that [9] active and [10] passive powers are always only other-directed. Those who argue that substances are active in producing their own proper powers reject [12] the claim that no part can be an efficient cause of the *per se* or *per accidens* unified whole of which it is a part. These facts, too, can hardly have escaped Godfrey's notice.

To uncover what Godfrey was so exercised about, I want first to examine the challenge and riposte between Godfrey and Henry, and then a similarly provocative sequence between Scotus and his opponents. These discussions will equip us to return to the heart of the matter: the theme of cosmic design.

3. Henry of Ghent versus Godfrey of Fontaines on Self-Actuation

3.1 Henry's Rejection of Godfrey's Arguments

Henry is firmly convinced not only of the metaphysical possibility but also of the actuality of self-actuation. To neutralize Godfrey's Contrariety and Part-Whole Arguments, Henry forwards a distinction between *being virtually-F versus being formally-F*.[11] Premiss [5] of the Contrariety Argument declares that a cause cannot give what it doesn't have. But there are two ways for a cause to "have" what it gives: X can be a cause of F-ness by being formally-F (so that X is actually-F) or by being virtually-F. Henry explains that for X to be virtually-F is for X to be formally-G, where G is not identical

---

[11] Henry of Ghent's *quodlibetal* questions are cited here from two very different printed editions, as explained in this book's Bibliography, Primary Sources. The present reference is to Henry of Ghent, *Quodl.* X, q.9 (Leuven XIV.221–2, 230–1).

with and does not include F, and where by virtue of being G, X is able to cause something to be formally-F, just as much as X would be able to do if X were itself formally-F. This situation obtains in all cases of equivocal causation. The sublunary quality of heat does not actually inhere in the sun, but the sun has other features G that includes formal active principles to produce heat in heatable sublunary objects. For that matter, the sublunary quality of heat does not actually inhere in God, but Omnipotence includes power to produce heat in sublunary heatables. Thus, premiss [5] does not entail step [6]. Moreover, if [2] being potentially-F and being formally-F are clearly contraries, being potentially-F and being virtually-F (= being formally-G, where G is not identical with or inclusive of F) are not. That takes away any principled reason for accepting premiss [12] of the Part-Whole Argument as well.

Godfrey construes premisses [9] and [10] of the Other-Directedness Argument to require that active and passive powers be housed in things that are not only really distinct but distinct in place and subject (*à la* Part-Whole Argument). Henry finds these claims counter-exampled both in nature and in spiritual beings. Going back to an idea forwarded by Godfrey and in places by Aquinas and Giles—that the generator produces both the substance nature and its proper accidents—Henry distinguishes two kinds of cases. In the first, the production of the substance and its proper accidents or motion towards its proper place are simultaneous: e.g., the iron and its heaviness are produced at the same time and at that very time the iron begins its downward motion to the center of the earth; the water and its coldness are produced at the same time. Here, Henry is willing to grant that the generator of the substance is the *per se* efficient cause of the proper accidents and of the heavy's downward motion. There is no self-actuation.

In the second, however, the substance is produced but an obstacle prevents the simultaneous production of the proper accidents and/or launching of motion towards its proper place. In this case, Henry says, the generator of the substance endows the substance with power to produce the accidents and/or to begin the motion as soon as the obstacle is removed. When the obstacles are removed, both the heavy's downward motion and the water's cooling itself off would have the substance itself as the *per se* efficient cause. The substance would be the *per se* efficient cause of its own actuation.

Even in this second type of case, there is a real distinction between that by which the composite (the iron or the water) is a mover (viz., its substantial form) and that by which the composite is moved (viz., its prime matter). The formal active and the formal passive principles would be housed in really distinct things, but—*contra* Godfrey—they would not be distinct in place or subject.[12]

Turning to spiritual things, Henry agrees with Giles that the intellect cannot be self-actuating with respect to its first act, but must initially be actuated by an external object. But the intellect *qua* actuated by the first act of understanding can actuate itself *qua* bare potency to receive any and every act of understanding. Henry reckons that here the difference between the former and the latter, between actuator and actuated, would be less than that between matter and substantial form in a composite.

For Henry, will-power goes intellect one better: will-power is self-actuating in the production of its first act. Will-power is naturally consequent upon the human substantial form, and obstacle-removal is required for will-power to be in a position to act. But no volition (nolition) is naturally consequent upon obstacle-removal except where the object is presented by the intellect as good without qualification.[13]

Moreover, where will-power is concerned, there is no real distinction but only an intentional distinction between the formal passive principle of receiving will-acts and the formal active principle of producing will-acts. Even though active and passive powers have distinct *rationes*, Henry denies that the distinction between them can be reduced to a distinction of reason. For Henry, the will's acts are the paradigm case of self-actuation.[14]

3.2 Godfrey's Counter-Challenge

Godfrey reacts to Henry's formal-versus-virtual distinction by demanding a criterion: under what conditions will X's being formally-G (where G is not identical with and does not include F) count as X's being virtually-F? Henry maintains that the water which is formally-hot and potentially-cold is nevertheless—by virtue of being water—virtually-cold and so causes itself to become cold, and that the will which is potentially willing is also virtually willing and so is self-actualizing with respect to willing. What is to keep us, by the same token, from saying that a piece of wood which is formally-cold

---

[12] Henry of Ghent, *Quodl.* IX, q.5 (Leuven XIII.113–19); *Quodl.* X, q.9 (Leuven XIV.223–4, 231); *Quodl.* XI, q.6 (fol.453rO, R, 453vY and 454rD).
[13] Henry of Ghent, *Quodl.* IX, q.5 (Leuven XIII.119–20, 131–2, 137–8); *Quodl.* X, q.9 (Leuven XIV.226, 231); *Quodl.* XI, q.6 (fol.453rT); *Quodl.* XII, q.26 (Leuven XVI.154–7).
[14] Henry of Ghent, *Quodl.* XI, q.6 (fol.453vAB, 454vQ); cf. *Quodl.* X, q.9 (Leuven XIV.226, 231); cf. Godfrey of Fontaines, *Quodl.* VIII, q.2 (*PB* IV.21).

but potentially-hot, is virtually-hot and so is the active cause of its own becoming hot?

Aquinas and Giles restrict the emanation of accidents from substantial forms or substances to inseparable accidents. But Henry cannot consistently rule out the idea that being wood is tantamount to being virtually-hot on the ground that heat is not an inseparable accident of wood. For cold is not inseparable from water, because water can be heated. Yet, Henry is implying that being water includes being virtually-cold. Likewise, no volition is an inseparable accident, yet Henry is insisting that will-power is active power to produce volitions.

To distinguish the wood from the water, Henry might appeal to the fact that Aristotelian causes are obstructable. Aristotelian natural causes act to the limit of their power to produce their effects unless there is an obstacle. On the Aristotelian explanatory model, what removes the obstacle is not a *per se* efficient cause of the effect. Rather obstacle-removal is a *sine qua non* of the effect's being produced. Thus, being water is being virtually cold, but the operation of this cold-producing power can be obstructed by placing the water near an over-powering heat (say, in the kettle on the lighted stove). The human being who takes the kettle off the stove and pours the water into a mug removes the obstacle, whereupon the formal active principle in the water takes over and the water cools itself off. Likewise, the will is not always in a position to will anything (say, when no object is shown to it). Henry maintains that the intellect's presenting the object produces no effect in the will, but is merely a *sine qua non* condition that removes an obstacle to willing. When the object is presented, the formal active principle in the will can get to work. By contrast, the results of Aristotelian science show that wood includes no formal active principle for heating itself up. Likewise, matter includes no formal active principles for producing substantial forms in itself but only a formal passive principle for receiving substantial forms. In the latter two cases, an external agent is required.[15]

Godfrey renews his complaint. Combining the two distinctions— between being formally-F versus being virtually-F, and between *per se* efficient causes versus causes *sine quibus non*—makes the problem all the more obvious. What is to keep us from saying that each and every substance is virtually all of the accidents that it is potentially? What principled reason stands in the way of claiming that each and every substance is self-actuating

---

[15] Henry of Ghent, *Quodl.* X, q.9 (Leuven XIV.238–9, 248–52); *Quodl.* XI, q.6 (fol.454rEFG); *Quodl.* XII, q.26 (Leuven XVI.156–7).

with respect to all of its accidents: some it emanates inseparably, regardless of what external conditions obtain; others flow from it only in the presence of relevant *sine quibus non* causes. Thus, wood would be active power to heat itself in the presence of fire and chill itself in the presence of snow. Human being would include active power to bronze its body in the presence of the sun and make it grow pale under winter clouds. But no creature other than the substance itself and/or what inheres in it would be an efficient cause of the accidents of that substance.[16]

Henry tries to meet this worry. A *sine qua non* cause is not a do-nothing cause. Rather if Y is a *sine qua non* cause of an effect E (say, X's being/becoming formally-F), Y is a *per se* cause of some other effect E*, where E*'s existence removes an obstacle to the production of E. The object does not do anything *to the will* to bring about the act of willing, but the object does do something *to the intellect*, insofar as it is a *per se* cause of knowledge in the intellect, and knowledge in the intellect removes an obstacle to the will's freely willing or nilling the object.[17] Likewise, when I remove the kettle from the stove and pour the water into a mug, I *do* something: I move both the kettle and the water to different places. But nothing that I do makes an active causal contribution to the production of cold in the water. Henry seems to be saying that, for Godfrey's threatened generalization to menace, he would have to identify something else for the external *sine qua non* cause to *do*, the doing of which would be a credible candidate for obstacle-removal.

Unfortunately for Henry, it doesn't matter for Godfrey's objection whether we are dealing with *sine qua non* causes that *do* something or *sine qua non* conditions that do not. The proximity of the water to the fire doesn't *do* anything, but it is a necessary condition of the water's heating up. Alternatively, the fire near the wood could be said to do something: say, brighten itself or move itself upward. Godfrey's challenge is this: if self-actuation is allowed anywhere, what principled reason do we have for not turning every case of a putative external cause of F in X into a *sine qua non* condition of X's self-actuation with respect to F? What principled reason do we have for not recognizing X's substantial form as being all of X's accidental properties *virtually*—and thus being the only active cause here below of any and all of them?

---

[16] Godfrey of Fontaines, *Quodl.* VIII, q.2 (*PB* IV.21–2).
[17] Henry of Ghent, *Quodl.* X, q.9 (Leuven XIV.238–9, 248–51).

4. Scotus on Self-Actuation

4.1 Undoing Godfrey's Arguments

In his *Quaestiones super libros Metaphysicorum Aristotelis*, Book IX, Scotus makes some of Henry's points with greater clarity. Scotus begins by distinguishing between potency (*potentia*) as mode versus potency (*potentia*) as principle or causal source. Potency as mode contrasts with necessity, impossibility, and actuality. This way, F in potency is incompatible with F in actuality; F cannot be merely potentially extant and actually extant at one and the same time. Potency as mode of being does not survive its reduction to act![18] But—Scotus maintains—"potency as principle is not—by reason of being a principle—opposed to act."[19] All parties to the dispute agree: there is no incompatibility in X's housing a formal active principle for producing F and X's being actually-F (formally-F) at one and the same time. After all, premiss [6] of Godfrey's Contrariety Argument asserts exactly that!

Scotus also distinguishes *objective* from *subjective* potency. Objective potency is "the whole insofar as it is in potency to existence" and as such is—like potency as mode—compatible with objective actuality or the whole in actual existence. Every being is in objective potency unless and until and while it actually exists. Subjective potency does not pertain to every being, but only to what is apt to receive (what has a formal passive principle of receiving) some further act. Any non-white body is in subjective potency to being white. Sleeping Socrates is in subjective potency to acts of thought and choice.[20]

Self-actuation presupposes that a thing includes a formal active principle for producing F and a formal passive principle for receiving F—put otherwise, that what is in subjective potency with respect to being F is also potency as efficient causal principle with respect to being F. Scotus acknowledges that a univocal formal active principle for producing F is not compatible with a formal passive principle for receiving F, because a univocal cause is or has power to produce F by virtue of being actually-F (formally-F) already. But the same thing can act on itself by *equivocal* action (where the formal active principle to produce F is formally-G where G is neither identical with nor inclusive of F).[21] These observations undercut Godfrey's Contrariety and Part-Whole Arguments.

---

[18] Scotus, *QM* IX, q.1–2, nn.14–15, 21–2 and 27 (*OPH* IV.512, 515, 518–19).
[19] Scotus, *QM* IX, q.1–2, nn.14–15, 21–2 and 27 (*OPH* IV.512, 515 and 518–19).
[20] Scotus, *QM* IX, q.1–2, nn.14–15, 21–2 and 27 (*OPH* IV.512, 515 and 518–19).
[21] Scotus, *QM* IX, q.14, n.24 (*OPH* IV.631–2).

Against Godfrey's Other-Directedness Argument—that active and passive causal powers are essentially powers to act and to be acted upon by *something else*—Scotus sets his own Generic Adequate Object Argument. He begins with an Aristotelian common-place:

[P] active and passive powers have generic adequate objects: active power is power to produce effects of a certain kind; passive power is power to be affected by agents of a certain kind in a certain kind of way.

Calefactive power is power to heat heatables in general and not power to heat this kettle of water as opposed to that. Calefactible power is power to be heated by any heater whatever and not power to be acted upon by this particular heater as opposed to that. From (P) Scotus infers

[C1] whatever is contained under the first object of a power is a *per se* object of that power.

Since calefactive power has the calefactible as its *per se* generic object, it has each and every particular calefactible as a *per se* object. Since the passive capacity is power to be heated by heaters in general, then—for each and every particular heater—it is the passive capacity to be heated by this heater in particular. Since an equivocal potency-as-principle for F is compatible with subjective potency for F in the same subject, it is possible that X be active with respect to F the same way that other F-productives are active with respect to F, and that X be passive with respect to F the way other F-receptives are passive with respect to F. In that case, given that F in X falls under the generic object of F-productive power, where both X and Y have F-productive power, X would be just as able to produce F in X as Y would be able to produce F in X. Therefore, X would be able to act on itself as much as on any other. Because powers are defined by generic objects, they cannot be essentially other-directed after all![22]

4.2 Presumptions of Perfection

Having defused Godfrey's arguments to his satisfaction, Scotus seizes the offensive by applying the presumption of perfection to natures.

---

[22] Scotus, *QM* IX, q.14, nn.24 and 30 (*OPH* IV.631 and 633-4).

[Q]   Nature always does its best, when this is possible, and is never wanting in anything necessary.

from which he infers the practical principle governing theory-making:

[R]   One ought not to deny any nature something which—if posited—would contribute to its perfection, unless such can be shown to be lacking on other grounds.

But self-actuation and the capacity for it are excellences: creatures would be absolutely more perfect if endowed with an active principle for what they are suited to have, because they would be less dependent on outside help. Scotus concludes that when it is not obvious that a given nature lacks an active principle regarding a given perfection, it should be granted that it has one.[23] All creatures—not only rational free creatures—should be presumed to have some measure of self-actuating power!

[Q] is an expression of the cosmic optimism that infects Platonic and Aristotelian philosophy alike. But the trouble with presumptions of perfection is that they easily "prove" too much. Scotus' first objector reasons that if capacity for self-perfection is an excellence, wouldn't immediate full and complete perfection *ab initio* be an even greater excellence? Shouldn't [Q] and [R] drive Scotus to conclude to that instead? Doesn't the fact that things are not fully and completely perfected from the first moment of their existence (e.g., animals and plants begin smaller and grow up to optimal species size) cast doubt on [Q] and [R]?

Taking a page from Henry, Scotus replies that if creatures came into existence fully and completely perfected from the beginning, the producer of those creatures would get full causal credit for that perfection. Holding fixed the results of Aristotelian science according to which the universe is populated by things of different natural kinds that form an excellence hierarchy, Scotus explains that the capacity for self-actuation that can be fitted into (as non-repugnant to) less excellent kinds is a capacity for progressive perfection. In Scotus' estimation, when there is a forced choice, aseity trumps temporal immediacy. A creature's participating in its own perfecting is worth the delay in gratification![24]

---

[23] Scotus, *QM* IX, q.14, n.63 (*OPH* IV.649–50).
[24] Scotus, *QM* IX, q.14, n.67 (*OPH* IV.651).

The objector presses: if self-actuation is the trumping excellence, why not maximize it and assign to each thing self-actuating power with respect to all of its perfections, so that all connection through causal interaction is taken away?[25] Here again, Scotus relies on definitions accepted as results of Aristotelian science: among the less excellent natures here below, some of the powers needed to actuate their perfections cannot be packed into them because they would be formally repugnant to those natures.[26]

4.3 Self-Actuation and the Unity of the Universe

Thoughts of what self-actuation might do to the connection of things, raise a neighboring issue in the objector's mind. Where presumptions of perfection are concerned, is it only natural kinds and individuals that stand to be perfected? What about the universe as a whole? To be perfect, doesn't it have to be perfectly connected?

In *Quaestiones super Libros Metaphysicorum Aristotelis* IX, q.14, Scotus' response is cryptic. But in his extracted treatise *De Primo Principio*, we find Scotus himself insisting that a *uni*verse is not just a heap or an aggregate of extant things. Rather he maintains that uniting many individuals in a *uni*verse is possible because natural kinds are essentially ordered to one another, and he specifies certain *a priori* features that essential orders properly ought to have. First and foremost, the ordering relations in an essential order are *prior* and *posterior*; equality is not a third ordering principle.[27] It follows that essential orders are *not reflexive*: nothing is essentially ordered to itself.[28] Neither are they *circular*, because then everything would be both prior and posterior to itself and to everything else thereby ordered.[29] But essential orders are *transitive*: what is not posterior to the prior is not posterior to the posterior.[30] Likewise, Scotus insists, they are *bounded*: not every being is posterior (the first is prior without being posterior) and not every being is prior (the last is posterior without being prior to anything else).[31]

---

[25] Scotus, *QM* IX, q.14, n.66 (*OPH* IV.650–1).
[26] See Scotus, *QM* IX, q.14, n.73 (*OPH* IV.652).
[27] Scotus, *De Primo Principio*, c.II, n.1 (Wad III.214); c.III, n.7 and n.11 (Wad III.232 and 234); *Ordinatio* I, d.3, p.3, q.2, nn.495–8 (Vat III.293–5); *Op.Ox.* IV, d.1, q.2 n.14 and d.13, q.1, n.37 (Wad VIII.55 and 807).
[28] Scotus, *De Primo Principio*, c.II, n.1 (Wad III.214).
[29] Scotus, *De Primo Principio*, c.II, n.1 (Wad III.214).
[30] Scotus, *De Primo Principio*, c.II, n.1 (Wad III.214).
[31] Scotus, *De Primo Principio*, c.III, n.14 (Wad III.235).

In *De Primo Principio*, Scotus identifies two non-congruent essential orders: the order of eminence and the order of dependence. Eminence is a function of intensive actuality.[32] In the order of eminence, essences with more of it are more perfect and nobler and hence prior, and those with less of it are less perfect and noble and hence posterior. Since the domain of natures constitutes a universe, Scotus contends, that for every pair of natures Nm and Nn, either Nm is more perfect than Nn or Nn is more perfect than Nm. Against the modern estimate that horse appears no more superior to cow than the other way around, Scotus appeals to Aristotle's authority in *Metaphysics* 8: where species under a common genus are concerned, "forms are like numbers" thereby generating a hierarchy of perfection.[33] If some nature were not ordered to every other nature as prior or posterior in eminence, then it would not be a member of the universe, but a stray or a left over[34]—which is impossible. Scotus thus subscribes to the idea that the essential order of eminence is comprehensive over the domain of natures, and so unifies them by ordering each and every nature.

Scotus' objector in *Quaestiones super Libros Metaphysicorum Aristotelis* ignores the order of eminence to focus on the order of dependence. The objector protests that what connects individuals with one another is causal interaction: effects essentially depend for their existence on the causes that exercise their powers to produce them. Maximizing the unity and perfection of the universe would require producer- and product-natures with exclusively other-directed active and passive causal powers. Self-actuation would decrease the range of interactions and so detract from cosmic perfection.[35]

Scotus responds by reasserting his own doctrine of essential orders, according to which the essential order of dependence is not constituted by the relation between *per se* causes and their effects, but relations among multiple equivocal causes—the dependence of one upon the other(s)—in causing their common effect.[36] Scotus famously forwards three criteria for distinguishing between accidentally and essentially ordered causal chains:

[a] in essentially ordered causes, the posterior cause depends on the prior cause *in causing* and not for its existence or something else; but in

---

[32] Scotus, *Op.Ox.* IV, d.12, q.2, n.12 (Wad VIII.732).
[33] Scotus, *De Primo Principio*, c.III, n.9 (Wad III.233).
[34] Scotus, *De Primo Principio*, c.III, nn.7 and 11 (Wad III.232 and 234).
[35] Scotus, *QM* IX, q.14, n.65 (*OPH* IV.650).
[36] Scotus, *QM* IX, q.14, n.69 (*OPH* IV.651).

accidentally ordered series (e.g., the series of fathers and sons) the posterior may depend on the prior for its existence or something else;

[b] in essentially ordered causes, the prior is of *another* order and is *higher* and *more perfect* than the posterior, whereas this is not necessarily the case in accidentally ordered series;

[c] in essentially ordered causes, all of the causes are required to *act simultaneously in causing* the caused item, but this is not so with accidentally ordered series.[37]

Thus, God, the sun, Ferdinand the bull, and Elsie the cow all act simultaneously, each its own order, the lower depending on the higher in acting to produce Beulah the cow. Univocal causal series—Abraham, Isaac, Jacob, Judah...—in which each is a *per se* effect of the prior and a *per se* cause of the posterior link, does not constitute an essential order but only an accidental order of dependence. The posterior depends on the prior for existence, but not in *per se* causing the next effect. Causes are simultaneous with their effects. Fathers often die before their son's reproduce![38]

The causal aptitudes that give rise to essentially ordered causal series—i.e., the causal aptitude for individuals of nature Nm to depend on individuals of nature Nn in causing an individual of nature Nj, so that the Nn-individual is the prior and the Nm-individual is the posterior cause of the Nj-individual—also pertain to natures essentially.

Scotus' objector can accept this correction—that it is collaboration among equivocal causes, not links between effects and the causes that exercise power to produce them, that essentially orders individuals into a universe—without ceasing to press the original point. Scotus himself has said that self-actuation is possible only where the formal active principle is equivocal. Self-actuation thus takes the unifying relations away from the arena of the inter-substantial and packs them into an individual substance. Maximizing the unity and perfection of the universe would dictate keeping those orders of equivocal causes, so to speak, "in the public sphere."[39]

Scotus concedes that it might be metaphysically possible to locate an essential order of causes of a common effect in an individual substance. Perhaps a single nature could contain an excellence hierarchy of formal active principles with respect to a given effect. Perhaps the excellence

---

[37] Scotus, *De Primo Principio*, c.III, n.2 (Wad III.230).
[38] Scotus, *De Primo Principio*, c.III, n.2 (Wad III.230); QM IX, q.14, nn.69 and 71 (*OPH* IV.651–2).
[39] Scotus, *QM* IX, q.14, n.70 (*OPH* IV.651).

hierarchy would include not only formal active principles in the nature but also formal active principles in the proper and inseparable accidents of the nature. Think of how Aquinas and Giles would see the substantial form of human being and the proper accident of will-power as part of an essentially ordered series involved in producing a volition.[40]

Scotus cautions, however. Self-actuation isn't an everywhere-and-always or not-at-all issue. Yes, the perfection of the universe involves essential orders of dependence among distinct substance individuals. But recognizing some essential ordering within an individual substance does not take away all of the external ordering. Why suppose that self-actuation removes the possibility of perfect and comprehensive cosmic ordering? Once again, Scotus takes the results of Aristotelian science for granted. Some of the efficient causal powers required to actuate the perfections of an individual substance are formally repugnant to the nature of that individual substance and so have to be housed in something else! How could the sun's power to heat the earth's surface differentially be packed into the essence of a mating bull?[41]

5. Cosmic Design

What is really at stake in this dispute among Godfrey of Fontaines, Henry of Ghent, Duns Scotus, and miscellaneous others is fundamental issues of cosmic design.

5.1 Self-Actuation versus Causal Interaction

First, revisit their points of agreement. They all concur that

[T1] the world as we know it exhibits non-trivial always-or-for-the-most part regularities.

They were not paleo-Pierceans who thought that any sequence could count as a regularity of some kind. Likewise, none disputes that

[T2] non-trivial always-or-for-the-most-part regularities require to be explained by causal powers.

---

[40] Scotus, *QM* IX, q.14, n.73 (*OPH* IV.652).
[41] Scotus, *QM* IX, q.14, n.73 (*OPH* IV.652).

They were not proto-Humeans. So far from eliminating causal powers or giving reductive analyses of talk about them, they would insist that no individual substance could exist without them, indeed, that individual substances are constituted mostly by them. Moreover, all agree that

[T3] there is a distinction between active and passive causal powers (between formal principles to act and formal principles to be acted upon),

and so recognize that the question, "where are the powers to be housed?" splits in two. In his controversy with Averroes, Aquinas insisted on what became another point of consensus among medieval Latin thinkers: viz., that

[T4] the formal passive principle for receiving F must be in the thing that is characterized by F.

On these points, and at this level of abstraction, our thinkers are of a common mind.

When it comes to housing the active causal powers, subsequent history of philosophy makes three theoretical options obvious to us.

[Option 1] Assign all of the *active* powers to a single transcendent being (God) and assign only passive powers to everything else,

as earlier Muslim theologians may have done; as later Malebranche almost did.[42]

[Option 2] Package active and passive causal powers together into distinctive natural kinds and distribute them among the plurality of macro-objects here below in such a way as to make them causally interactive with one another,

as Aristotle was understood to do.

[Option 3] Assign a transcendent being active powers to make things here below exist and to cause them to exist no longer, while assigning each

---

[42] "Almost" because—for Malebranche—mental substances are self-actuating with respect to their own free choices. But such choices are not causally necessitated by, and do not causally necessitate, anything else. See Adams, "Malebranche's Causal Concepts."

individual substance active powers of self-actuation sufficient to explain all of its accidents,

as most interpreters think that Leibniz did in his mature works.[43]

Christian Aristotelians did not take [Option 1] seriously, partly because—as Aristotelians—they could not conceive of macro-objects without natures and could not conceive of substance natures that did not include active powers. This seemed so obvious to Aquinas that he thinks Moslem theologians must have meant that creatures have active causal powers, but God everywhere-and-always obstructs their use. In the background, there is an appeal to the Presumption of Perfection. Aquinas suggests that God creates out of generosity, to share the goodness. But causal activity is an excellence.[44] Likewise, Scotus maintains that productive power is a pure perfection and efficient causal power is an excellence.[45]

Godfrey of Fontaines feels an urgency to give principled metaphysical reasons for—if we may speak anachronistically—siding with Aristotle instead of Leibniz, for preferring [Option 2] to [Option 3]. Godfrey believes that he has identified such reasons, and he sets them out in his Contrariety, Other-Directedness, and Part-Whole Arguments. What acts and what is acted upon must be not only really distinct but distinct in place and subject. Powers to act and to be acted upon are essentially other-directed. Godfrey insists that these principles are necessary and unexceptionable. Individually and together they rule out self-actuation as impossible and thereby guarantee that the universe here below will—by the nature of things and by metaphysical necessity—be a scene of causal interaction. For Godfrey, a less exalted account of free choice is not too big a price to pay for this benefit.

Objectors to Scotus share Godfrey's sense that self-actuation must be ruled out entirely, if causal interaction is to be preserved. They are convinced that causal interaction is the metaphysical glue that unites multiple individual substances into a universe. Admitting the possibility of self-actuation threatens to dissolve cosmic connection and collapse the universe into a heap.

By contrast, Henry of Ghent and Duns Scotus do not so much *defend* the Aristotelian model as take it for granted. Their more modest aim is to argue

---

[43] See Adams, *Leibniz*, chs. 3 and 13, pp. 75–110 and 378–99; and Garber, "Leibniz: Physics and Philosophy."
[44] Aquinas, *De Potentia*, q.3, a.7 c; *Summa Theologica* I, q.105, a.5, c.
[45] Scotus, *Ordinatio* I, d.2, p.1, q.1–2, n.53 (Vat II.158–9).

that some self-actuation is compatible with [Option 2]. Their predecessor Peter John Olivi (1248–98) had focused on free will, and insisted that both empirical observation[46] and the theoretical exigencies of moral and religious evaluation require us to posit Divine and created wills as self-actuating powers.[47] Henry of Ghent argues that self-actuation is also the best interpretation of some natural phenomena, while Scotus appeals to the Presumption of Perfection to posit self-actuating power in every individual substance and substance-kind. Despite the widening scope of their claims, they insist, the inference from "some self-actuating powers" to "only self-actuating powers" is still invalid. Their contention is that self-actuating powers are packaged into natural kinds together with many active and/or passive powers that have generic adequate objects and so are partly other-directed, roughly in the manner that Aristotelian science would indicate. Scotus agrees with his objectors that such partly other-directed generic powers play a key role in organizing a universe out of the many individual substances of many and diverse natural kinds.

5.2 Non-Obvious Essential Orders

Suppose we agree with Scotus that some self-actuation does not automatically take away whatever causal interaction and causal cooperation were supposed to contribute to the order of the universe. There is a cosmic-design question left-over: *are Scotus' essential orders sufficient to unify the cosmos in a comprehensive way?*

Even if the essential order of eminence is comprehensive over the domain of *natures*, it will not be enough to unite all of the *individuals* that actually exist here below, because sublunary natural kinds are regularly shared by many individuals that are therefore equally eminent in nature. But—for Scotus—the essential ordering relations are prior and posterior, not equal.

Nor is it the case that—for any pair of natures—either individuals of the one are apt to *per se* cause individuals of the other, or individuals of the one are naturally apt to depend on individuals of the other in *per se* causing a common effect. Platypuses and giraffes do not depend on each other in

---

[46] Olivi, *Sent.* II, q.57, c (Quaracchi II.324–5 and 327–9).
[47] Olivi, *Sent.* II, q.57 c and ad 22, and q.58 ad 14 (Quaracchi II. 317–23, 330 and 437–8).

reproducing platypuses and giraffes, respectively. For a time, they did not even exist on the same continent!

Scotus recognizes that eminence and "obvious" essential dependence will not be enough for comprehensive cosmic ordering. In *De Primo Principio* and his *Sentence*-commentaries, Scotus supplements these with a category of "non-obvious" essential dependence in which the essential order between X and Y is *essential* because it is underwritten by the ordered intentionality of causal powers, but *non-obvious* because it is underwritten, not by their own active and/or passive causal powers, but by the ordered intentionality of the active causal power of something else Z.

In *De Primo Principio*, Scotus posits non-obvious essential dependence among multiple effects of a single cause. [Case 1] Suppose some cause X is naturally apt to cause two caused items E1 and E2, but is naturally apt to cause them in a certain order—viz., E1 immediately and E2 only after having caused E1. E1 is the prior caused item and E2 is the posterior caused item; and both were caused by X. Scotus argues that even if E1 neither has nor exercises any causal power to produce E2, E2 still essentially depends on E1, because E2 cannot exist unless E1 exists. This is because the ordered intentionality of X's causal power is by nature such that X cannot produce E2 without first producing E1. E1 and E2 have an essential order of dependence to one another, not because either has or exercises any causal power in relation to the other's existence or causal activity, but because E1 and E2 are related to a third X that is the common cause of both. E2 is not related to X *simpliciter*, but to X *qua* having first produced E1. Thus, X can be said to be the remote cause of E2 and E2 the posterior effect of X, not because there is some other active causal power that intervenes to act together with X in producing E2, but insofar as X is first ordered to the prior caused item E1 and then to the posterior caused item E2.[48]

[Case 2] Suppose E1 and E2 are essentially ordered to a common third Y, where Y is a proximate *per se* cause of E1, but Y is essentially ordered to X and X is the proximate *per se* cause in producing E2, and Y's causal power is by nature ordered in such a way that Y does not cooperate with X to produce E2 without first having acted immediately to produce E1. Once again, Scotus declares, E2 will be essentially dependent on E1, because E2 cannot exist unless E1 exists.[49]

---

[48] Scotus, *De Primo Principio*, c.I, nn.2–3 (Wad III.210–11).
[49] Scotus, *De Primo Principio*, c.I, n.4 (Wad III.211).

In *Opus Oxoniense*, Scotus also recognizes non-obvious essential connections among effects of multiple causes.[50] [Case 3] Suppose that C1 is a *per se* cause of E1 and C2 is a *per se* cause of E2, but the intentionality of C2's causal power is so ordered that C2 would not act to produce E2 unless C1 had acted to produce E1. The ordered intentionality of C2's causal power makes it the case that the production of E1 by C1 is a necessary condition for the production of E2 by C2, even if neither E1 nor E2 has or exercises efficient causal power in relation to each other.

Where C2 is a natural cause, E2 follows by natural necessity when C1 produces E1. Thus, in Aristotelian optics, colored objects produce sensible species in nearby air, if and only if the air is illuminated. The sun (= C1) does the illuminating (= E1); the colored object (= C2) produces the sensible species (= E2). Here the illumination inheres in the air and is a "receptive basis" (*ratio receptiva*) that makes the air suitable for receiving further forms, namely sensible species. Thus, the illumination of the air is a necessary *sine qua non* condition of the air's receiving sensible species. But when the air is illumined, the production of sensible species in it by relevantly positioned colored objects follows by natural necessity.

Again, a rock (= C1) may knock a piece of wood from its place, moving it (= E1) relevantly close to the fire (= C2) that burns it up (= E2). Proximity to the fire is a *sine qua non* of the wood's being burned up by it, and—given the wood's proximity to the fire—its combustion follows by natural necessity.

Illumination of the air and the motion of the wood are *sine quibus non* disposing conditions, which—given the presence of other relevant causal factors—naturally necessitate the second effect. But the naturally necessary sequencing of the effects—illumination and sensible species; motion and combustion—is explained not in terms of any active causal power of the prior effect (= E1) or of its cause (= C1) with respect to the posterior effect (= E2), but in terms of the suitably situated active causal power of the second cause (= C2).

Where C2 is a voluntary cause, however, E2 follows the production of E1 by C1 because of the freely and contingently established ordered intentionality of the will. Thus, free and contingent Divine volition establishes a non-obvious essential order between the priest's performance of the

---

[50] For a more detailed discussion of Scotus' texts on this point, see my *Some Later Medieval Theories of the Eucharist*. ch.3, 51–79, esp. 68–76.

sacramental rite and the real presence of Christ under forms of bread and wine, and between the believer's reception of the sacrament and grace in the soul. Neither the priest nor the sacramental acts have any efficient causal power to make Christ to be really present on the altar. The believer's receiving the consecrated host does not have or exercise causal power to produce grace in the soul. Freely and contingently established Divine policy establishes the essential order between what priests and believers do and what Divine power effects, so that the former are *sine quibus non* conditions of the latter.

Does the addition of non-obvious essential dependence put Scotus in a position to affirm a unified cosmos? In general, it is not the case that every pair of individuals is such that either [a] they are related to each other as *per se* cause to *per se* effect, or [b] they are essentially ordered causes cooperating to produce a common effect, or [c] one is the *sine qua non* of the other because of the ordered intentionality of some *natural* power. For Scotus, the contingency of free choices is empirically evident, and he infers from this that there must likewise be contingency in the first cause. Contingencies can be tucked into the essential order only if some are *sine quibus non* conditions of others by virtue of the freely and contingently ordered intentionality of a voluntary cause—to wit, Divine providence or the freely and contingently ordered intentionality of the Divine will.

Of course, Divine providence brings in its wake *another essential order*, not among efficient- but *among final-causal sequences*, among ends and the proximate and remote means chosen thereto. Scotus argues vigorously that final causation comes into play only where there are voluntary agents who love something X and for its sake produce Y, Z, etc. Right reason dictates that God ought to be loved above all and for God's own sake. According to Scotus, reason demonstrates that God is the ultimate end or first final cause. Moreover, Scotus describes God as the maximally well-organized lover, who makes nothing without a purpose and selects apt means to Divine ends. In several works, Scotus offers a general sketch of God's means-end calculations in creation. Thus, Scotus explains: God loves Godself above all and for God's own sake, and for that reason wants others to love God above all and for God's own sake, too: pre-eminently the soul of Christ. Then God wills that the soul of Christ should be the head of many co-lovers of Godhead, and so wills to create angels and other human souls. Then, having willed to create human souls, and being consistent of purpose, God wills the material world so that human souls can be united with bodies to make a complete substance and so that they can exercise their distinctive functions as material beings.[51]

Even so, given the universe as it is, no "obvious" essential order of means and ends looks to be comprehensive. It is not the case that for each pair of creatures Cm and Cn, either Cm is a means to Cn or Cn is a means to Cm. Comprehensive Divine providence will order all things to the same ultimate end (= God), but there will be non-obvious essential orders among multiple hierarchies of remote and proximate means. Whether it is efficient causality or final causality, Divine providence will have to use non-obvious essential orders to fit everything in.

5.3 Obvious Essential Dependence, Necessary or Superfluous?

Scotus' objector insists that other-directed causal powers are necessary to unify the universe. Scotus replies that obvious essential dependence is required and can help unify distinct individual substances into a universe, because some of their causal powers are generic and hence partly other-directed. Scotus and his objectors agree that causal powers that are at least partly other-directed are necessary for ordering the universe.

Consideration of Scotus' category of non-obvious essential dependence, however, suggests that they were wrong. Ultimately, what guarantees that each and every individual is essentially ordered into the universe is comprehensive Divine providence, the ordered intentionality of the Divine will that makes some individuals and causal sequences that don't causally interact with each other to be *sine quibus non* conditions, some of one thing, some of another.[52] But if Divine providence and/or nature can make C1's producing E1 a *sine qua non* condition of C2's producing E2, where neither C1 nor E1 has or exercises any active causal power on C2 or in the production of E2, then why couldn't Divine providence and/or nature do this even in a world of individual substances each of which was self-actuating with respect to all of its accidents—i.e., a world in which [Option 3] obtained?

---

[51] E.g., Scotus, *Ordinatio* III, suppl. dist. 32 (Assisi com.137, fol.174ra–va), in McElrath, *Franciscan Christology*, pp. 154–7.
[52] Allan B. Wolter emphasizes that—for Scotus—Divine providence wills the actual universe holistically and so underwrites the coordination of causal sequences. See his "The Unshredded Scotus," esp. 326–7, 336–41, and 346.

On some standard readings,[53] Leibnizian monads are united into a universe by pre-established harmony. Picking up on neo-platonist themes, Leibniz speaks of each monad expressing the whole universe from its own point of view. One way of interpreting this claim would be to say that the ordered intentionality of the monad's substantial form involves infinitely many connections of the following sort: M1 will produce S1 in M1 only when M2 produces S2 in M2 and M3 produces S3 in M3…M2's producing of S2 in M2 is essentially ordered to M1's producing S1 in M1, not because either M2 or S2 exercises efficient causal power to produce any effect in M1, but because the ordered intentionality of the force in M1 is such that it won't produce S1 unless the force in M2 produces S2 in M2. Presumably, any possible world would contain windowless monads ordered to one another by non-obvious essential dependence relations. While Leibniz does recognize an excellence hierarchy among monads, Leibniz's God—in exercising Divine providence—is more focused on the excellence of fit between them and hence on the excellence of the cosmos as a whole.

5.4 Why Prefer [Option 2]?

If Godfrey's arguments are to be rejected, if causal interaction and partly other-directed causal powers are not necessary for cosmic unity, why privilege [Option 2] over [Option 3]? One pragmatic answer is that these medieval Latin scholastics were too entrenched in Aristotelian research programs for either [Option 1] or [Option 3] to seem live to them. Slightly more principled is that [Option 2] reflects the common sense position, because it most obviously saves the appearances (many macro-objects *seem* to be causally interactive).

Venturing beyond this, I suspect that medievals were motivated, not so much by unexceptionable metaphysical principles as by explanatory desiderata. Aristotelians aimed for science that was both *real* and *perspicuous*: real in the sense of burrowing down to the metaphysical fundamentals, and perspicuous in the sense of rendering the connections between phenomenal patterns and metaphysical roots intelligible. Intelligibility required the root properties to be definite (genus and differentia) and so (they believed) finite. But the price of intelligibility is limited explanatory scope. The "real

---

[53] E.g., Adams, "The Pre-established Harmony and the Philosophy of Mind."

definition" of human nature—rational animal—might explain why humans have intellect and will, sensory and vital powers, indeed why humans are risible. But rational animal cannot explain why Socrates is pale or chose to drink the hemlock. Explanatory factors beyond human nature—external causes such as the sun or an internal free power such as the will's power of free choice—must be called upon for that.

By contrast, all of a Leibnizian monad's accidents are naturally consequent upon its substantial form. It is not clear whether Leibniz thinks the substantial form is a mega-conjunction of properties, or whether he conceives of it as a neo-platonic one-over-many, some overarching property from which the infinite sequence flows. What Leibniz does make plain is that neither substantial forms, nor the infinite analyses it would take to show how each and every accident emanates from them, are wholly intelligible to us. Leibniz does appear to make room for phenomenal science, whose laws are cognitively accessible to us. But merely phenomenal science would not have met the Aristotelian demand for real science, with perspicuous demonstrations based on real definitions. For this, Aristotelians gladly pay the price of limited self-actuation and causal interaction.

3
Debates about Potentialities and their Relations to Being

1. Thomas Aquinas on Really Distinct Soul and Soul-Powers

Debates of the 13th and 14th century about soul-powers were attended with many and various ambiguities of *potentia*. Thomas Aquinas maintained that soul-powers are really distinct from the human intellectual soul and from one another. This is true in general for all created substances and their essential powers. For instance, intellect and will in an angel are really distinct from one another and from the angelic substance,[1] just as much as calefactive power is from fire substance and visual power is from bovine substance.

1.1 Arguments from the Division *Potentia* (power or potentiality) vs *Actus* (actuality)

Aquinas is driven to this conclusion, not least, by his reflection on Aristotle's dictum that being and every genus of being is divided by *potentia* versus *actus*.[2] Where F-ness is concerned, we can consider F-ness *in potentia* and we can consider F-ness *in actu*. The house *in potentia* is conceived by the builder's mind; the house *in potentia* comes to be in act, when the builder cuts and fits wood and stones to build the house. When the builder is finished, buyers move into the house *in actu*. House-building is a "transient" act that is located in the finished house. But understanding is an "immanent" act that remains within the agent. When the builder is asleep, he

---

[1] Aquinas, *Summa Theologica* I, q.54, article (henceforward, a.)1–3.
[2] For a thorough examination of Aquinas' doctrine of potency and act, see Wippel, *The Metaphysical Thought of Thomas Aquinas*. For its application to substance and accident, and to the soul and its powers, see especially ch. VIII, pp.238–94.

Housing the Powers: Medieval Debates about Dependence on God. Marilyn McCord Adams, Oxford University Press.
© Marilyn McCord Adams 2022. DOI: 10.1093/oso/9780192862549.003.0003

understands the house *in potentia*. But when he wakes up and starts thinking about it, he understands the house *in actu*.

Aquinas uses cosmological arguments to conclude that God is pure act. God is in no way *in potentia* for existing or functioning. God's essence is identical with God's actual existence (= God's *esse*); and God's essence is identical with God's immanent functioning (= God's *intelligere* [understanding] and *velle* [willing]).[3] By contrast, a creatable nature of itself is only a being *in potentia*: its actual existence (*esse*) is neither identical with nor does it necessarily follow from the defining principles of its nature. Rather, God as first efficient cause actualizes creatable natures by conferring actual existence upon them: bovinity *in potentia* becomes bovinity in *actu*, when God creates Beulah the cow. *Esse* is really distinct from bovinity in Beulah the cow.

1.1.1 Argument

Aquinas reasons that bovinity *in potentia* and bovinity *in actu* are in the same Aristotelian category: viz., substance. Likewise, understanding *in potentia* and understanding *in actu* are in the same category. Since the builder does not always actually understand, the builder's act of understanding is an *accident* in the category of quality. Aquinas concludes, the builder's power to understand must be in the same category: viz., the category of quality. By contrast, the builder's intellectual soul is a substantial form and so—insofar as it is an essential part of something that is in the category of substance, viz., the builder—it is in the category of substance, by reduction. Therefore, intellectual soul-power cannot be identical with the intellectual soul.[4]

1.1.2 Argument

Drawing on the same potency versus act considerations, Aquinas forwards the following proportional equation: *potentia* is to *operari* as essence is to *esse*. In each pair, the second is the act of the first. Aquinas infers—by transposition—that *potentia* is to essence as *operari* is to *esse*. But in God alone is actually understanding (*intelligere*) identical with actual existence (*esse*). Therefore, in God alone is *potentia* identical with essence. Because no creature's actually understanding is identical with its actual existence, no creature's

---

[3] Aquinas, *Summa Theologica* I, q.3, a.1, c; a.4, c; a.5, c; a.6, c; a.7, c; I, q.14, a.4, c. See also *De Ente et Essentia*, c.4.

[4] Aquinas, *Summa Theologica* I, q.77, a.1, c; see also I, q.54, a.3, c.

intellect is identical with its essence. The soul's functional powers are really distinct from the soul.[5]

Aquinas' next two arguments make explicit some of his assumptions about *immediate* functional principles.

1.1.3 Argument
This argument assumes that

[P1]   if the immediate functional principle of A-ing is actually in X, then that is sufficient for X to be actually A-ing.

Aquinas reasons that if a soul-power for A-ing were really the same as the soul, then the soul would be the immediate functional principle of A-ing. But—so long as it exists, the soul-haver is always actual with respect to having its soul. Therefore, if the soul itself were the immediate functional principle, the soul-haver would always be actually functioning—which is not true where human beings and their soul-functions are concerned. Therefore, the soul, which is the soul-haver's substantial form, cannot be the immediate principle of its functions.[6]

1.1.4 Argument
This argument rests on the claim that

[P2]   No formal functional principle can be the immediate principle of more than one kind of act.

Where creatures are concerned, actual functioning (*operari*) is not the same as actual existence (*esse*). But the creature's essence is the immediate principle of its actual existence (*esse*). Therefore, by [P2], the creature's essence cannot be the immediate principle of its actual functioning (*operari*). Rather the immediate principles of a creature's functioning must be really distinct from its essence.[7] This argument is distinctive for treating actual existence as if it were a function of the creature's essence. But Aquinas also combines [P2] with the observation that all living creatures have many vital functions (e.g., nutrition as well as reproduction, seeing as well as hearing, willing as

---

[5] Aquinas, *Summa Theologica* I, q.54, a.3, c; I, q.77, a.1 c.
[6] Aquinas, *Summa Theologica* I, q.77, a.1, c.
[7] Aquinas, *Summa Theologica* I, q.54, a.2, c; a.3, c. Cf. *Quodlibet* 10, q.3, a.1.

well as reasoning) to draw the same conclusion: the soul cannot be their immediate formal functional principle.[8]

1.2 Cosmic Recapitulation?

In developing his positive thesis, Aquinas models the metaphysical structure of an individual substance on the neo-platonic cosmos. The One necessarily emanates Intelligence which necessarily emanates Soul which necessarily emanates the sublunary world in a Great Chain of Being and Goodness that "bottoms out" with prime matter. Each higher level is at once the efficient cause and the proximate end of the next lower level: the One is the efficient cause of Intelligence and Intelligence seeks to return to the One; likewise, Intelligence, and Soul; etc.

Analogously, living things have many functions. If the soul cannot be their *immediate* functional principle, it is nevertheless their *first* functional principle[9] and *root*.[10] The soul emanates and is somehow the active cause[11] of the soul's many powers, which flow from it,[12] and these are the soul's *immediate* and *proximate* functional principles. The soul is also the end or final cause of the soul-powers, because the soul-powers essentially perfect the thing whose substantial form the soul is. As in the neo-platonic universe,

[P3] many can proceed from one only according to a certain order.

The many soul-powers by nature form an excellence hierarchy, so that the more perfect is naturally prior to the less perfect (e.g., intellect to sense, sense to vegetative powers, vision to taste). Higher powers are somehow an end and active principle with respect to lower powers (e.g., sense exists for the sake of the intellect).[13] Besides this, there is the reverse order of generation in which the less perfect come to be earlier in time than the more perfect.[14] This way, the temporarily prior may be part of the receiving subject with respect to the later powers: e.g., the soul with sensory powers is the receiving subject with respect to the intellect.[15]

---

[8] Aquinas, *Summa Theologica* I, q.77, a.2, c; a.3, c.
[9] Aquinas, *Summa Theologica* I, q.77, a.1, ad 4um.
[10] Aquinas, *Summa Theologica* I, q.77, a.8, c.
[11] Aquinas, *Summa Theologica* I, q.77, a.6 ad 2um.
[12] Aquinas, *Summa Theologica* I, q.77, a.6, c.
[13] Aquinas, *Summa Theologica* I, q.77, a.7, c.
[14] Aquinas, *Summa Theologica* I, q.77, a.4, c; a.6 ad 1um; a.7, c.
[15] Aquinas, *Summa Theologica* I, q.77, a.7, c.

Aquinas explains that such soul-powers are *accidents*, so far as Aristotle's categories are concerned, because they do not exist *per se* but in a subject. Nevertheless, so far as the five types of predicables distinguished by Porphyry[16] are concerned, soul-powers are not accidents but *propria*, inherent qualities that are naturally consequent upon the essence.[17] In what subject do soul-powers inhere? Fundamental Aristotelian methodology moves from function to a formal functional principle in the functioner. Put otherwise, *potentia* and its corresponding *actus* are in the same subject. Aquinas observes how many vital functions are organic. Just as the functions exist in the corporeal organs, so vegetative and sensory soul-powers exist in the composite substance as in a subject. Other vital functions—notably, understanding and willing—are inorganic, not depending on corporeal organs. Thus, the subject of intellect and will-power is the intellectual soul alone.[18] Aquinas reasons that when the soul is separated from the body at death, the qualities that inorganic soul-powers are survive and continue to exist in the soul as in a subject. But the qualities that the organic powers are do not survive the destruction of the organs that are their proximate subject. Accidents do not migrate from subject to subject. The soul-power qualities that formerly existed in the composite do not come to exist in the soul alone, instead. Nevertheless, vegetative and sensory soul-powers continue to exist in the separate soul as "in their principle and root" in the sense that when the soul is introduced into matter, it is naturally apt to emanate them into the composite.[19]

Aquinas' First Way of proving the existence of God famously turns on Aristotle's thesis that

[P4] whatever is in motion is moved by another,

which in turn rests on Aristotle's act/potency axiom,

[P5] the same thing X cannot be both in act and in potency in the same respect at the same time.[20]

---

[16] A 3rd-century-CE neo-platonist philosopher and disciple of Plotinus; in his *Isagoge* he distinguished five types of predicable: genus, species, difference, proprium, and accident.
[17] Aquinas, *Summa Theologica* I, q.77, a.1, ad 5um.
[18] Aquinas, *Summa Theologica* I, q.77, a.5, ad 1um and ad 2um; q.77, a.6, c.
[19] Aquinas, *Summa Theologica* I, q.77, a.8, c.
[20] Aquinas, *Summa Theologica* I, q.2, a.3, c.

Yet, here, Aquinas firmly declares that—with respect to inorganic soul-powers—the soul is not only a "somehow active" cause and final cause, the soul is also their receiving subject. Thus, whether by itself or as part of the composite, the soul is somehow in potency to receive them and somehow in act to produce them at one and the same time.[21] Evidently, Aquinas assumes that the respect in which the soul is passive—the formal passive principle of receiving—and the respect in which the soul is active—the formal active principle of emanating—are distinct in a way that keeps them from violating [P5].

2. Giles of Rome: More Neo-Platonic Modeling

The neo-platonic analogies that backdrop some of Aquinas' arguments, are brought front and center in Giles of Rome's account of the structure of created substance, which in turns forms the basis of Giles' assertion that the soul is really distinct from its powers.

2.1 Great Chain of Excellence in Being

Giles[22] begins by positing an excellence hierarchy: substance has more entity and actual existence (*esse*) than accidents; permanent accidents than non-permanent and/or successive accidents. Non-permanent accidents are accidents that don't persist as long as their substance-subject does. Successive accidents (allegedly, motion and time) are accidents that are divisible into parts not all of which can exist at once.

Giles endorses (what we may call) "the Gradual Differentiation" Principle:

[P6]   In those that are of the same nature, those that differ more from the nature flow from those that differ less.[23]

The grounding causal intuition is that "like produces like" (bovines produce bovines; heat produces heat). But in so-called equivocal causation, where

---

[21] Aquinas, *Summa Theologica* I, q.77, a.6, c; q.77, a.7, c.
[22] Known in his own time, and in some contexts even now, by the Latin form of his name, *Aegidius Romanus*.
[23] Giles of Rome, *Quodlibet* III, q.11, 158.

causes are not of the same kind, the cause is more perfect than the effect. Gradual Differentiation says that this transition cannot be abrupt. Rather, if X emanates Y and Y emanates Z, there is some feature F that X and Y share and some feature G that Y and Z share, although X may not share G.

According to Giles, substance is permanent: that is, substance is not a successive and substance persists through a duration always-or-for-the-most-part characteristic of its natural kind. Powers that naturally belong to a nature are permanent accidents: that is, they are not successives and they persist as long as the substance does. Immanent functional acts (e.g., understanding and willing) are non-permanent accidents: although they are not successives, they do not exist as long as the substance does. Giles concludes—by [P6] Gradual Differentiation—that immanent functional acts cannot flow immediately from substance. Rather, permanent accidents flow immediately from substance, while non-permanent accidents (which include immanent functional acts) flow immediately from permanent accidents and flow from substance only by means of the permanent accidents.[24]

From this general portrait of created substance, Giles infers that spiritual beings such as angels or souls are not really the same as their soul-powers. Rather, cognitive and appetitive powers are really distinct from and permanent accidents of the angelic substance or the soul.[25] Giles declares that no action immediately flows from a substantial form, because the substantial form does not have the aspect (*ratio*) of a power.[26] Nevertheless, Aristotle's *Categories* forwards the Substance-Agent Assumption that substance is the primary and principal agent. Moreover, like Aquinas, Giles reads Aristotle as holding that the substantial form is the root principle of all of the substance's proper powers and their acts. The functional act flows *principally* from the substance but *immediately* from the power.[27] Giles styles the power as an "organ" or "instrument" by which the substance acts. But in living things the soul is the root principle of all of the substance's acts.[28]

At the same time, Giles wants to say that a substance gets its permanent accidents, its *propria*, from the agent that generates it. On the one hand, the *propria* are necessarily consequent upon the nature. On the other hand, the *propria* have an external cause, because the substance itself has an external

---

[24] Giles of Rome, *Quodlibet* III, q.11, 158.
[25] Giles of Rome, *Quodlibet* III, q.11, 160; see also *loc. cit.*, 159.
[26] Giles of Rome, *Quodlibet* III, q.11, 160.   [27] Giles of Rome, *Quodlibet* III, q.11, 160.
[28] Giles of Rome, *Quodlibet* III, q.11, 160; V, q.23, 334.

cause in what generates it. Conversely, where corruption is concerned, Giles insists that an agent that has power over the *propria* of a substance—over those accidents that are immediately founded on the substance—has the power to corrupt the substance.[29]

2.2 Ordered Emanation

Like Aquinas, Giles endorses a version of [P3]:

[P3*] those that naturally flow from one thing must flow according to a certain order, so that one flows by means of another.

Giles read the Islamic philosopher Avicenna as taking this principle strictly and claiming that one and only one effect can immediately proceed from God[30]—a conclusion Christians felt bound to reject. All the same, Giles applies [P3*] to the soul's emanation of its non-organic powers, to conclude that the intellect flows from the soul immediately and the will flows from the soul by means of the intellect. He gives three arguments.

2.2.1 From the Soul's Powers
Natural things are understood to have form prior to having an inclination consequent on the form (i.e., a natural inclination). But intellect and will in the soul are like form and the inclination consequent on form. Therefore, the intellect is prior in nature and origin.[31]

2.2.2 From the Soul's Acts
The act of intellect is naturally prior to the act of will, because the object of the will is the *apprehended* good. Thus willing presupposes the intellect's act of apprehension.

2.2.3 From the Object
The end is last in being and first in intention. A thing *qua* object of the intellect is prior to a thing *qua* object of the will. Therefore, the intellect flows from the essence prior to the will.[32] Aquinas seemed to equate natural

---

[29] Giles of Rome, *Quodlibet* III, q.11, 159.
[30] Giles of Rome, *Quodlibet* V, q.23, 334.
[31] Giles of Rome, *Quodlibet* V, q.23, 334–5.
[32] Giles of Rome, *Quodlibet* V, q.23, 335.

priority with priority in perfection. Giles probably understands "X is naturally prior to Y" to mean "Y depends on X for Y's existence but not vice versa," when he remarks that the intellect is prior to the will in nature and in origin, but not necessarily in perfection.[33]

2.3 Self-Actualization?

Giles endorses the Aristotelian principles [P4] and [P5]. Nothing actualizes itself. When the act is really distinct from the patient, it is necessary that something really distinct from the patient causes it. Nevertheless, Giles maintains, it is not problematic that something act on itself indirectly and through its accidents (e.g., the soul moves the body and by moving the body moves itself indirectly and *per accidens*). If the soul is the passive receiver of the soul-power, then the naturally consequent powers can be attributed to something really distinct from the soul: viz., the external cause of the soul's existence. Likewise, even if an angel's substance were its power (which some supposed, but which Giles' model of created substance would deny), then either the angel's act of self-understanding would be naturally consequent upon the angel's essence, which is identical with the angel's power; or it would be partly voluntary. If natural, then it would be attributed to the external cause that produced the angel in existence. If voluntary, then it would be a cause of indirect self-actualization, because the intellectual cognition would be dependent on the free and contingent will-act.[34]

3. Henry of Ghent on the Ontology of Powers

3.1 Powers as Relational

If Aquinas' account rests on his general metaphysics of act and potency, and if Giles of Rome is primarily driven by a cosmic-recapitulation hypothesis about the metaphysical structure of substances, Henry of Ghent begins with his distinctive understanding of the metaphysics of powers.[35] Of Aristotle's *Categories*, the first three—substance, quantity, and quality—are essentially

---

[33] Giles of Rome, *Quodlibet* V, q.23, 335.
[34] Giles of Rome, *Quodlibet* III, q.11, 159.
[35] For an extensive analysis of Henry of Ghent's understanding of powers, see Paasch, *Divine Production in Late Medieval Trinitarian Theology*, ch.9, 117–26.

"absolute." Each has a distinctive kind of thing (*res*) corresponding to it. Moreover, they do not essentially involve any relatedness to other things. The other seven categories are all essentially relational modes of being. Powers, Henry declares, are essentially relational. Therefore, no merely absolute thing considered in itself is a power. But relations require to be ultimately grounded on absolutes as their foundations. And, Henry argues, real relations are not really distinct from their foundations.[36] The upshot is that a power is an absolute thing *qua* related in a certain way to a determinate object or determinate activity. The power is really the same as its absolute foundation, but intentionally distinct from it. Henry understands this analysis to apply both to active and to passive powers.[37]

3.2 Henry's Critique of Aquinas

Henry rejects Aquinas' contention that functional power is identical with essence in God alone.

3.2.1 Henry's First Argument against Aquinas

Henry agrees with Aquinas that God alone and no creature is always actually functioning. But against Aquinas' argument 1.1.3, Henry denies that if the substance or essence were the power, the individual would be always actually functioning. There is a difference between Divine power and created power, but it is not that Divine powers are identical with their essence, while created powers are really distinct from theirs. It is rather that because created natures are participations of Divine power, created power is not sufficient in itself for action.[38]

Henry recalls Aristotle's distinction between transient acts where the act the agent causes is outside itself (e.g., when fire heats the water in the tea kettle), and immanent acts where what is caused is some act in the agent itself (e.g., its own functional activity, say, understanding or willing). Henry explains that where transient acts are concerned, created powers are not sufficient for action, because such powers require a proximate subject on which to act, and it is not always the case that any such subject is nearby. Where

---

[36] For a thorough examination of Henry of Ghent's theory of relations, see Henninger, *Relations: Medieval Theories 1250–1325*, ch.3, 40–58.
[37] Henry of Ghent, *Quodlibeta* III, q.14 (fol.67vR).
[38] Henry of Ghent, *Quodlibeta* III, q.14 (fol.68rX).

immanent acts are concerned, the essence itself is indeterminate with respect to many kinds of acts and to many individual acts of a given kind. The essence itself becomes a power only when it comes to be related to a determinate act or object. Where sensory powers are concerned, there is a double layer: the soul is related to an organ that is naturally disposed to be affected by sensible species of a certain kind, but it requires a further determination to a particular act or object, which happens when the species is received. Where intellectual acts are concerned, the soul has no standing relatedness to disposed corporeal organs. Rather the soul becomes a power when it receives an intelligible species that determines it to a determinate act or object. Thus, what accounts for the fact that creatures are not always actually functioning is not that the functional power is really distinct from the soul, but that the created essence is insufficient in itself and requires something external to determine it to a determinate object or act. This also means that Aquinas' argument 1.1.2 fails, because the transposed proportional equation—*potentia* is to essence as *operari* is to *esse*—doesn't hold either.[39]

3.2.2 Henry's Second Argument against Aquinas

Aquinas and Giles of Rome have focused on arguing that the proper powers of a substance must be really distinct from the substance and from its substantial form. Henry charges that even Aquinas and Giles will have to concede that some created essences are not really distinct from their powers. Henry has in mind qualities of the second species (e.g., the heat in fire).[40] The essence of heat *is* really the same as calefactive power. Otherwise, if each absolute thing were active only through another thing really distinct from it, there would be an infinite progression.[41]

3.2.3 Henry's Third Argument against Aquinas

Henry wants to argue that Aquinas and Giles were wrong about substantial forms as well. Henry rejects Aquinas's claim [P2] that different species of act require different formal principles located in really distinct absolute things. On Henry's ontology, what makes an absolute thing a power is its relatedness to a determinate act or object. But the same absolute thing can be the foundation of multiple relations, and so could in principle be the foundation of relations to determinate acts and objects of different species.

---

[39] Henry of Ghent, *Quodlibeta* III, q.14 (fol.68rX–68vZ).
[40] On "qualities of the second species," see note 52.
[41] Henry of Ghent, *Quodlibeta* III, q.14 (fol.66vO).

In argument 1.1.4, Aquinas argued that the same form couldn't be the immediate formal principle of a composite's actual existence (*esse*) and the composite's functioning (*operari*). Henry distinguishes substantial forms that are "immersed" in matter (i.e., forms that root only functions that are functions of the composite) from "non-immersed" substantial forms (i.e., forms that root some functions that the body cannot share). "Immersed" forms are naturally producible while "non-immersed" forms are not naturally producible. Working from his own ontology of powers, Henry argues against Aquinas that the same "immersed" substantial form fire is in one respect a formal principle of the fire's actual existence (*esse*) and in another respect a formal principle of fire's functioning (*operari*). Thus, Henry contends, the substantial form fire is a formal principle of fire's functioning to heat, because fire heats, not only by means of its proper quality heat but also by means of its own substantial form. Likewise, the substantial form of fire is a formal principle of the actual existence (*esse*) of fire, because the substantial form of fire is the principal agent in the generation of (another) fire; its proper quality heat is merely an instrumental disposing cause that produces the necessary alterations preparing the way for generation.[42]

"Non-immersed" substantial forms are not formal principles of the production of souls or angels in actual existence (*esse*) at all, because the latter are not naturally producible. They are created by God. If what was supposed to disqualify substantial forms from being immediate formal functional principles was that they are already busy being formal functional principles for their own actual existence (*esse*), Henry thinks that reason has just been removed! Henry insists that the intellectual soul is apt to act of itself, but it doesn't actually act (or actually become the power to act) unless and until it is rendered determinate by an intelligible species.[43] Put otherwise, what empowers the intellectual soul is not some emanated really distinct power quality, but an intelligible species that relates it to a determinate act and a determinate object!

---

[42] Henry of Ghent, *Quodlibeta* III, q.14 (fol.66vO–Q). So far as Henry's critique of Aquinas's argument is concerned, there is a certain amount of talking at cross-purposes. Henry fails to note that [P2] speaks of *immediate* functional principles. Aquinas does not deny that the substantial form is the principal formal principle in fire's heating, but rather that it can be an *immediate* functional principle, given that the substantial form is the immediate principle of the substance's actual existence (*esse*). Again, Aquinas was talking about the substantial form's being a formal principle of the substance's own actual existence (*esse*). It is a clever twist on Henry's part to ask whether the same thing could be a formal principle of generation (the production of something else in actual existence) and heating. Since generation and heating are functions of different species, Henry's example should still serve as a challenge to [P2].

[43] Henry of Ghent, *Quodlibeta* III, q.14 (fol.66vQ).

3.2.4 Henry's Fourth Argument against Aquinas

Finally, for the sake of completeness, Henry contends, the supposition that passive power is an absolute thing, really distinct from its subject, would lead to an infinite progression. Take the passive power in fire to receive heat. If that passive power were really distinct from the fire, it couldn't belong to the fire unless the fire had another passive power to receive the passive power to receive heat. And if that second passive power were really distinct from fire, it wouldn't belong to the fire without a third passive power to receive it, and so on.[44] Rather, matter *is* really the same as the power to receive the substantial form. The composite substance *is* really the same as the power to receive accidental forms. Forms separate from matter (separate souls and angels) are really the same as their receptive power to receive accidents.[45] Not that such absolute things (matter, composite substance, separate substantial forms) are of themselves the powers. Once again, the powers are these things *qua* related and so are really the same as but intentionally distinct from the absolute things themselves.[46]

4. John Duns Scotus: Critiques and Positive Proposals

When it comes to the real distinction or sameness of soul(s) and soul-powers, Aquinas, Giles of Rome, and Henry of Ghent focus on the philosophical. Aquinas draws on his metaphysics of act and potency, while Giles of Rome features his model of Cosmic Recapitulation, to defend the claim that the soul is really distinct from its proper powers. Henry of Ghent counters with his distinctive metaphysics of powers to undermine their arguments philosophically and to clear the ground for his opposite claim. All agree that soul-powers are somehow really distinct from each other: Aquinas and Giles, because soul-powers are really distinct absolute accidents; Henry, because different powers are distinguished by distinct real relations.

By contrast, Scotus raises the question in a theological context, in the face of Augustine's claim to find the best image of the Trinity in the soul. Taking soul and soul-powers—particularly, the intellectual soul and its powers of intellect and will—to be really distinct might seem to make it easier to

---

[44] Henry of Ghent, *Quodlibeta* III, q.14 (fol.66vR–67rR).
[45] Henry of Ghent, *Quodlibeta* III, q.14 (fol.67rR).
[46] Henry of Ghent, *Quodlibeta* III, q.14 (fol.67vR–S).

construct such an image. Scotus begins by dismantling the philosophical case offered by Aquinas, Giles, and others in favor of the thesis that intellect and will—as proper powers of the intellectual soul—are (Aristotelian) accidents flowing from the soul. He then raises philosophical objections against Henry of Ghent's metaphysics of power, before coming to his own tentative positive resolutions of the problem.

4.1 Scotus' Critique of Aquinas and Giles

Aquinas and Giles base their arguments for a real distinction on bed-rock metaphysical convictions with which Scotus disagrees.

4.1.1 Scotus' First Argument against Aquinas

Scotus begins by attacking the following argument (from act and potency) by Aquinas:

[i]   *Potentia* and *actus* pertain to the same genus.
[ii] The acts of the powers—understanding and willing—are accidents.
[iii] Therefore, the powers of the soul are accidents.

Scotus declares that this application of Aquinas' act/potency axiom rests on an equivocation on the term "*potentia*." [a] Taken one way, "*potentia*" stands for a functional principle (*principium operandi*). The class of such principles subdivides into formal active principles and formal passive principles, in this sense into active and passive powers. [b] Taken another way, "*potentia*" is contrasted with act. This way *potentia* and *actus* (F *in potentia* and F *in actu*) are not only specifically the same, they are numerically the same.[47]

For Aquinas' argument to be relevant, he needs to take "*potentia*" [a] the first way. But where "*potentia*" is taken [a] the first way, it is false that *potentia* and *actus* are of the same genus. Substance is a passive power immediately to receive accidents. That passive power is in the category of substance, but the accidents are not. Again, Aristotle in *Metaphysics* 7, suggests that substance is an immediate *efficient* cause of all of its accidents—quantity and quality. But that formal active power will be in the category of substance, while what is actually produced will not be.

---

[47] Scotus, *Op. Ox.* II, d.16, q.u, n.5 (Wad VI.2.762).

Nor can Aquinas consistently maintain the opposite, because Aquinas holds that the essence of the soul itself is somehow an active power (*virtus*) from which the soul-powers—which he identifies as (Aristotelian) accidents—flow. If so, the substantial form would be a *potentia* that is not in the same genus as the acts it causes. Likewise, Aquinas holds that the soul itself is an immediate proximate principle receptive of the powers that are (Aristotelian) accidents. Thus, it follows that the receptive power is not always in the same genus as what is received.[48]

Scotus' complaint looks so reasonable, one wonders how Aquinas could have overlooked it. Some of the language in Aristotle's *De Anima* and the commentary tradition upon it, helps to explain how cognitive power understood [a] the first way came to be taken to be power [b] the second way. In the *De Anima*, Aristotle forwards the view that human cognition involves the reception of the object into the cognitive power. Cognitive power (*potentia*) is in potency (*potentia*) with respect to receiving its objects. But Aristotle's metaphysics of act and potency lays it down that if X is in potency with respect to F, then X is not actually F. Aristotle concludes that cognitive powers must lack the features that they are powers (*potentiae*) to receive. Thus, Aristotle teaches that visual power can exist in the eye only because its operative part (the acqueous humor) is colorless. Likewise, Aristotle reasons that, because the human intellect is *potentia* to understand bodies, it must lack every bodily nature.[49] In one place, Aristotle goes so far as to say that—because our intellect is in potency with respect to intelligible objects and capable of being affected by them, "its nature is simply to be open to all things."[50] All natures are intelligible. If intellectual power (*potentia*) were one of the natures it is in power to understand, then it would be actually that nature and so no longer *potentia* with respect to that nature.

In fact, Aristotle was still talking about our intellect's lacking all bodily natures. But one strand of the commentary tradition picks up the language of this passage, and combines it with a distinctive reading of Aristotle's cognitive psychology to conclude that the intellectual power is like prime matter: pure potency with no actuality of its own. That is, intellect is *potentia* in sense [b], and in sense [b] *potentia* is in the same genus as act! When the form of bovinity actualizes the potency of prime matter, the result is

---

[48] Scotus, *Op. Ox.* II, d.16, q.u, n.5 (Wad VI.2.762).
[49] Aquinas summarizes this reasoning in his *Commentary on Aristotle's* De Anima, III.VII, n.680, p. 206. He also endorses a version of this argument in *Summa Theologica* I, q.75, a.2, c.
[50] Aquinas, *Commentary on Aristotle's* De Anima, Book III, Lecture VII, nn.680–81, p. 206.

bovinity actually existing in reality (i.e., an actual cow). When the form of bovinity actualizes intellect, the result is bovinity actually understood, and "thought is identical with its object when it thinks"!

For his part, Scotus finds the resulting view ridiculous. Pointing to symptoms, he quips that if the intellect were pure potency, there would be as many actual intellects in a human being as there were actual thoughts![51]

More fundamentally, Scotus insists that only what is actually something can be a receiving subject. Put otherwise, a formal passive principle to receive can exist only in what is actually something already. Prime matter has an actuality of its own and is in potency to receive further actuality from substantial forms.[52] Every cognitive power is actually something, and only because it is actually something is it in potency to receive species. The act that receives the act of understanding bovinity is not in the same genus, since the act of understanding is a quality, while the soul is in the genus of substance at least by reduction (the soul itself is not a substance but a substance fragment, which combines with other constituents to make something that is one *per se* in the genus of substance).[53] The language of traditional texts may explain how conflations arise, but it does nothing to make them philosophically tenable!

Happily, Scotus thinks, such readings mistake Aristotle's meaning. Scotus interprets Aristotle as agreeing with Aquinas' considered opinion: that soul-powers are accidents in "the second species of quality" and therefore are not pure potency but actually something![54]

4.1.2 Scotus' Second Argument against Aquinas

Scotus thinks that Aquinas' argument—that if the soul according to its essence were an immediate functional principle, the human being would always actually function—also rests on an equivocation, this time on an "immediate functional principle." For immediate functional principles come as formal and as efficient causes. The soul itself is an immediate formal

---

[51] Scotus, *Op. Ox.* II, d.16, q.u, n.7 (Wad VI.2.763).

[52] For a discussion of the disagreement between Aquinas, on the one hand, and Scotus and Ockham on the other, over the nature of prime matter, see my *William Ockham*, ch.15, 653–69.

[53] Scotus, *Op. Ox.* II, d.16, q.u, nn.5–7 (Wad VI.2.762–3).

[54] Scotus, *Op. Ox.* II, d.16, q.u, n.7 (Wad VI.2.763). In using the phrase, "the second species of quality," Scotus alludes to chapter 14 of Book Delta of Aristotles *Metaphysics* (1020b13–18), which (in Latin and English translations) offers philosophical definitions of "quality." Aristotle offers a quadripartite and a bipartite array of definitions; but in both of them the second species consists of affections of things that are moved or change, as such, and the differentiating properties of motions and changes.

principle (viz., the substantial form) by means of which living things are alive. The soul is also a functional principle (*principium operationis*) and as such is reduced to the genus of efficient cause. The facts that throughout its existence the composite is always in first act (i.e., always is an intelligent substance), and that the soul is *an* immediate efficient cause of its being in second act (e.g., actually understanding) do not show that the soul is always in second act (always actually understanding). As Scotus explains elsewhere, the soul is a partial cause and the object is also a partial cause of actual understanding.[55] In any event, God alone acts or can act independently of everything else; everything else depends on Divine concurrence for its action.

4.1.3 Scotus' Third Argument against Aquinas

Against arguments mounted by Aquinas and others based on Aquinas's principle,

[P2]   No formal functional principle can be the immediate principle of more than one kind of act,

Scotus flatly denies it. If the same simple thing could not be an immediate active functional principle of specifically different effects, then the intellectual soul would not be able to emanate specifically distinct soul-powers (e.g., memory, intellect, and will) the way Aquinas says it can. Neither would the essence of fire be the immediate principle of emanating its proper accidents, heat and lightness.

Suppose Aquinas and Giles appeal to the Ordered Multiplicity Principle

[P3]   many can proceed from one only according to a certain order,

to rationalize saying that only the first proceeds immediately and the others mediately (see section 2.2 above). Scotus switches our attention to passive formal principles. Even if [P3] applied to active functional principles so that active production would be sequential, that doesn't mean that the second would be received into the first, and the third into the second as into a receiving subject. No matter what the order in which fire emanated its proper accidents, heat and lightness, neither would exist in the other as in a subject: heat would not exist in lightness, and lightness would not exist in

---

[55] Scotus, *Op. Ox.* II, d.16, q.u, n.5 (Wad VI.2.762).

heat. Even if understanding were received before willing, both would exist immediately in the intellectual soul as in a subject. [P2] and [P3] are not true where formal passive principles are concerned.[56]

Scotus likewise rejects Giles' argument based on [P6] the Gradual Differentiation Principle that non-permanent or variable accidents pertain to the soul only by means of permanent accidents. Scotus protests that—on Giles' view—there is no difference between the soul and soul-powers when it comes to permanence. If permanence is a barrier to the immediate inherence of non-permanent accidents in the soul, why would it not be an obstacle to their immediate inherence in permanent soul-powers? Giles would, of course, reply that the problem is not merely that the soul is permanent while the soul's functional acts are not. The problem—by [P6]—is that the difference between permanent substance and non-permanent accident is not gradual. Hence, it is necessary to posit something—viz., a permanent accident—in between. The bottom line is that Scotus sees no good philosophical reason to accept [P6] and the picture of cosmic recapitulation on which it rests.[57]

4.1.4 Scotus' Fourth Argument against Aquinas

Scotus rejects Aquinas' proportionality argument as resting on a false premise: "*potentia* is to *operari* as essence is to *esse*." Scotus rejects Aquinas' idea that creatable essences are to *esse* as potency is to acts that it limits, with the result that a creatable essence and its *esse* are somehow really distinct. Unlike Aquinas, Scotus takes separability to be a criterion of real distinction: i.e., X and Y are really distinct only if it is logically possible for X to exist without Y and/or logically possible for Y to exist without X. But it makes no sense to suppose that human nature exists without its actual existence or that human nature's actual existence exists without human nature. Thus, on Scotus' view, a created essence and its *esse* are really the same, while its *potentia* and its *operari* are not really the same. Rather, created functional acts are producible by and so really distinct from their functional powers.[58]

Scotus' overall verdict is that the philosophical arguments mounted by Aquinas and Giles are not compelling, because their act/potency metaphysics and their cosmic-recapitulation model of the structure of created substances are not compelling.

---

[56] Scotus, *Op. Ox.* II, d.16, q.u, n.9 (Wad VI.2.763).
[57] Scotus, *Op. Ox.* II, d.16, q.u, nn.4, 10 (Wad VI.2.761–3).
[58] Scotus, *Op. Ox.* II, d.16, q.u, n.10 (Wad VI.2.763).

4.2 Scotus contra Henry of Ghent

Henry of Ghent drew on his metaphysics of powers and real relations to defend the thesis that soul-powers are really the same as the essence of the soul, but distinguished from one another by real relations. Powers are essentially relatives because they essentially involve an order to an object or act. The soul is essentially absolute and so not essentially relative and not essentially a power. Rather the soul *qua* relevantly related to an object or act is a power. The same absolute thing can be the foundation of many respects to many different objects. Thus, many soul-powers (e.g., intellect and will) will be really the same as the soul but intentionally distinct from it. Moreover, the many soul-powers will be distinguished by distinct real relations.[59]

Scotus grants that Henry's account would, if true, be theologically advantageous. For it would make it easy to find an image of the Trinity in the intellectual soul. Just as in the Godhead there is one essence and the three persons are distinguished by three real relations; so in the intellectual soul there would be one soul-essence and three soul-powers (memory, intellect, and will) distinguished by three real relations.[60] Unfortunately, Scotus contends, Henry's account is not true, because both his metaphysics of power and his theory of relations are mistaken.

First of all, Scotus challenges, respects do not turn an essence into a power. True, one can use the word "*potentia*" to signify a respect to an act or object. But what is at stake metaphysically is the location of the formal functional principles, both active and passive. Scotus merely follows Aristotle, when he insists that

[P7] formal functional principles do not reside in relations or respects themselves, but rather in their absolute foundations.

The question under discussion has been whether the proximate foundation of those respects is the soul-essence or some other absolute things really distinct from it.

Nor will it do for Henry to reply that the formal functional principles do not reside in the respects alone or in their foundations alone, but in the foundation under the respect to an act or object. Scotus insists that a formal

---

[59] See section 3.1 above. See also Scotus' summary in *Op. Ox.* II, d.16, q.u, n.12 (Wad VI.2.768).
[60] Scotus, *Op. Ox.* II, d.16, q.u, n.13 (Wad VI.2.768).

functional principle is one *per se*. But the absolute foundation and the respect would be in different Aristotelian categories. If X and Y are in distinct Aristotelian categories, X and Y cannot unite to form something one *per se*.[61]

Moreover, Scotus argues, Henry's analysis of powers gets the natural priorities backwards. For the power or *per se* functional principle is naturally prior to its functional acts. Powers can exist unexercised, when no functional acts exist. On Henry's view, however, an absolute thing counts as a power only when it comes to be relevantly related to a determinate act or object. And a real relation of something can neither exist nor be understood without the other term of the relation, which in this case is the functional act. Thus, on Henry's view, powers or functional principles would depend for their existence on the existence of functional acts and so would not be naturally prior to them.[62]

Again, Henry stresses that to be a power, the absolute thing must be rendered *determinate* by a relation to a *determinate* object or act. But that means there will be a distinct relation for each functional act, and so there will be a distinct power for each functional act—e.g., not a single power to understand, but one power to understand human nature and a numerically distinct power to understand bovine nature.[63]

Again, Henry defends the claim that the will is nobler than the intellect. Yet, on Henry's understanding, real respects or relations are really the same as their foundation and only intentionally distinct from it. If intellect and will are alike really the same as the soul, and if real relations to acts of understanding and willing are not really distinct from the soul, how can one power be nobler than the other?[64]

4.3 A Philosophically Defensible Opinion

So far, Scotus has considered both Aquinas' and Giles' thesis that

[T1] soul-powers as *propria* of the soul are really distinct from the essence of the soul and flow from it by natural necessity,

---

[61] Scotus, *Op. Ox.* II, d.16, q.u, n.13 (Wad VI.2.768).
[62] Scotus, *Op. Ox.* II, d.16, q.u, n.13 (Wad VI.2.768).
[63] Scotus, *Op. Ox.* II, d.16, q.u, n.14 (Wad VI.2.769).
[64] Scotus, *Op. Ox.* II, d.16, q.u, n.13 (Wad VI.2.768–9).

and Henry of Ghent's counter-thesis that

[T2] soul-powers are really the same as the essence of the soul but distinguished from one another by real relations.

He does not take himself to have disproved the theses [T1] and [T2] themselves, but rather to have shown that the philosophical cases made for them are not compelling, because they rest on confused and/or contentious philosophical assumptions. At this juncture, Scotus forwards the alternative thesis that

[T3] intellect and will are not really distinct from one another and not really distinct from the essence of the soul

as philosophically more defensible. Scotus does not think he can demonstrate the truth of [T3], but he defends it with an array of philosophical arguments or "persuasions."

[Argument 1] First, Scotus offers a razor argument. Economy is a good-making feature of a theory. Plurality should not be posited without necessity. But it is not necessary for the powers to be absolute or relative accidents in the soul. Neither is it necessary for the powers to be essential or integral parts of the soul. Therefore, one should not posit that soul-powers are absolute or relative accidents really distinct from the soul-essence and/or one another.[65]

[Argument 2] Again, Scotus maintains, order to an end is nobler to the extent that it is more immediate. The soul-essence is ordered to an end. Therefore, the more immediately the essence attains that end, the nobler the order. But the soul-essence attains its end more immediately if it functions and acts from itself immediately and not by means of accidents that are really distinct from it.[66]

[Argument 3] Again, on the hypothesis that the powers are really distinct from the soul, the powers would be the proximate subject of the soul's functional acts. Aquinas and Giles agree and maintain that—although the remote subject—substance is always the *per se* and principal subject of its functional acts. Scotus contends, on the contrary, that acts belong *per se* to their proximate subjects of inherence, and to their remote subjects only *per*

---

[65] Scotus, *Op. Ox.* II, d.16, q.u (Wad VI.2.770).
[66] Scotus, *Op. Ox.* II, d.16, q.u, n.15 (Wad VI.2.770).

accidens. Thus, if soul-powers were really distinct from the soul-essence, acts of beatific vision and enjoyment would belong to intellect and will *per se* and to the soul-essence only *per accidens*.[67]

[Argument 4] Again, all agree that activity is a measure of nobility. Otherwise, it would not pertain to God to function immediately through the Divine essence. But an act or form less excellent than the soul's essence can be an immediate principle of activity: e.g., heat and other active qualities. A *fortiori* the soul-essence ought to be capable of functioning immediately.[68]

[Argument 5]   All agree to the Causal Nobility Principle that
[P8]   the cause must be as noble or nobler than its effect.

Aquinas and Giles conclude that qualities alone cannot generate a substance. But they also maintain that a substance acts only through its qualities. They try to accommodate [P8] with the claim that substance is the first but not the proximate principle of generation. Scotus counters with an alternative formulation:

[P8*]   the *immediate* cause must be as noble or nobler than its effect.

Scotus concludes that accidents cannot be immediate principles in the generation of substance. Where the generation of plants and animals is concerned, the substantial form must be an immediate cause. Where the human intellectual soul is concerned (which is not naturally producible), Divine agency is the immediate cause.[69] To Aquinas' and Giles' reply that the proper accidents of a substance are instruments of the substance in producing its effects, Scotus counters with an alternative understanding of instrumental cause: "You say that an accidental form is not a principal agent, but an instrumental agent. But I say the opposite... For an instrumental cause does not move anything, without being moved. Therefore some immediate efficacy must be ascribed to a superior agent, that is, to a substance."[70] Principal agents must be *immediate* agents, and when immediate agents use an instrument they use the instrument to produce the effect. But Aquinas and Giles

---

[67] Scotus, *Op. Ox.* II, d.16, q.u (Wad VI.2.770).
[68] Scotus, *Op. Ox.* II, d.16, q.u, n.16 (Wad VI.2.770).
[69] Scotus, *Op. Ox.* II, d.16, q.u (Wad VI.2.770).
[70] Scotus, *Op. Ox.* II, d.16, q.u, n.16 (Wad VI.2.770).

see the accidents as disposing causes that do not reach the effect but qualify the subject in ways required for the effect to be produced.

From arguments [1] to [5] above, Scotus draws the conclusion, not that [T3] is true, but that it is philosophically coherent and defensible to hold that the essence of the soul is neither really distinct nor distinct in reason from its soul-powers, and that the soul-essence is an immediate principle of many actions prior to and independently of any real distinction of soul-powers either as parts or as accidents. Contrary to [P2], the Species Diversity Principle, it is not necessary that species-variety in real effects posits plurality in the cause, because plurality can proceed immediately from one unlimited thing.[71] Divine creation itself is a counter-example both to [P2], the Species Diversity Principle, and to [P6], the Gradual Differentiation Principle, because one simple Godhead is an immediate cause of each and every creature, in fact creatures of many different kinds.[72]

Nor—Scotus insists—would distinctions of reason help to explain how a plurality of effects can proceed from one simple thing. The reason is that a real production must be explained by a real functional principle. But distinctions of reasons are productions of the mind and as such have no bearing on real causal connections.[73]

4.4 Theological Revision

Medieval philosophical theology does not work with philosophical data alone. It seeks to integrate theological and philosophical desiderata into a coherent and defensible theory. Taken by themselves, Scotus thinks, philosophical considerations commend [T3]. But [T3] does not answer to theological tradition that finds the best image of the Trinity in the intellectual soul. To accommodate it, Scotus concludes that it is necessary to posit some distinction among the soul-powers. Scotus has argued that real distinction is philosophically spend-thrift, while distinction of reason is philosophically confused; so his proposal is unsurprising:

[T4] the soul-essence and its soul-powers are really the same but distinct formally.

---

[71] Scotus, *Op. Ox.* II, d.16, q.u, n.16 (Wad VI.2.770).
[72] Scotus, *Op. Ox.* II, d.16, q.u, n.16 (Wad VI.2.771).
[73] Scotus, *Op. Ox.* II, d.16, q.u, n.16 (Wad VI.2.771).

By contrast with distinctions of reason, formal distinctions exist independently of and prior to any activity of the intellect. Moreover, Scotus claims that while real sameness takes away separability, formal distinction preserves the natural priorities and posteriorities. Thus, even though the soul-essence is really the same as its soul-powers, nevertheless, the soul-essence (with its genus and differentia) is naturally prior to the soul-powers that are its *propria* (intellect and will). Thus, there is a natural sequence—

n1: the soul is of such and such a nature

n2: the soul is capable of functioning (is possessed of the soul-powers intellect and will)

n3: the soul actually functions (actually understands, actually wills)

—which rationalizes traditional language of powers flowing from the essence and being intermediaries between essence and act.[74] Although more of a stretch, one could accommodate Aristotle's talk of parts picked up by Bonaventure. One could say that soul-powers are quasi-partial because either contains the whole perfection of the soul.[75]

Having arrived at this analysis of natural priorities and posteriorities, Scotus uses it to resolve an issue that adherents of [T3] might find more difficult. Intellect and will are functional powers both in the human intellectual soul and in angels. If human intellect and will-power are really the same as the human intellectual soul, and angelic intellect and will-power are really the same as the angelic form, are human and angelic intellects and will-powers necessarily of a different species? Scotus denies it. Nature is naturally prior to functional powers. What in the first instance makes the archangel Gabriel really distinct from Socrates is not a difference in their functional powers, but that Gabriel's angelic nature is distinct in species from human nature of which the intellectual soul is the dominant substantial form. Any distinction in their functional powers is naturally consequent upon their natures, not the other way around.[76] Nevertheless, specific difference between natures does not entail that all of the functional principles consequent upon them will be distinct in species. Scotus' own view is that the formal principle of understanding in Gabriel is *not* specifically different from the formal principle of understanding in Socrates, any more than

---

[74] Scotus, *Op. Ox.* II, d.16, q.u, n.18 (Wad VI.2.773).
[75] Scotus, *Op. Ox.* II, d.16, q.u, n.19 (Wad VI.2.773).
[76] Scotus, *Op. Ox.* II, d.1, q.5, nn.4–5 (Wad VI.1.112).

visual power in a cow is specifically different from visual power in an eagle. Scotus thinks we will find this conclusion less startling if we remember that the *propria* of being (one, good, true) do not differ in species in a stone and a human being![77]

4.5 Sensory Powers

With Scotus, the sensory soul-powers get shorter shrift. Because there is one and only one soul-form in human beings, formal functional principles of vision, hearing, etc., perfect the intellectual soul. Moreover, *pace* Aquinas and Giles, they are really the same as the intellectual soul and not really distinct accidents consequent upon and inhering in it. But visual power is not to be identified with the soul's formal principle of vision taken by itself. Rather visual power is a conjunct of the soul's formal principle of vision and a corresponding perfection of a mixed body (of the eye) that suits it for their common function. Sensation pertains primarily to the whole body-soul conjunct, so that the immediate and proximate subject of sensations is neither the intellectual soul alone nor the sense organ alone, but the form of the whole composed of the two. Scotus concludes that the form of the whole is the sensory power, just as it is the immediate and proximate subject of sensory acts. This way, even though there is only one soul-form, and even though sensory soul-powers are not really distinct accidents inhering in the soul-form, sensory powers can be said to be really distinct from each other, insofar as different powers are partially constituted by perfections in sense organs that are really distinct from one another.[78]

5. Real Distinctions, Relocated by William Ockham

5.1 Overviewing the Strategies

Recall how Aristotelian method moves from function to formal functional principle within the functioner. Next comes a distinction between essential and non-essential functions, along with the observation that essential

---

[77] Scotus, *Op. Ox.* II, d.1, q.5, n.5 (Wad VI.1.112–13).
[78] Scotus, *Op. Ox.* IV, d.44, q.2, nn.5–6 (Wad X.129–30).

functions travel in packages. Substantial forms are posited as the root-explainers of why they travel together.

Aristotelian substances have many essential functions. Aquinas and Giles of Rome mount general metaphysical arguments [P2] that functions of different kinds require distinct formal functional principles, and that these must necessarily be housed in proper accidents that are really distinct from the soul-essence and from one another. Henry of Ghent forwards general metaphysical arguments that different kinds of soul-powers are grounded in the soul-essence with which they are really the same, but are really distinguished from one another by really distinct respects.

Scotus counters that from a philosophical point of view, there is no need to house the formal functional principles of understanding and willing in anything really distinct from the soul, and no need to house them in things really distinct from each other. Theological desiderata drive him to conclude that soul-powers are distinct formally from one another and from the essence, and that the essence is naturally prior to the functional principles.

Ockham follows Scotus' philosophical analysis where the intellectual soul and its soul-powers of intellect and will are concerned. Ockham maintains that "intellect" and "will" directly signify the same thing—viz., the intellectual soul—but they connote different functional acts—viz., acts of understanding and acts of willing respectively. Indeed, one can say that the will wills as much through the intellect as through the will, because "will" and "intellect" denominate the same thing: viz., the intellectual soul. Ockham's metaphysical bottom line is that intellect and will-power are not really distinct from the intellectual soul; there is no need to house the formal functional principles involved in understanding in anything really distinct from what houses the formal functional principles of willing.[79]

But what about vegetative and sensory functions? Ockham argues for the conclusion that the formal functional principles of sensory functions are to be metaphysically housed in something really distinct from what houses the formal functional principles of understanding and willing.

For Aquinas and Giles: unity of substantial forms is a given. Species-variety in the functional acts of a given individual or kind of substance leads them to posit a plurality of proper accidents emanated by the single soul-form and inherent in it.

Ockham argues for a plurality of substantial forms in living things—some soul-form and the form of corporeity—because the living body and

---

[79] Ockham, *Quaest. in II Sent.*, q.20 (*OTh* V.437–40).

the corpse are arguably the same.[80] Turning to vital functions themselves, Ockham sees no reason why vegetative and sensory principles could not be housed together,[81] but argues that intellectual and sensory principles cannot be. Against Aquinas and Giles, Ockham sees no reason to posit a real distinction between soul-essence and soul-powers. If some soul-powers must have really distinct housing from others, this will be in really distinct substantial forms!

5.2 Ockham's Case for Really Distinct Soul-Forms

Aquinas, Giles, and Henry of Ghent marshal their metaphysical resources and assert their conclusions with confidence. By contrast, Scotus warns that these issues cannot be settled with demonstrations. Ockham admits that conclusions in this subject-matter are difficult to prove, but advances five arguments for a real distinction between sensory and intellectual soul-forms. The first three take one premise from metaphysics and the other from ordinary experience of our appetitive acts.

5.2.1 Argument from Contrary Acts

[i] It is impossible that contraries exist in the same subject at once.

[ii] But pro- and con-appetitive acts with respect to the same object are contraries.

[iii] Therefore, if they exist simultaneously in the nature of things, they exist in different subjects.[82] ([i] and [ii])

[iv] Such acts *do* exist simultaneously in a human being.

[v] Therefore, the pro-act and the con-act will exist in different soul-forms as in a subject. ([iii] and [iv])

[i] is advanced as a self-evident first principle. [iv] is obvious from experience: e.g., when we have a strong desire for chocolate and at the same time will against eating it. Ockham concludes that the sensory soul-form in which the strong desire exists must be really distinct from the intellectual soul-form in which the will-act exists.

---

[80] Ockham, *Quaest. in II Sent.*, q.7 (*OTh* V.137); *Quodlibeta* II.11 (*OTh* IX.163–4).
[81] Ockham, *Quodlibeta* II, q.11 (*OTh* IX.164).
[82] Ockham, *Quodlibeta* II, q.10 (*OTh* IX.157).

The vulnerable point of the argument is [ii]. Ockham's contemporaries countered [ii] by appealing to Scotus' distinction between *formal* and *virtual* contraries. Formal contraries are formally incompatible, so that it is metaphysically impossible that they exist in the same subject simultaneously. But virtual contraries are not formally incompatible. Rather F and G are virtually incompatible if [a] F and G are formally compatible but [b] F is or includes a tendency to produce effect E and G is or includes a tendency to produce effect E*, where [c] E and E* are formally incompatible. Thus, the strong desire for chocolate inclines us to eat it, but the will-act against it inclines us not to eat it. Virtual contraries can exist in the same subject, even though formal contraries cannot.[83]

Ockham snaps back that if so, volition and nolition would also turn out to be virtual contraries, and there would be no way to prove appetitive acts to be contraries.[84] But Ockham regards the latter as a dialectical consideration and not an evident proof.

5.2.2 Argument from Duplicate Acts

[i]   The same subject cannot have two pro- (two con-)appetitive acts with respect to the same object at once.

[ii]   Humans frequently will (nill) what they have a strong desire for (revulsion towards).

[iii]   Therefore, in humans there are two subjects of appetitive acts.[85]

Ockham does not expand on [i], but Scotus explains that one pro-act (one con-act) at a time is "adequate" to the power (i.e., constitutes the full expression of the power for a given time). [ii] is obvious from experience: e.g., we sometimes desire to eat something because we like the taste of it, and also will to eat it because we believe it is good for our health.

5.2.3 Argument from Contrasting Functional Modes

[i]   Numerically the same form does not elicit one act of natural appetite and another act of a free appetite towards the same thing at the same time.

---

[83] Ockham, *Quodlibeta* II, q.10 (*OTh* IX.157).
[84] Ockham, *Quodlibeta* II, q.10 (*OTh* IX.157).
[85] Ockham, *Quodlibeta* II, q.10 (*OTh* IX.158).

[ii] Humans often have a free volition and a strong natural sensory appetite for the same thing at the same time.

[iii] Therefore, the same thing cannot be simultaneously the subject of both the natural act and the free act.[86]

Notice: [i] does not make the strong claim that no single functional principle can explain both *natural* acts and *free* acts. Ockham thinks that the same Divine will-power explains the natural will-act to produce the Holy Spirit and the free will-act to create the world. The claim in [i] is more restricted: the same formal functional principle does not explain the production of both a natural will-act and a free will-act *regarding the same object at the same time*. Insofar as Scotus and Ockham think it is evident to experience that we will freely, they would find [ii] obvious: e.g., when we freely will to eat the chocolate we strongly desire.

Here below, substantial forms exist in prime matter as in a subject; accidental forms exist proximately or remotely in substances as in a subject. Ockham is fundamentally convinced of

[P9] for a form F to exist in something X as in a subject, there has to be a proper proportion between F and X,

and its corollary

[P10] an accident cannot be simpler than its proximate subject.[87]

These principles underwrite his next argument.

5.2.4 Argument from Proportional Inherence

[i] A sensation is simpler than a composite.

[ii] Therefore, a sensation does not exist in the composite as in a subject but in the soul alone.

[iii] Any act that is in the intellectual soul as in a subject is an act of understanding.

---

[86] Ockham, *Quodlibeta* II, q.10 (*OTh* IX.158).
[87] Ockham, *Quodlibeta* II, q.10 (*OTh* IX.158).

[iv] Therefore, if a sensation were in the intellectual soul it would be an act of understanding—which is absurd.

[v] Besides the intellectual soul there is a really distinct soul-form in which a sensation exists as in a subject.

Alternatively, Ockham draws conclusion [v] by means of an alternative premise:

[iv*] If sensation were in the intellectual soul, God could conserve sensations in separate souls and separate souls could sense.[88]

Aquinas and Giles would reject Ockham's inference of [ii] from [i]. On the contrary, they defend not-[ii] the claim that sensory powers exist in the composite as follows: Powers are that according to which power-havers do or suffer something. But the subject of the action is the subject of the power. Some functions are inorganic—i.e., functions that the body does not share—and so do exist in the soul as in a subject. Other functions are organic—i.e., completed only by means of a body. Hence they maintain, contrary to Ockham, that organic powers exist in the composite as in a subject.[89]

Scotus and Ockham maintain that the inherent form must be what it is and have whatever quantity it has (if any) prior to and independently of its inherence in its subject, so that a form can exist in a subject only if their quantities (if any) are relevantly proportionate. By contrast, Aquinas[90] and Giles hold that what is simple in itself can be rendered divisible by the inherent form (e.g., prime matter is indivisible in itself, but it is—they hold—rendered divisible by the inherence of quantity). Conversely, Aquinas and Giles locate sensory function and hence sensory powers in bodily organs. Oddly, even Scotus holds that sensations exist in sense organs as in a subject—contrary to [P10].

5.2.5 Argument from Different Kinds of Subjects

[i] Numerically the same form cannot be both extended and not extended, material and immaterial.

---

[88] Ockham, *Quodlibeta* II q. 10 (*OTh* IX.158–9). The motivating proposition [P10], and the premises [i], [ii], [iv], and [iv*] are all more or less explicit in the text, as is the conclusion [v]; premiss [iii] was left for the reader to supply.
[89] Ockham, *Quaest. in III Sent.*, q.4 (*OTh* VI.131).
[90] See Ockham, *Quaest. in III Sent.*, q.4 (*OTh* VI.133.)

[ii]   The sensory soul in humans is extended and material.

[iii]   The intellectual soul in humans is not extended but whole in the whole and whole in each part.

[iv]   Therefore, the human sensory soul and the human intellectual soul are really distinct. ([i], [ii], [iii])

Defending that conclusion [iv], Ockham argues that it is obvious that our faculties of sensuous desire and of intellectual judgment often disagree with each other about what we should want and what we should go for. In a *quodlibital* debating context, that evokes an appeal to the authority of St. Augustine condemning the idea of two souls in a human being. But Ockham squelches that by pointing out that what Augustine was condemning in the book referred to was the idea of two intellectual souls in one human being, of which one was from God and the other from the devil.[91]

5.3   The Real Distinction of Sensory Powers

It is one thing to argue that the subject of sensory functions is really distinct from the subject of intellectual functions. It is another to ask whether sensory powers are really distinct from their soul-form and/or from one another.

Having rejected Aquinas' contention that sensory soul-powers are really distinct accidents that flow from the soul-form, Ockham reconsiders whether there is any sense in which sensory soul-powers are really distinct from the soul-form. He distinguishes: "soul-power" can be taken either [i] for everything necessarily required for each vital act as a partial cause, or [ii] for the soul eliciting an act as a partial principle. Taken [i] the first way, vital acts involve many partial causes, including the dispositions in bodily organs, and dispositions needed for the sense of sight, for example, may be lost without impairment of the dispositions needed for hearing; and therefore some partial causes of vital acts will be really distinct from the soul. Taken [ii] the second way, the soul and its powers are not really distinct. One sensory soul, altogether without distinctions in itself, is the eliciting principle by which all sensory functions are elicited.[92]

Nevertheless, the latter thesis—that one sensory soul is the eliciting principle of all sensory functions—does not settle the question of whether

---

[91] Ockham, *Quodlibeta* II, q.10 (*OTh* IX.157–60).
[92] Ockham, *Quaest. in III Sent.*, q.4 (*OTh* VI.136).

the soul-powers are really distinct from one another. Reviving Aristotle's *De Anima* talk of soul-powers as parts, Ockham notes that the sensory soul-form is extended. It is—like the parts of the continuum—divisible into really distinct parts of the same kind that unite to make *per se* one sensory soul-form. (By contrast, two intellectual souls or two angels cannot unite to make *per se* one individual.[93]) The sensory soul-part that perfects the eye is the visual power; the sensory soul-part that perfects the ear, auditory power; etc. Thus, what makes one soul-power visual and the other auditory is not that they are different kinds of forms (or part-forms), but that they are located in different sense organs. The presence of the soul-power in the organ is not enough by itself to guarantee sensory function, however. The organs must also be properly disposed as they are not in the deaf and the blind.[94]

6. Adam Wodeham on Soul-Form(s) and Soul-Powers

6.1 Wodeham's Critique of Scotus

Ockham's *socius*[95] Adam Wodeham arrives at his own views about soul-form(s) and soul-powers by way of a critique of Scotus. Wodeham summarizes Scotus' position in four theses:

[T1] there is a single soul-form in living things;

[T2] it is not the case that soul-powers are really distinct either from one another or from the soul;

[T3] soul-powers are distinct realities of the same simple thing (viz., the soul-form);

[T4] what immediately receives sensations is not a soul-form but the composite of the soul-form and the vital organ.[96]

Behind [T2] and [T3] is Scotus' understanding of formal distinction: if X and Y are really the same but distinct formally, then X and Y are not

---

[93] Ockham, *Quaest. in III Sent.*, q.8 (*OTh* VI.246–7).
[94] Ockham, *Quaest. in III Sent.*, q.4 (*OTh* VI.138–9).
[95] A *socius* in this context was, as it were, a graduate student teaching assistant: a junior member of a religious order who was assigned to assist a somewhat more senior member who was giving a course of lectures. Wodeham had assisted Ockham in that capacity. That was some years before Wodeham gave the lectures cited here.
[96] Wodeham, *Lectura 2 in I Sent.* Prologue, q.1 (vol. I, p.11).

separable, but otherwise the order among them (e.g., of natural priority and posteriority) is preserved just as much as if they were really distinct. Wodeham maintains, on the contrary, that if two passive realities are separately changeable and perfectible, so that one can be perfected by what is naturally active without the other, they are not merely two formalities or realities, but two beings (*entia*) and two things (*res*). Intellect, memory, and will-power are soul-powers that include formal passive principles to receive their corresponding acts. But the intellect can actually receive an act of understanding without memory or will-power receiving any act. Wodeham concludes that [T3] entails not-[T2].

Wodeham adopts Ockham's argument against [T4]: no simple form is primarily received into what is essentially composite. But every sensation is a simple form. Therefore, every sensation is received immediately into a simple form.[97]

6.2 Unity of Soul-Form

Wodeham agrees with Scotus about [T1] that there is one and only one soul-form for each living substance. Where human beings are concerned, the single soul-form is the intellectual soul. Having accepted Ockham's argument against [T4], Wodeham bites the bullet to conclude that all sensations and for that matter all vital acts are received into and exist in the intellectual soul as in a subject.[98]

In reply to Ockham's Argument from Contrary Acts, Wodeham appeals to Scotus' distinction between formal and virtual contraries. The sensory pro-act (con-act) and the intellectual con-act (pro-act) are not formally incompatible but only virtually contrary (e.g., when the sensory appetite inclines to a pursuit that is incompatible with the act of will that efficaciously wills not to follow it).[99] To the objection that pursuit and flight in the appetite should be as contrary as assent and dissent in the power of judgment, Wodeham responds that there is a disanalogy because of differences in how such acts are caused. Acts of assent and dissent are both produced by natural causes. But in the case of the appetites, one is produced by a real change in a

---

[97] Wodeham, *Lectura 2 in I Sent.* Prologue, q.1 (vol. I, pp.12–13).
[98] Wodeham, *Lectura 2 in I Sent.* Prologue, q.1 (vol. I, pp.15–16).
[99] Wodeham, *Lectura 2 in I Sent.* Prologue, q.1 (vol. I, p.17).

corporeal organ, while the soul freely causes the other in itself.[100] Moreover, "pursuit" and "flight" signify not the appetites themselves, but their execution. The contrariety is in their executions and not in the soul-acts.[101]

For those who (like Ockham) are leery of such appeals to Scotus' distinction between formal and virtual contrariety, Wodeham offers an alternative response: that while the pro- and con-appetites seem *prima facie* to be contraries, they are not because their objects are not altogether the same. Simultaneous pro- and con-appetites arise because—unlike sense appetite—the will is guided (and/or misguided) by reason. Thus, sense appetite may desire an object and the will-act that precedes deliberation may will that object under the very same aspect as that under which sense desired it. But after deliberation the will-act wills against the object under the aspect of being contrary to right reason or displeasing to God or insofar as pursuing the object is incompatible with honor or deserving of punishment.[102]

6.3 Distinguishing Sensory from Intellectual Acts

For Aquinas, Giles, and Scotus, sensory and intellectual acts are distinguished by the fact that the former are acts of sense organs and so exist in the composite as in a subject, while the latter are acts that the body does not share and so exist in the intellectual soul as in a subject. But Wodeham accepts Ockham's Proportional Inherence Argument based on [P9] and [P10] and concludes that sensory acts are immediately received into the soul and exist in the soul as their proximate subject. At the same time, Wodeham agrees with Aquinas, Giles, and Scotus that [T1] there is a single soul-form in a human being. This makes it urgent for Wodeham to show cause why all soul-functions do not turn out—as Ockham charged—to be intellectual acts. Put otherwise, if—for Wodeham—a single soul-form is the proximate subject of all soul-acts, how does Wodeham distinguish sensory from intellectual acts?

Wodeham's criteria point primarily to intentional objects and causes.[103] Thus, [i] external sense is only of determinate singulars and has determinate singulars as a partial cause.[104] Likewise sensory imagination is of determinate

---

[100] Wodeham, *Lectura 2 in I Sent.* Prologue, q.1 (vol. I, pp.18, 20).
[101] Wodeham, *Lectura 2 in I Sent.* Prologue, q.1 (vol. I, p.18).
[102] Wodeham, *Lectura 2 in I Sent.* Prologue, q.1 (vol. I, pp.18–19).
[103] Wodeham, *Lectura 2 in I Sent.* Prologue, q.1 (vol. I, pp.21–2, 30).
[104] Wodeham, *Lectura 2 in I Sent.* Prologue, q.1 (vol. I, pp.21–2).

singulars. We can imagine only things of which we sensed or mix-matched parts (e.g., a golden mountain).[105] By contrast, [ii] the intentions in the intellect are no more of one sensible singular than another, but are common and universal in what they represent. Intellectual imagination is imagination that is not of a determinate singular.[106] Likewise, [iii] things that don't fall under sense (e.g., soul-acts and qualities themselves), whether universal or singular, are cognizable by the intellect alone.[107]

Subjects are denominated from the forms that are received into them. The objection arises, if [T1] the same indivisible principle in us immediately receives every sensation and every act of intellect and every vital act, then it will be true to say that sense receives universals and the intellect receives particulars, and that whatever is received into sense is likewise received into the intellect, and vice versa.

Wodeham grants the conclusion, but refuses to find it absurd. Rather, he takes a page from Ockham's semantics to explain that "the intellect senses" and "sense understands" are true but *per accidens*. They are *per accidens* because the soul is called "intellect" from an act of intellect and not from sensation; "sense" from an act of sense and not from an act of intellect. X may be denominated "Y-cause" from an act Y and "Z-cause" from an act Z. But "Y-cause is a cause of Z" is not *per se*; rather "Y-cause is a cause of Y" is. Thus, "the intellect understands" and "sense senses" and "the will wills" are somehow *per se*.[108]

Alternatively, Wodeham suggests that sensations can still be distinguished from the intellect and from one another by their receiving subjects. Despite his claim that all vital acts are *immediately* received into [T1] a single receiver, acts could be said to have different *mediate* receivers: viz., the corporeal organs by means of which they are received. Thus, acts of seeing would "determine themselves" to the eyes; acts of hearing to the ears; acts of understanding and sensory imagination, to the organ of sensory imagination. Wodeham suggests that differences in mediate receivers would make it false that whatever is received in sense is received in the intellect, and false that whatever is received into one sense is received into the others.[109]

Wodeham could be clearer about what it would mean to say that an act "determines itself" to an organ or that an organ "mediately" receives an act.

---

[105] Wodeham, *Lectura 2 in I Sent.* Prologue, q.1 (vol. I, pp.22–3).
[106] Wodeham, *Lectura 2 in I Sent.* Prologue, q.1 (vol. I, p.23).
[107] Wodeham, *Lectura 2 in I Sent.* Prologue, q.1 (vol. I, p.21).
[108] Wodeham, *Lectura 2 in I Sent.* Prologue, q.1 (vol. I, p.24).
[109] Wodeham, *Lectura 2 in I Sent.* Prologue, q.1 (vol. I, pp.24, 30).

He seems to be thinking that since the soul-form would be whole in the whole body and whole in each part, the acts that are immediately received into the soul-form are mediately received into the body in which the soul exists. Likewise, when he says that an act determines itself to the organ involved in causing it, Wodeham seems to mean at least that the act is *located* in that organ in particular and not in the others.

Wodeham considers the obvious objection. The single human soul-form is simple and unextended. If so, any act that exists in the soul as in its immediate subject would seem to be located wherever the soul is located. But the soul-form is whole in the whole and whole in each part of the body. It seems to follow that whatever acts exist in the soul as in an immediate subject, are located everywhere in the body, and not just in some determinate organ.[110] If a subject W were divisible into extended parts P1, P2, P3, and P4, then each part could be the immediate subject of different forms F1, F2, F3, and F4, and the subject-whole W could exist somewhere F4 doesn't exist because P1 is a part of W and exists in a different place than P4. But how could an indivisible subject be somewhere without taking all of the acts of which it is the immediate subject with it?

Wodeham declares that the major premise—that an indivisible immediate subject takes all of the acts of which it is an immediate subject with it wherever it goes—can be denied. Wodeham follows Scotus and Ockham in affirming a plurality of substantial forms in living composites: corporeity as well as soul. The soul perfects the body which is perfectible by it. Since the soul exists whole in the whole and whole in each part, the perfecting soul-form will exist somewhere that its perfectibles do not. For example, the soul that perfects the right hand will also exist in the left hand. But the right hand will not be in exactly the same place as the left hand. Wodeham seems to be suggesting that there will be no problem the other way around either: viz., if the perfectible exists somewhere the perfecting form does not exist. Soul-acts that exist immediately in the soul-form perfect it the way second act perfects first act. Wodeham invites us to find it unproblematic to conclude that soul-acts do not exist everywhere the soul exists.[111] Interestingly, Ockham also toys with this idea by way of interpreting Averroes: perhaps when the separate possible intellect "couples" with Socrates, not all of its acts of understanding are coupled with Socrates but only those for which

---

[110] Wodeham, *Lectura 2 in I Sent.* Prologue, q.1 (vol. I, p.24).
[111] Wodeham, *Lectura 2 in I Sent.* Prologue, q.1 (vol. I, pp.24–5).

Socrates has relevantly sorted phantasms. But even Ockham finds this notion very difficult indeed![112]

6.4 Disputed Cognitive Psychological Consequences

Ockham defends the conclusion that there are two soul-forms in human beings: a sensory soul-form and an intellectual soul-form (see section 5.2 above). When he turns to cognitive psychology, Ockham distinguishes simple acts of apprehension from complex acts of forming and assenting to (dissenting from) propositions, where the former are presupposed for the latter. No one can formulate the proposition "Socrates is white" without first having acts of simple apprehension of Socrates and his whiteness. Following consensus, Ockham agrees that human cognition begins with sense-experience of sensible objects, while formulating propositions and judging their truth-value are activities of the intellect. Ockham reasons that *sensory* apprehension of Socrates and his whiteness will not be enough to put the intellect in a position to do its work of proposition-formation and evaluation. The intellect itself must have a simple apprehension of Socrates and his whiteness. In general, Ockham posits that when the senses have an intuitive cognition of a sensible object, the intellect has an intuitive cognition of the same object under the same aspect at the same time.[113]

Wodeham explains that Ockham was driven to posit this "extra" intuitive cognition in the intellect, because he believed that there are two soul-forms. Ockham's underlying assumption was

[P11] the soul-form that is the immediate and proximate subject of proposition-formation and evaluation should also be an immediate proximate subject of relevant acts of simple apprehension.

Wodeham counts it an advantage of his own position that he is able—by affirming [T1] a single soul-form—to avoid this putative redundancy.[114]

Walter Chatton, a contemporary of Ockham and Wodeham, and a fellow Franciscan, rejects [P11]. He contends that even if there were two

---

[112] Ockham, *Quaest.*, q.6, a.vii (*OTh* VIII.238); cf. *Quodlibeta* I.12 (*OTh* IX.70).
[113] For a fuller discussion of Ockham's cognitive psychology, see my *William Ockham*, ch.13, pp.495–550.
[114] Wodeham, *Lectura 2 in I Sent.* Prologue, q.1 (vol. I, p.25).

soul-forms, the sensory intuitive cognition would still suffice, because the role of the sensory intuitive cognition is to be an efficient cause of the judgment. If an external object can be an efficient cause of an intuitive cognition in the sensory soul, why can't a sensory intuitive cognition be an efficient cause of an act of proposition-formation in the intellectual soul? True, Aristotelian causes must be proximate to the subjects on which they act. But even if the sensory soul were extended, whole in the whole and part in the parts of the human body, no proximity problems would arise, because the intellectual soul is whole in the whole and whole in each part of the body. Hence, the intellectual soul would be present in the organ of each sense where a sensory cognition is located.[115]

Wodeham agrees that proximity between causal agent and patient is not a problem. Ockham does hold that the sensory intuitive cognition is an efficient partial cause of the intellectual intuitive cognition of the same object under the same aspect. But—against Chatton—Wodeham reads Ockham aright: efficient causal connection is not all that was at stake. Ockham's intuition is that no subject can form a proposition from its terms unless that very subject itself has a simple apprehension of those terms. Your intuitive cognition of Socrates and his whiteness would not be enough for my intellect to form the proposition "Socrates is white." Intuitive cognitions of Socrates and his whiteness in my sensory soul wouldn't be enough either.[116]

---

[115] Wodeham, *Lectura 2 in I Sent.* Prologue, q.1 (vol. I, pp.25–6).
[116] Wodeham, *Lectura 2 in I Sent.* Prologue, q.1 (vol. I, pp.29–30).

4
Outsourcing the Subject
Whose Thought Is It?

By Marilyn McCord Adams and Cecilia Trifogli

1. Aristotelian Conundrums

Aristotelian research programs move from *function* to *ontology* (or metaphysical structure). More precisely, observed function demands an explanation, which is furnished by positing a theoretical entity: *the formal principle of the function* (the *ratio agendi* or the *ratio formalis operandi*), which gets identified as *the form*. Against Platonism, Aristotelian research programs insist that the formal principle that explains the activity must be *in, not separate from*, the subject of the activity. Analytical attention to the function exposes what characteristics a thing must have to be the subject of such functioning. Natural kinds are, or naturally give rise to ordered arrays of formal functional principles, so that every member of that kind by nature possesses a certain complex of active and passive causal powers.

In a perfectly good sense, Aristotelian philosophy is also common-sense philosophy. It begins with experience and common-sense interpretations of experience, which are treated as "givens" that any adequate theory must explain or explain away. Herein lies the rub. Common-sense beliefs often assign many functions to a single subject. Abstractly considered, the possibility thus arises: what if X were said to G and to K, and theoretical investigations revealed that being the subject of G-ing was incompatible with being the subject of K-ing and vice versa?

This is precisely the predicament in which 13th- and 14th-century Aristotelians found themselves in their efforts to produce a coherent account of human nature and psychology. They begin with an alleged datum of experience:

[Exp Datum 1]   every adult human being experiences that s/he her/himself both [a] senses and [b] understands,

which was already philosophically enshrined in Aristotle's definition of human nature:

[Phil Datum 1]   human being is rational animal.

[Exp Datum 1] seemed and still seems *prima facie* unassailable. Given the gravity of Aristotle's corpus in their philosophical canon, [Phil Datum 1] enjoyed presumptive weight. Functional analysis is, or quite quickly becomes theory-laden. Aristotelian reasoning told them that the subject of sensation had to be or involve an organic body, while interpretations of Aristotelian cognitive psychology passed down through the Arab commentators implied that the subject of understanding had to be immaterial. Sensing occurs. An animal is sensing. Philosophizing happens. There must be something or someone that is engaging in abstract thought. But whose thought is it? How is it metaphysically possible for the subject of sensing and the subject of abstract thinking to be the same?[1]

Some 13th- and 14th-century Aristotelians grappled with this problem in the context of their engagement with Averroes (Ibn-Rushd), "the Commentator" whose 12th-century interpretations of Aristotle had also become part of their philosophical canon. Averroes' contended that there was one and only one ("possible" or "material") intellect or intellectual substance for the human race, which all of us had to share, as it was the only possible home for human intelligence—though no mere individual human could share all the knowledge that was in the human intellect.

Thomas Aquinas, Guido Terreni, Thomas Wylton, and William Ockham stretched their theoretical imaginations in different directions to answer the question, how and why Averroes could or could not be right.

In the middle ages, authorities had wax noses. That is, canonized texts and tags could be twisted to mean what those who appealed to them regarded as true or plausible. Our authors do not read Averroes the same way. Our focus here is not on the "real" Averroes, but on what our authors

---

[1] This Aristotelian problem is not the Cartesian puzzle about how to unite *res cogitans* to *res extensa*, but rather a cousin of it. Both worry about the union of mind to body. The difference lies in their conceptions of body. Descartes' *res extensa* is lifeless and merely mechanical. Aristotelian interest is in animal bodies—bodies that are not only extended, but animated; bodies that essentially include the formal principles of vital and sensory functions.

made of him and the resultant contributions to the conceptual map of our problem.

2. Aquinas and Aquinas' Averroes on Intellectual Functioning

2.1 In-formation

Aquinas' argument in *Summa Theologica* I, q.75, a.2 turns on an analysis of cognitive function that he finds in Aristotle and in the Arab commentators (Averroes included), according to which

[P1]   form is that by which things are cognized, and
[P2]   cognition involves the reception of the form into the cognitive power.

From an Aristotelian point of view, [P1] seems reasonable, because Aristotelian science aims at the natures of things, and the forms in a thing are that through which the thing has its being and through which it functions. If only being is knowable, the form of a thing should be that through which the thing is knowable as well.

[P2] asserts that cognition literally involves in-formation. Thus, in *Summa Theologica* I, q.14, a.1 c, Aquinas declares that knowers differ from non-knowers in this: that knowers not only have their own form but are able to have the forms of other things ("alien forms"). In his discussion of angelic knowledge in the *Summa Contra Gentiles*, Aquinas explains that—where the natures of material things (e.g., stones and oak trees and cows) are concerned—the forms (e.g., the form of bovinity) can be received into subjects of two kinds: into individual matter to produce really extant individual material things (e.g., Beulah the cow, Ferdinand the bull), and into the intellect to make possible a thought of the nature (e.g., of what it is to be a cow). Likewise, the accidental form of redness may exist in the wall to make the wall really red, and the accidental form of redness may be transmitted through the medium to the living eye with the result that its possessor *sees* red.[2] Aquinas often speaks as if it is the same form (at least specifically the same) that exists in the matter and in the cognitive powers.

---

[2] See Aquinas, *Summa Contra Gentiles* II.50.

What makes the difference is the nature of the subjects: in the one case a cognitive power, and in the other case individual matter.

2.2 Immaterial Subject

To this general cognitive psychological analysis, Aquinas' Averroes adds then common-place philosophical assumptions that

[P3] it is a/the function of the intellect to cognize universals,[3]

[P4] forms in matter are only potentially intelligible and become actually intelligible only when they are abstracted from matter,[4] and

[P5] what is received is received after the manner of the receiver.[5]

On the basis of these, Aquinas' Averroes reasons that

[C1] the subject of understanding is immaterial.

For if the understanding into which the form is received were a matter-form composite, then the form would be received into individual matter so that—by [P4]—it would not be actually intelligible[6] and—by [P5]—it would be individuated and so no longer universal—contrary to [P3].[7]

2.2.1 Not the Form of a Material Subject
Aquinas' Averroes goes further to defend a second conclusion that

[C2] the subject of understanding must not be the form of some matter.

He reasons that

[P6] if the form that is the functional principle of A-ing exists in some matter, then the form is not itself the subject of A-ing; rather the matter-form composite is the subject of A-ing[8]

---

[3] Aquinas, *Summa Contra Gentiles* II.59 [2].
[4] Aquinas, *Summa Contra Gentiles* II.50 [2].
[5] Aquinas, *Summa Contra Gentiles* II.50 [5]; II.51 [3 and 4].
[6] Aquinas, *Summa Contra Gentiles* II.50 [2].
[7] Aquinas, *Summa Contra Gentiles* II.50 [5], II.59 [2].
[8] Aquinas, *Summa Contra Gentiles* II.50 [3] and [5].

—which is a principle that purports to draw out the implications of Aristotle's *Categories*-doctrine that,

[C3]   properly speaking, only primary substances (or supposits) act.

Properly speaking, it is not the formal functional principle that does the acting. Rather the proper subject of functional activity is the primary substance in which the formal functional principle exists. Consequently, being the form of some matter would make the subject of understanding just as material as if the intellect were itself a matter-form composite.

Aquinas' Averroes concludes that the subject of understanding must be immaterial, incorporeal, "separate" in the sense of not being the form of any matter, and subsistent in the sense of not depending for its existence on existing in anything else. But—Aquinas and Aquinas' Averroes agree—forms are numerically distinguished and multiplied within a species by inhering in numerically distinct hunks of matter.[9] If the human intellect is neither partly constituted by matter nor the form of some matter, it follows that'

[C4]   the human intellect is one and numerically unmultipliable.

For Aquinas' Averroes, [C4] also follows from [P3] and [P5]. For if the intellectual soul were numerically multiplied (say in Socrates, Plato, and Aristotle), then—by [P5]—the intelligible species would be numerically multiplied in the three intellectual souls and so would be individual and not universal—contrary to [P3].[10]

2.3 Merely Functional Union

So far, Aquinas' Averroes seems committed to the idea that a single separate immaterial substance is or houses the formal principle of understanding and so is the proper and proximate subject of understanding. How, then, can abstract thoughts in any way pertain to individual human beings here below? Aquinas' Averroes finds his answer in some further claims of

---

[9] Aquinas, *De Ente et Essentia*, c.2; Roland-Gosselin ed., 11–12; *Summa Theologica* I, q.75, article (henceforward, a.)7 c, I, q.76, a.6, ad.2um, III, q.77, a.2 c.
[10] Aquinas, *Summa Theologica* I, q.76, a.1, arg.3.

Aristotelian cognitive psychology. Of itself, the "possible" (or what Averroes refers to as the "material") intellect does not actually understand anything. Its potential for understanding gets actualized when the agent intellect (the separate intellect next higher up the scale of metaphysical eminence) illumines phantasms relevantly sorted by an individual human's imagination, with the result that an intelligible species is abstracted from them, and impressed upon the possible intellect. When this happens, Aquinas' Averroes contends, *numerically the same species* exists in two subjects at once—in the possible intellect and in the individual human's imagination, so that the shared species serves as a link that "couples" the two subjects. Because the same form, whose inherence in the possible intellect brings on its act of understanding, also exists in the individual human's imagination, the individual human is also said to understand. For example, Socrates can be said to understand what it is to be a cow, when his relevantly sorted cow phantasms are the ones from which the intelligible species of bovinity is abstracted; Plato can be said to understand what it is to be an oak tree, when it is his phantasms from which the intelligible species of oak tree is abstracted; etc.[11] Thus, Aquinas' Averroes sees such functional union as licensing the attribution of acts primarily and properly belonging to one linked substance to the other linked substance.

2.4 Aquinas' Critique of Merely Functional Union

Aquinas is convinced this approach will never do. First, same-species coupling can't be the answer because the species in the intellect and the species in the phantasms are not one and the same. Contradictories cannot be predicated of one and the same thing simultaneously. But the species in the intellect are actually intelligible while the species in the phantasms are not.[12]

Second, Aquinas cites Aristotle as saying that phantasms are related to the intellect the way color is to vision. But color is the object of vision. The fact that color in a wall propagates sensible species of itself to the eye doesn't turn the wall into a seer, but rather into the object seen. Phantasms or sense images function (in lieu of the actual object) to make the *object* present. If intelligible species are abstracted from them, that does not turn the phantasms or the imaginative power or the individual human being into a

---

[11] Aquinas, *Summa Contra Gentiles* II.59 [5–6]; *Summa Theologica* I, q.76, a.1 c.
[12] Aquinas, *Summa Contra Gentiles* II.59 [11].

subject of understanding, but rather an *object* of understanding.[13] Same-species coupling has it backwards: an individual human being is not joined to a cognitive power through its object; it is joined to an object through its cognitive power![14]

Third, even if the first two difficulties are left aside, Averroes' philosophical commitments seem to imply that—however far back in time you go—there has been no need for such couplings. The reason is that Averroes believes in the eternity of the world, the eternity of the separate agent and possible intellects, and the eternity of the human species. However far back in time you go, the possible intellect's potential to receive species would already have been fully actualized, so that no further abstractions from the phantasms would be needed. However far back in time you go, no couplings would occur and no abstract thoughts would be attributable to individual humans.[15]

2.5 Principal vs Instrumental Cause?

A seemingly more charitable construal would take Averroes to be identifying the single separate intellect as the principal agent, the individual humans with their relevantly sorted phantasms as instrumental causes of abstract thoughts. By Aquinas' own account, the formal principle of the principally intended action is in the principal agent, not the instruments. But while the action is going on, the instruments enjoy a temporary and transient participation in the causal power of the principal agent and its intended action. In many cases (where the instrument is not merely a disposing cause but "reaches" the principally intended effect), both the power and the resultant action can be attributed to them.[16]

Aquinas would reply that appearances deceive, first and foremost because—unlike locomotion or heating—understanding is an action that "remains inside" and does not pass on to external things. If the single separate intellect is the primary and proper subject of understanding, it cannot share that activity with really distinct things, no matter how many of them it uses as instruments.

---

[13] Aquinas, *Summa Contra Gentiles* II.59 [7–8]; *Summa Theologica*, I, q.76, a.1 c.
[14] Aquinas, *Summa Contra Gentiles* II.56 [9].
[15] Aquinas, *Summa Contra Gentiles* II.73 [36].
[16] Aquinas, *De Veritate* 27.4.c; *Summa Theologica* III, q.62, a.1 c and ad a.2um.

Second, what cognitive powers use as instruments are organs of cognition: vision uses the eyes as instruments of seeing, hearing the ears as instruments of hearing. If the possible intellect used relevantly sorted phantasms in human imaginations as instruments, they would be the organs of understanding. But understanding is an immaterial function. There are no organs of understanding, and understanding is not an organic activity.

Third, even leaving these aside, this proposal will not save the phenomenon that when Socrates and Plato both understand what it is to be a cow, there are two thinkers and two thoughts, two agents and two acts of understanding. For agents are numbered as the principal agents are numbered and actions are numbered as the instruments are numbered. One agent and many instruments make for many actions (one man touching with two hands yields two touchings); many agents and one instrument, one action (many sailors pulling one ship yield one pulling). One intellect and many individual humans with relevantly sorted phantasms of different things will yield one agent and many thoughts, where common sense posits many thinkers and many thoughts of different things. One intellect and many individual humans with relevantly sorted phantasms of the same sort will yield one intelligible species and one action, where common sense posits many thinkers and many thoughts of the same nature.[17]

2.6 Aquinas' Own Position

These reflections return Aquinas to the Aristotelian bottom line: nothing acts as principal agent through a formal principle that is external to it; rather the principal and proper agent acts through its own form. Moreover, where the function is essential to an agent, the form through which it acts is its substantial form or powers naturally consequent upon its substantial form. Aquinas is further convinced that common sense and philosophical givens—

[Exp Datum 2]   numerically distinct human beings are numerically distinct understanders and willers with numerically and often specifically distinct acts of understanding and willing

—require that each human being has its own substantial form. Aquinas thinks that this could be the case only if the substantial form of intellectual

[17] Aquinas, *Summa Theologica* I, q.76, a.2 c.

soul were numerically multiplied in numerically distinct individuals. But on Aquinas' theory of individuation, numerical multiplication of form within a species can occur only through a relation to matter. We are back where we started. How can the formal principal of understanding exist in and be the form of a material subject such as the animated human body?

From an Aristotelian point of view, Aquinas' explanation is nothing less than a startling piece of conceptual innovation. He begins by distinguishing between substantial forms and the powers consequent upon them. The intellectual soul is the substantial form of a human being, and—like other substantial forms of some matter—exists in matter unextended, whole in the whole and whole in each part.[18] The agent intellect and the possible intellect are powers that—like vital powers—are necessarily consequent upon it. Because vegetative and sensory powers are organic powers—e.g., digestive powers belong to the stomach and intestines, visual power to the eye—their corresponding functions are attributed to the relevantly empowered organ as to their proximate subject and—via [C3]—to the individual substance as their proper but remote subject. What Aquinas takes Aristotelian cognitive psychology to prove is that the power for abstract thought is inorganic; intellectual powers are not extended in matter any more than the intellectual soul itself is. In consequence, understanding is an activity of the soul alone, an activity that the body does not share.[19]

Thus, for Aquinas, [i] the intellectual soul is the formal principle by which prime matter is organized into a human body and flooded with vegetative and sensory powers. [ii] The intellectual soul is also the formal principle that emanates inorganic intellectual powers of understanding and willing. And [iii] the intellectual soul is also the proximate subject of intellectual functions. The fact that the intellectual soul is the form of some matter and the source of organic powers does not keep it from being the immaterial proximate subject of understanding in the way the visually empowered eye is a material proximate subject of vision. The fact that the intellectual soul is the form of some matter also allows it—contrary to [C4]—to be [iv] numerically multiplied in numerically distinct human beings.

Aquinas takes his points of divergence from Averroes (namely, [i] and [iv]) to allow him to say that the intellectual soul is the form of the body, numerically multiplied in numerically distinct human beings. But Aquinas

---

[18] Aquinas, *Summa Theologica* I, q.76, a.8 c.
[19] Aquinas, *Summa Theologica* I, q.75, a.2 c.

understands his point of agreement with Averroes (namely, [iii]) to put him in a position to endorse Averroes' conclusion that

[C5] the proximate subject of human understanding (for Aristotle, the "possible" intellect, for Averroes the "material" intellect; for Aquinas, also the intellectual soul) subsists.

Aquinas applies the principle

[P7] a thing has its being (*esse*) the same way as it has its functioning (*operari*),

to infer that if there is enough to something for it to function independently, there is enough to it to exist independently.[20]

Aquinas insists—*pace* Averroes' [P6]—that the mere fact that X might have other functions that are not independent (of which X is not alone the subject) but are shared with Y (in the sense that the X-Y composite is not only their remote but their proximate subject) does not keep X from existing *per se*. Thus, Aquinas wants to claim[21] that the intellectual soul is the form of the body, and that—because it is the only substantial form of humans[22]—it is the formal principle behind many composite functions (e.g., sensation, digestion) which it shares with corporeal organs (e.g., eyes, ears, stomach, intestines). But the human intellectual soul exists *per se* all the same, because intellectualizing is a function it engages in all by itself.

2.7 Insufficient Independence?

Yet, Aquinas' contemporaries did raise the challenge: how can Aquinas claim functional independence when his Aristotelian cognitive psychology makes human understanding dependent on abstraction from phantasms, which are modifications of corporeal organs and get sorted by the power of sensory imagination?[23] Doesn't Aristotle's method dictate that the subject of a function has to have built into it all of the powers necessary for that

---

[20] Aquinas, *Summa Theologica* I, q.72, a.1 c.
[21] Aquinas, *Summa Theologica* I, q.76, a.1 c.
[22] Aquinas, *Summa Theologica* I, q.76, a.4.
[23] Aquinas, *Summa Theologica* I, q.78, a.4 c, I, q.79, a.4 c.

function (that is, necessary for bringing it up to first actuality with respect to engaging in the function)?

In *Summa Theologica* I, q.75, a.2 ad3um, Aquinas warns us to distinguish different sorts of functional dependence. Sense images do for the human intellect what external bodies do for the senses: they make the object present. Vision is the power to see colors, but the eye has that power whether or not any colored objects are present and whether or not there is enough light in the medium to see. The eye has visual power-to-see-proximate-visibles-when-the-medium-is-appropriately-illumined, independently of whether or not the proper objects of vision are in fact present. Likewise, the human soul has power to understand whether or not its objects (the quiddities of material things) are made present through its access to appropriately sorted sense images. *The objects don't have to be built into the subject of the power for the subject to have the power!*

What is key for Aquinas is that the intellect alone (not the soul-body or form-matter composite) is the subject of the power-to-understand-when-objects-are-present. It alone is the subject of that power, and it has that power whether or not any objects are present. And it is the independent possession of that functional power (viz., power-to-understand-when-objects-are-present) that—Aquinas supposes—is sufficient for independent existence. In this, Aquinas and Aquinas' Averroes are in agreement.

3. Terreni's Turns

3.1 The Soul as the Form of the Body?

In his *Quodlibet* VI, q.6,[24] Guido Terreni declares that it should be easy for Aristotelians to prove that the rational soul is the form of the human body and the substantial form of human beings. Condensing Aristotelian method into two principles—

[P8] if an act/function A is properly attributed to a subject X, the formal principle of A-ing is properly attributed to X and the formal principle of A-ing is attributed to X insofar as it is the formal principle of A-ing;[25]

---

[24] See Nielsen and Trifogli, "Guido Terreni and His Debate with Thomas Wylton," which includes the edition of four of Terreni's *quodlibetal* questions: *Quodlibet* 2, q.13; 3, q.3, q.6; 6, q.6.
[25] Terreni, *Quodlibet* 6, q.6, sec. 2.9.4.2, p.659.

[P9] the principle of the proper function of a thing arises immediately from its proper *passio* or from an informing quality that arises from the proper principles of the species of the subject

—he simply adds that

[Exp Datum 1b] understanding is properly attributed to individual human beings such as Socrates,

and Aristotle's definition

[Def 1] the soul is and/or gives rise to the formal functional principle(s) within animals,

to conclude that power to understand exists in Socrates and that power to understand either *is* the soul or is a quality to which the soul immediately gives rise.

3.2 Christological Complications

What is important for present purposes is the way Terreni acknowledges and explores certain complications. Within Aristotle's own metaphysics, [C3] primary substances are the agents properly speaking. Within Medieval Latin interpretations of Aristotle, Aristotle thought (or would have thought had he considered the question) that primary substances (e.g., Socrates the human, Brownie the donkey, Beulah the cow) are really identical with individual substance natures (e.g., this humanity, that donkeyhood, that bovinity). If so, [P8] and [P9] would seem to imply that

[P8*] where X is an individual substance, the formal principles of X's functioning, are not to be found in an individual substance nature really distinct from X.

On this understanding, Averroes' mistake was to place the formal principle of understanding in a substance nature (the possible or "material" intellect) *really distinct* from Socrates.

Christology was, however, seen to complicate Aristotle's metaphysics with the claim that "alien suppositing" is possible. That is, for each and every primary substance, there is an individual substance nature that exists in it (or *is* it) and constitutes it as the very thing it is. But it is metaphysically possible that a primary substance also "assumes" or "supposits" an additional individual substance nature that is really distinct from it and which it could exist without. The alien supposit makes the assumed nature its own and functions through it as well as through the individual substance nature that constitutes it. Thus, the alien supposit functions through two power-packs: that of the nature it couldn't exist without, and that of the nature it has contingently assumed as its own.

Standard Christian belief has it that the Incarnation of God the Son is the only case in which this has actually happened. God the Son is essentially Divine and couldn't exist without being Divine. Divinity is a principle that (along with the personal property of Filiation) constitutes God the Son as the very individual supposit He is, and through Divinity God the Son exercises a variety of intra-Trinitarian and cosmic functions. But God the Son also assumes and thereby supposits an individual human nature. Even though God the Son did and still could exist without the individual substance nature, so long as God the Son does supposit the individual substance nature, He functions through it (e.g., walking and talking, eating and sleeping, besting rivals in Torah disputations, etc.). Ockham and other 14th-century philosophers speculate that it would be metaphysically possible (accomplishable by Divine power) for Socrates to become an alien supposit of bovine nature. In that case, Socrates would function both through human nature (the nature he can't exist without) to do philosophy and bovine nature (the nature he assumed) to moo and chew cud.

Thus, hypostatic union is a type of union that—contrary to [P8*]—allows an alien supposit to have functions (be the subject of actions) whose formal principles exist in an individual substance nature that is really distinct from it. In general, Terreni explains, hypostatic union licenses a *communicatio idiomatum* according to which "the properties of one nature in the concrete are predicated of the other nature."' "Divine essence," "Divinity," "Godhead," "humanity," "humankind," "human nature" are abstract terms; "God" and 'man"/"human being" are concrete terms. Hypostatic union does not mean—*pace* Luther[26]—that the predicates that belong to one nature can be

---

[26] Martin Luther, *That These Very Words of Christ, "This is my body"*, stand Firm against the Fanatics, in Luther, *LW* 37.95–96, 212–13; WA 26, 324. See Lienhard, *Luther: Witness of Jesus Christ*, esp. chs.4–5, 195–267; and Adams, "Eucharistic Real Presence: Some Scholastic Background to Luther's Debate with Zwingli."

predicated of the other in the abstract: e.g., "Divinity is mortal and passible" or "humanity is omnipotent" are false. This is because the abstract terms name the natures. But their corresponding concrete terms stand for supposits of those natures. Where alien suppositing has occurred, one individual supposit can be referred to by the concrete terms corresponding to both natures. Thus, predicates that pertain to one nature can be truly predicated of the concrete term that connotes the other nature: e.g., 'this man is impassible and the Creator' (that is, a supposit of human nature is impassible and the Creator when functioning through Its essential Divine nature), "this God was seen walking the earth," "God the Son suffered and died on the cross" (that is, one of the Divine supposits exercises these functions through Its human nature).[27]

3.3 Two Types of Action-Attributing Unions

Terreni's Christological detour makes clear that—contrary to [P8*]—there are two types of *metaphysical* union that license action-attribution:

[P8**]   X can be said to A, if the formal principle of A-ing is a form that exists in X, *or* if X is hypostatically united to something in which the formal principle of A-ing exists.

Forms are related to their subjects as potency-actualizers: the substantial form actualizes a potency in prime matter to be a metaphysical constituent of a human being; heat actualizes a potency in the fire for being hot. By contrast, in hypostatic union, the assumed nature does not actualize any potency in its alien supposit or in the nature that the alien supposit couldn't exist without. Humanity does not actualize any potency in God the Son, much less in Divinity. Bovinity would not actualize any potency in Socrates, much less in his humanity. In Aquinas' sometime accounts, the assumed nature merely shares the act of existence (*esse*) of the alien supposit, and so has *its* potency for existing actualized by the act of existing (*esse*) of the alien supposit. For Scotus, the alien supposit is merely the term of a non-efficient causal dependence relation which has its foundation in the nature assumed.[28]

---

[27] Terreni, *Quodlibet* VI, q.6, sec. 1.4.3.1, p.654.
[28] See Cross, *The Metaphysics of the Incarnation*, ch.5, 121–43; Adams, *Christ and Horrors*, ch.5, 108–43.

Bringing this "amplified" Aristotelian metaphysics to bear on debates about the soul, Terreni contends that

[P10] hypostatic union is the only kind of union in which the formal principle of an action properly belonging to a subject is to be found in an individual substance nature really distinct from the subject.

Thus, Socrates could be said to understand even though human beings are hylomorphic composites with top-of-the-line sensory souls and the formal principle of understanding exists in a really distinct "separate" substance or intelligence, only if they were hypostatically united, so that there was one supposit of both substance natures. Accordingly, Terreni concludes, *no matter how else they might be united, if Socrates and the separate intellect are two supposits, the properties of the separate intellect could not be predicated of Socrates.* Terreni takes it that Averroes regards the possible intellect and Socrates, not merely as really distinct, but as two supposits. That was Averroes' mistake.[29]

4. Wylton's Averroes

4.1 Functional Dependence, Revisited

Wylton's Averroes agrees: it would be a mistake to locate the human intellect and the human body in distinct supposits. To show why this is not his view, Wylton's Averroes returns to functional arguments. From the fact that intellectual activity involves understanding universals, he infers that [C4] the human intellect is universal, one, and numerically unmultipliable.[30]

[P5] What is received is received after the manner of the receiver.

Wylton's Averroes rejects Aquinas' contention that a species might be universal in representing but numerically multiplied in being.[31] Likewise, [C1] the human intellect must be immaterial and subsistent. The intellectual soul

---

[29] Terreni, *Quodlibet* VI, q.6, secs. 1.5 and 2.1 (pp.64–5).
[30] Wylton, *On the Intellectual Soul*, secs. 85–7 (pp.56 and 58), 90–4 (pp.58 and 60), 115 (p.70), 119 (p.72), 132–3 (pp.80 and 82), 136 (p.84). In sections 124 and 177–9, Wylton is particularly clear in identifying topics on which he holds by faith what he believes to be Christian views, but thinks as a philosopher that Averroes, "the Commentator," has stronger arguments.
[31] Wylton, *On the Intellectual Soul*, secs. 91 (pp.58 and 60), 187–8 (pp.112 and 114), 194–6 (pp.114 and 116).

is not a material form, educed from the potency of matter and extended in it.[32] It differs from forms immersed in matter in that it does not inhere in any subject in such a way that it could not exist without inhering in that subject.[33] Likewise, it is eternal, both ingenerable and incorruptible, insofar as no natural cause could make it come into being or cease to exist.[34]

Nevertheless, Wylton's Averroes denies—contrary to Aquinas—that the human intellect can exist separately from the human body. Aquinas and Wylton's Averroes agree that it is essential to human understanding (as opposed to that of higher-up intelligences) to understand by abstracting intelligible species from aptly sorted images.[35] Where Aquinas contends that the subjects of cognitive powers do not have to have their *objects* built into them (e.g., the colored wall and its species-propagating power do not have to exist in the same supposit as the seeing eye), Wylton's Averroes counters: the subject of a cognitive function must have built into its supposit all of the *cognitive* powers needed for that function. Where human understanding is concerned, that includes imagination. By [P8]–[P10], it follows that the human intellect must exist in the same supposit as the human body to which imaginative power belongs, and cannot exist separately from it.

4.2 The Intellectual Soul as Form of the Body

If we ask *how* the human intellect exists in the same supposit as the human body, Wylton's Averroes gives the standard Aristotelian answer: the human intellect is *the form* of the human body. Like Aquinas, Wylton's Averroes forwards a distinction between *inhering* and *subsisting* forms. Both inhering and subsisting substantial forms (e.g., bovine soul and the human intellectual soul, respectively) fulfil the Aristotelian functions of combining with their corresponding matter to make something one *per se* and of being that through which the composite is located in a determinate species. But—Wylton's Averroes maintains—while an inhering form informs the corresponding matter by inhering in it (by "being educed from and actualizing some potency in its matter"), a subsisting form informs the corresponding matter in virtue of its natural inclination or order to the corresponding

---

[32] Wylton, *On the Intellectual Soul*, secs. 88–9 (p.58), 116 (p.70), 141 (pp.88 and 90).
[33] Wylton, *On the Intellectual Soul*, sec. 124 (pp.74 and 76).
[34] Wylton, *On the Intellectual Soul*, sec. 112 (p.68).
[35] Wylton, *On the Intellectual Soul*, secs. 125 (pp.76 and 78), 136 (pp.84 and 86), 138 (pp.86 and 88).

matter and/or some sort of (functional) dependence upon it.[36] By contrast with higher-up intelligences, the human intellectual soul has a natural inclination toward the human body in the sense that it exercises its essential powers in functional collaboration with the human body's power of imagination. This means that—unlike higher-up subsistent intellects—the human intellect is not itself a species, but rather a principle (*principium*)—indeed the first formal and intrinsic perfection—of the species.[37] Yet, *how* can what is one and numerically unmultipliable be the form of the human body which is numerically multipliable and multiplied? Wylton is some sort of Aristotelian realist about common natures. He insists that what soul-forms perfect in the first instance is the natures themselves which they complete in the sense of making them to be natures of a determinate species. As Wylton's Averroes puts it, what the human (material, possible) intellect first perfects is the *species* humankind, which is one in itself and the quiddity of all human supposits.[38] Individual human beings or supposits such as Socrates are *secondary* perfectibles of the material intellect.[39] The material intellect is eternal, necessarily emanated (caused to exist) by higher intellects and only mediately by the first cause.[40] The human body is numerically multipliable by combination with distinct haecceities,[41] and the material intellect couples with each to make an individual human being that is one *per se* and in the genus of substance *per se*, and it couples more than one animate body at a time to make numerically distinct human beings.[42] There is only a *per accidens* efficient cause of the coupling between the material intellect and individual human bodies: viz., the efficient cause that brings the individual human body into being.[43]

How can the eternal human intellect be inseparable from the human with its imaginative power, when each and every human body is not only generable and corruptible, but acrually comes into being and passes away. Doesn't this mean that for each human body and imaginative power, the human intellect can exist without it?

---

[36] Wylton, *On the Intellectual Soul*, sec. 112 (p.68).
[37] Wylton, *On the Intellectual Soul*, secs. 85 (p.56), 120 (p.72).
[38] Wylton, *On the Intellectual Soul*, sec. 120 (p.72).
[39] Wylton, *On the Intellectual Soul*, sec. 133 (p.82).
[40] Wylton, *On the Intellectual Soul*, sec. 86 (p.56).
[41] Wylton, *On the Intellectual Soul*, sec. 122 (pp.72 and 74).
[42] Wylton, *On the Intellectual Soul*, sec. 136 (pp.84 and 86).
[43] Wylton, *On the Intellectual Soul*, sec. 134 (pp.82 and 84).

Wylton's Averroes replies to these questions that the primary perfectible of the human *soul* is the incomplete quiddity human nature; individual human *bodies* are merely secondary perfectibles.

The quiddity human nature does not come into being or pass away. On the contrary, Aristotle held that the species are eternal even though they exist, not as Platonic forms, but in individuals. The eternal human intellect can and does exist without Socrates' human body and without Plato's human body, but its essential function means that it cannot exist without any and every human body. There are, always have been, and always will be some extant human bodies or other, and—while they exist—the human intellect will function in collaboration with them.

What about the "eternity" problem? If the agent intellect, the material intellect, and the human species are all eternal, then, however far you go back in time, the human intellectual soul had a complete set of the intelligible species necessary for understanding the quiddities of material things, and so already had no need of phantasms from which to abstract them, and so already no need for the human intellect to be in the same suppositum as human bodies? However far back you go in time, the human intellect will have intelligible species corresponding to all of the quiddities of material things. We saw in section 2 that Aquinas noticed this.

Wylton's Averroes replies that human intellectual activity involves not only the intelligible species but relations to the phantasms. Intelligible species remain eternally the same, but the relations change, so that there are numerically distinct relations at different times.[44] This suggestion could be developed in two ways. What Wylton actually says is that the human intellect eternally needs phantasms from which to *abstract* intelligible species. Perhaps his idea is that although the intelligible species of bovinity abstracted from Abraham's phantasms could not be numerically distinct from the intelligible species of bovinity abstracted from Socrates' phantasms, nevertheless it has continually to be abstracted from some phantasms or other in order to conserve it in existence. Alternatively, Wylton's Averroes could recall the Aristotelian doctrine that the human intellect not only needs phantasms as the source from which intelligible species are abstracted; all human intellectualizing involves a "conversion" to the phantasms. Even if the human intellect is eternally supplied with intelligible species, it will always need sorted phantasms to which it can "convert" if actual thinking is

---

[44] Wylton, *On the Intellectual Soul*, sec. 57 (p.34).

to occur. It is on the basis of these relations to the phantasms that first Abraham and then Socrates are said to understand, and—because their sorted phantasms and the relations to them are numerically distinct—to have numerically distinct concepts or thoughts. Insofar as they sort different kinds of phantasms, they are said to have different thoughts.[45]

For Wylton's Averroes, functional dependence is what drives his conclusion that the human intellect is the form of the human body. Nevertheless, Wylton is keen to emphasize, his Averroes does not espouse merely functional union between the human intellect and individual human bodies. That would make the human bodies instruments and the connection as episodic as between my hand and the potato-slicing knife. The human intellectual soul is the form of the human body. The human body is its primary perfectible at the species level. Their essential connection is as eternal as they are, and maps down to any individual human beings (the secondary perfectibles) there may be. Thus, Abraham and Socrates were fully human from birth, before they reached the age of reason and were able to engage in abstract thought. Likewise, they are fully human even when—as adults—their minds idle. The nature of the function is what gives the human intellect its natural aptitude to be joined with the body. Actual functional collaboration is episodic. But the intellectual soul is the form of the individual human body (unites with it to make *per se* one substance) continually, between birth and the grave.[46]

5. A Fresh Look with Ockham

Aquinas' and Terreni's efforts to discredit Averroes' thesis—that there is one and only one human material/possible intellect for the whole human race—have charged that he cannot save the "givens" of action- and essential-power attribution. Ockham thinks it is necessary to distinguish.

5.1 Attribution-Securing Connections

There are three perfectly good relations that can couple Averroes' unitary intellect with human bodies (animated by vital and sensory powers) in such

---

[45] Wylton, *On the Intellectual Soul*, secs. 57–8 and 118–19 (pp.34, 70, and 72).
[46] Wylton, *On the Intellectual Soul*, secs. 131, 136, and 138 (pp.80, 84, 86, and 88).

a way as to guarantee that [Exp Datum 1b] Socrates understands and that [Phil Datum 1] the intellect is for humans an essential power. Ockham wonders, what obstacle would keep either of the two metaphysical relations—informing or hypostatic union—or even the coupling of mover-to-moved from being able to do that job?

[1] Not—according to Ockham—that *one-many metaphysical union* is impossible. Divine power can make one and the same, numerically unmultiplied form simultaneously to inform two discontinuous hunks of matter. Likewise, if it is metaphysically possible for one Divine person to be the alien supposit of an individual human nature, it is also metaphysically possible for all three Divine persons to be alien supposits of numerically the same individual human nature.[47] Whether the unitary intellect were united as substantial form or through hypostatic union, act- and essential-power attribution could be secured.

[2] Nor would the *real distinction* of Averroes' unitary intellect from the human bodies with which it unites be a barrier to act- and essential-power attribution. For Scotus and Ockham, normally and naturally, the matter and forms of hylomorphic composites are really distinct from one another.[48] But that does not keep them from having natural aptitudes to unite to make something one *per se*. Alien-assumed natures are always really distinct from their supposits. Being really distinct from human bodies would be no obstacle to Averroes' unitary intellect being joined to human bodies as their substantial form, or through hypostatic union, or as mover to moved.

[3] *Pace* Aquinas, the mover-to-moved hypothesis would also make Socrates an understander, so long as Socrates is identified with the whole—soul and body united by the former moving the latter—and not just with the body (animated by a sensory soul) which is a part.[49]

5.2 Accounting for the Differences

Where the metaphysical relations of informing or hypostatic union are concerned, Averroes' unity-of-the-intellect hypothesis falls short when it comes to explaining how different human individuals are the subjects of

---

[47] Ockham, *Quaest.*, q.6, a.vii (*OTh* VIII.239–40).
[48] Scotus, *Op. Ox.* II, d.12, q.1, n.11 (Wad VI.671). Ockham, *Quaest. in II Sent.*, q.20 (*OTh* V.429); *Quaest. in IV Sent.*, q.9 and q.13 (*OTh* VII.161 and 275). See also Adams, "What's Metaphysically Special about Supposits?"
[49] Ockham, *Quodlibeta* I, q.10 (*OTh* IX.63).

[Exp Datum 2] different and [Exp Datum 3] contrary intellectual acts. Ockham takes the principle

[P11] every absolute form that is the same as another form or denominates that form will equally denominate the subject of the form or anything to which the form is united.

Color denominates a substance, because it inheres in the surface of the substance (e.g., Socrates is white because whiteness inheres in his skin). If a single whiteness existed in three designated surfaces, each and all three would be denominated by it, because there would be no more reason why one should be denominated than another. Likewise, if a particular human nature were assumed by all three Divine persons (instead of by the Son alone), the properties that denominate the assumed nature would denominate each and all three supposits. Reasoning from [P11], Ockham continues

(ii) An act of understanding is an absolute form that either is the same as the intellect, or it informs the intellect as an accident does its subject.
(iii) Therefore, if the possible intellect is the same in all humans—whether through informing or through special union—if the act of intellect denominates the intellect in one, it will also denominate the intellect in them all.
(iv) Therefore, given [Exp Datum 2], the unity of the intellect will be impossible.[50]

To save [Exp Datum 2], what Averroes needs is some rationale for denying that [P11] is generally true.

As if to follow an intellectual Golden Rule, Ockham notes how Christian theology seems to counter [P11] when it insists that a substance may be present in places where its accidents are not present. For example, Christ's Body is extended in heaven but not on the altars where masses are said. Likewise, hypostatic union does not transfer the predicates from one nature to the other nature: Godhead is everywhere, but Christ's humanity is not thereby everywhere, although Christ (the supposit) is.[51] Perhaps Averroes could maintain that the possible intellect is united to Socrates who thereby understands what it is to be a cow and is simultaneously united to Plato who

---

[50] Ockham, *Quaest.*, q.6, a.vii (*OTh* VIII.238); see also *Quodlibeta* I, q.12 (*OTh* IX.70).
[51] Ockham, *Quaest.*, q.6, a.vii (*OTh* VIII.240).

does not, so that the possible intellect is somewhere (viz., united to Plato) where its act of understanding what it is to be a cow is not (viz., in Plato). Averroes could then appeal to efficient causality to explain why the *communicatio idiomatum* is selective: e.g., by claiming that both the intellect and the phantasm are partial efficient causes of the act of understanding, and hence that the act is present only in those human individuals in which that partial efficient cause is to be found.[52]

Having thus sought to present an Averroistic hypostatic union solution in its strongest form, Ockham points out two major disadvantages. First, Ockham thinks exceptions to [P11] where an accident and its subject are concerned would constitute "a maximal miracle": it is "scarcely intelligible that it could be done by God's power." It is theoretically disadvantageous to posit maximal miracles, much less invoke them to explain common everyday occurrences such as Socrates' and Plato's thinking different thoughts and making different choices.[53]

Second, even if the hypostatic union hypothesis found a way to save [Exp Datum 2], it would not allow Averroes to accomodate [Exp Datum 3] the fact that the cognitive and appetitive acts of one human individual are often contrary to those of another's at the same time. Ockham maintains that it is impossible for one and the same first subject to be both assenting to and dissenting from the same proposition, loving and hating the same, rejoicing and grieving over the same, etc. Yet, the possible intellect is the first subject of such acts. Hence, if there were only one possible intellect for the whole human race, it would be the first subject of contraries simultaneously—which is impossible.[54]

Nor, Ockham insists, can this argument be evaded by an appeal to different phantasms in different human individuals. For phantasms are at most *efficient* causes of intellectual acts. Phantasms are not *material* causes (i.e., first subjects) of intellectual acts. The fact that an intellectual substance bears different efficient causal relations to the same thing does not make it possible for it to be the *first* subject of contrary acts with respect to it. Nor can something other than the will be the first subject of acts of will. This last objection from contraries would also apply to Wylton's Averroes or to an

---

[52] Ockham, *Quaest.*, q.6, a.vii (*OTh* VIII.240).
[53] Ockham, *Quaest.*, q.6, a.vii (*OTh* VIII.241).
[54] Ockham, *Quodlibeta* I, q.11 (*OTh* IX.67).

Averroistic mover-to-moved theory. Ockham regards this not just as a plausible argument, but as fully demonstrative, an *evident* proof that the intellect cannot be one and the same, numerically unmultiplied, in each and all human beings.[55]

5.3 A Plurality of Souls

If—as the "catholic" position holds—intellectual souls are numerically multiplied as human individuals are multiplied, that still leaves the question of what their relation to individual human bodies would be. [1] Ockham thinks that while the mover-to-moved hypothesis cannot be refuted by an evident proof, it does suffer from explanatory superfluity. For what is supposed to join the intellect (which is the proximate subject of understanding and willing) to the human animal body is that the former explains some of the latter's motions. But the vital motions of human animal bodies are already explained the Aristotelian way: through formal functional (vegetative and sensory) principles that exist in them.[56] [2] Nor—according to Ockham—can natural reason take off the table the opinion of some Aristotelians, who think that the intellectual soul is a substantial form of the human body, but insist that it is a *material* form.[57] For them, the problem with which this chapter began does not arise. Their challenge would be to offer an alternative cognitive psychology that allows material acts to have immaterial or abstract contents, a suggestion which Scotus continues to find counter-intuitive.[58] [3] All who think human intellectual souls are numerically multiplied in numerically distinct human beings, will have to accept— *pace* Averroes and Wylton—some version of Aquinas' thesis that mental representations can be singular in being while universal in representing. Ockham is in any event committed to this idea, because he thinks that only singulars exist![59]

---

[55] Ockham, *Quodlibeta* I, q.11 (*OTh* IX.67–8).
[56] Ockham, *Quodlibeta* I, q.10 (*OTh* IX.64–5).
[57] Ockham, *Quodlibeta* I, q.10 (*OTh* IX.64).
[58] Scotus, *Op. Ox.* IV, d.43, q.2, nn.10–12 (Wad X.24–6).
[59] Ockham, *Ordinatio* I, d.2, q.8 (*OTh* II.290–1); *Quodlibeta* V, q.13 (*OTh* IX.532–4); *Summa Logicae* I, c.13 (*OPh* I.45–6).

6. Conclusions: Integrated "Anomalies" and the Great Chain of Being

The sense that human nature is mysterious is ancient and persistent. Hugh of St. Victor picks up on Augustine's asides, when he urges that Incarnation is no more remarkable than soul-body union. If God can unite such different substances as soul and body in a single suppost, why not Divinity and humanity?[60]

Our authors rise to the occasion by examining four candidate relations for uniting the human intellect to the human subject of sensation:

[1] functional union via phantasms;
[2] as mover to moved;
[3] as informing substantial form;
[4] via hypostatic union.

They examine three versions of the claim that [3] the human intellect is united to the human body as its substantial form. There is the view of some Aristotelians

[3a] that the intellectual soul is united to the human body as a material form that is educed from the potency of the matter, is numerically multiplied in numerically distinct bodies, and ceases to exist when the composite is dissolved.

Then there is what Wylton calls the "catholic" position

[3b] that the intellectual soul is united to the human body as an immaterial form that is functionally independent of the body in understanding and so subsistent and capable of existing without being united to a body to make something *per se* one, but numerically multiplied in numerically distinct particulars and created *ex nihilo* at the relevant stage of fetal development.[61]

Finally, there is the stand taken by Wylton's Averroes

---

[60] Hugh of St. Victor, *On the Sacraments of the Christian Faith (De Sacramentis)*, Bk.2, Pt One, ch.XI, pp. 246–9. Hugh may be thinking—contrary to later Aristotelians—that the soul itself is the suppost, and that the human body is a really distinct individual substance nature that gets hypostatically united to the soul-suppost.

[61] Wylton, *On the Intellectual Soul*, secs. 132–3 (pp.80 and 82).

[3c]   that the intellectual soul is united to the human body as an immaterial form that is functionally dependent on phantasms and so incapable of existing without being the substantial form of some human body or other, but is eternal and incapable of numerical multiplication.

Of these options, all but the [2] mover-to-moved and [3a] intellectual-soul-as-material-form hypotheses, posit (what are from an Aristotelian point of view) metaphysical innovations. Re [1] Aquinas' Averroes imagines numerically the same-species form existing in two subjects (one immaterial and the other material and extended) at once. Re [3c] Wylton's Averroes sees human nature as composed of one numerically unmultipliable and one numerically multipliable constituent, posits that one numerically unmultipliable soul combines to make one *per se* with numerically distinct and spatially distant human bodies, and holds that a form can be unable to exist without a human body, even though—for each human body—it can exist without that one. Re [3b] The so-called "catholic" view posits that the formal principle of understanding is also its proximate subject, that a subsistent intellect is also the form of some matter, and that some entities (human intellectual souls) are eternal into the future but not into the past. Moreover, the catholic view requires creation *ex nihilo* to account for what Aristotle would think ought to be naturally explicable (viz., the coming into existence of a complete individual human being). Both [3b] the catholic position and [3c] Wylton's Averroes hold that one and the same intellectual soul informs spatially distant hunks of matter simultaneously. For catholics say the intellectual soul is whole in the whole head and whole in the whole hand of a single human body, while Wylton's Averroes thinks the intellectual soul is simultaneously the form of numerically distinct whole human bodies located in different places. [4] Hypostatic union multiplies the big miracles required to get individual human beings who understand.

Certainly, proposals advanced [3b] by the catholics and [3c] by Wylton's Averroes go beyond the conceptual machinery developed to handle the merely immaterial and the merely material. That of [1] Aquinas' Averroes posits exceptions to the Aristotelian axiom that numerically the same form can't inhere in multiple discontinuous subjects at once, while [4] the hypostatic union theory violates the Aristotelian assumption that supposits can have only one nature.

Yet, metaphysical innovations are anomalies only if they lack systematic fit. Happily, our authors are able to domesticate such unusual features, because they stand heir to a cosmological theory that requires and predicts them: viz., the Great Chain of Being! The cosmos constitutes a Great Chain of Being and Goodness with Godhead at the top and other natures ordered under it in descending degrees of godlikeness. Moreover, the cosmos divides into two ordered realms: the more godlike immaterial substances and the less godlike material world. Hierarchical theory requires that for the two realms to constitute a *uni*verse, they be linked together by a "straddler" nature in which immaterial and material are joined.[62] It should be theoretically unsurprising, therefore, if the unity of human nature needs metaphysical apparatus not required to account for the unity of merely immaterial angelic natures or merely material natures such as oak tree or cow![63]

---

[62] Aquinas, *Summa Contra Gentiles* II.59 [1]; Wylton, *On the Intellectual Soul*, sec. 132 (pp.80 and 82).

[63] This chapter was first published in *Philosophy and Phenomenological Research*, Vol. LXXXV, No. 3 (November 2012), 624–47, under the title, "Whose Thought Is It? The Soul and Its Actions in Some Thirteenth and Fourteenth Century Philosophers." It has been reprinted here with minor revisions.

5
Outsourcing the Object: Divine Illumination I
Early Franciscans and Henry of Ghent

This begins a series of chapters about outsourcing the *object* rather than the *subject* of Divine illumination. In Chapter 4 we examined reasons that led Averroes to locate one or both in "separate" intelligences—that is, intelligences that are separate from matter in that they are neither matter-form composites nor the forms of any matter. By contrast, we saw how Aquinas and other Christian philosophers worked to save the phenomena: that individual human beings, such as Socrates not only sense but understand, are not only subjects with formal passive principles to receive but active causes with formal active principles that contribute to the production of acts of intellectual understanding of the quiddities of things.

Augustinian Platonism identified a different set of problems for human understanding—call them "Stability Problems." For—Augustinian Platonists contended—certain knowledge of the truth of things (i.e., of their quiddities) requires infallibility in the knowing subject and immutability in the known object. Divine power (whether cognitive or productive) is essentially infallible; the Divine essence is necessarily immutable. But among creatures here below, such natural stability is nowhere to be found. There is not enough to what they are essentially to make them infallible or immutable. To preserve the possibility of certain knowledge for humans, Augustinian Platonists draw on their metaphysical conviction that the same intelligible content can exist and be expressed at multiple ontological levels—most importantly for present purposes, in Divine exemplars, in reality in particulars, and in our intellects as the objects of our thoughts. To have certain knowledge of creatable quiddities, they insist, our minds must make contact with those objects where they exist immutably: in Divine exemplars. Because such transcendent objects exceed the reach of our purely natural powers, cognitive upgrades will be needed. Augustinian Platonists conclude: Divine illumination is required both for presenting the object and for empowering us as subjects to recognize it—if human beings are to have certain knowledge of the quiddities of creatable things.

Thirteenth-century advocates of Divine illumination had read their Aristotle and shared many commitments with their Inward-Principle/Same-Level Aristotelian opponents: that the object of knowledge properly speaking is immutable, that understanding creatable quiddities is an essential function of human beings, and that *ante-mortem* human understanding involves cognitive psychological processes that begin with the senses and involve abstraction from sense images. They also endorsed the methodological presumption that natural functions should not receive miraculous explanations such as those involved in prophetic inspiration or changing water into wine. They all acknowledged that many human beings have intellectual understanding, while experience and theological consensus insist that almost none sees God face-to-face or sees all things in God before death. In this chapter, we will examine three accounts of Divine illumination—those advanced by Bonaventure, Matthew of Aquasparta, and Henry of Ghent—to get a better feel for which explanatory gaps it is supposed to fill and how. Then in Chapter 6, turning to Duns Scotus' critique of Henry's position, we will try to sort out where those two are talking at cross-purposes and which are the root disagreements between them.

1. Bonaventure's *Viae Mediae*

1.1 Levels of Knowables and Knowledge

So far as soul-functions are concerned, Bonaventure's own interest is riveted on our ultimate end—to see God face-to-face and to enjoy God forever. Epistemologically, he is preoccupied with charting the developmental process, with outlining and implementing the *ante-mortem* pedagogy required to fit souls for eternal life. Nevertheless, Bonventure agrees that understanding creatable quiddities numbers among human natural functions. His account of how this is possible for us is premissed on an Augustinian-Platonist conviction that the truth of creatable quiddities exists at three levels of descending ontological perfection: in the eternal and immutable Divine ideas; in really extant particular things; and in concepts of created minds. Bonaventure emphasizes: the Divine ideas are the norms. A particular

F is more or less a true F insofar as it measures up to the Divine idea of F-ness, while our concept of F-ness is measured proximately by truth in really extant particular Fs and ultimately in the Divine idea of F-ness.[1]

Augustine distinguished *morning knowledge* in which the blessed will see the Divine essence and see all things in God in their eternal exemplars, from *evening knowledge* in which human beings know things and their quiddities insofar as they are found in really extant particulars. Bonaventure never tires of repeating: our end is union with God, and morning knowledge of creatable quiddities is the best knowledge of them for us to have. But experience shows that *ante-mortem* human beings do not—except for the human soul of Christ and perhaps a few saints—have direct knowledge of God[2] or the eternal reasons.[3] Likewise, experience shows that *ante-mortem* human beings don't see all things in God, but rather come to knowledge by a process starting from sense experience[4] and proceeding by abstraction.[5] Experience shows that *ante-mortem* human beings do not have free cognitive access to the eternal reasons.[6] In short, experience proves that (with a few exceptions) morning knowledge is not available to the vast majority of human beings *ante-mortem*. But are our natural powers sufficient for evening knowledge? Can we have certain knowledge of creatable quiddities through evening knowledge through our purely natural powers?

1.2 The Need for Divine Illumination

Bonaventure's short answer to these questions is "no."

1.2.1 [Argument 1] Stability Problems
These are front and center in his first argument:

[i] Certain knowledge requires [a] immutability in the object and [b] infallibility in the knower.

[ii] Just as not-[ia] created truth or created being is not immutable in itself, so not-[ib] created life is not infallible by its own power.

---

[1] Bonaventure, *DQX*, q.4, pro-arguments 3, 6, 7, 8, 18, 26 (pp.21–2).
[2] Bonaventure, *DQX*, q.4, con-arguments 1, 2, 5, 6 (p.17).
[3] Bonaventure, *DQX*, q.4, con-arguments 15, 16, 17 (pp.18–19).
[4] Bonaventure, *DQX*, q.4, con-argument 9 (p.18).
[5] Bonaventure, *DQX*, q.4, con-argument 12 (p.18).
[6] Bonaventure, *DQX*, q.4, con-argument 13 (p.18).

[iii] Therefore, certain knowledge requires a further light (beyond those that are natural to the created nature) to give [a] immutability to the object and [b] infallibility to the knower.

[iv] This light is the eternal reasons which are in God, who is eternal and immutable and infallible.[7]

Bonaventure is explicit: the problem is two-sided. Creatures are not stable enough to be objects of certain knowledge, and they are not stable enough to be subjects of certain knowledge either. Divine ideas are the essentially stable objects. But—Bonaventure observes—the mere presence of Divine ideas (eternal reasons) will not be enough for human beings to have certain knowledge. Visible objects are present to open-eyed sleepers and to the blind, who do not see what is before them because their cognitive powers are indisposed or damaged.[8] Bonaventure reasons that since like is known by like, if there is going to be any created knowledge of creatable quiddities, the created subject has to become more than naturally deiform. Bonaventure thinks that Divine power acts to make the human soul more deiform by infusing it with habits that "sensitize" it to receive inputs from the Divine ideas.[9] God alone is the motive or efficient cause that produces such habits. Because such habits in the soul are metaphysically as flimsy and unstable as the soul itself, God as motive cause must do more than merely *produce* them. God must also *conserve* such habits to keep soul-powers from weakening and to counter subject-side functional imperfections. Relative to those who say that the presence of the Divine ideas is enough, and those who maintain that the deiformity of the soul is enough, Bonaventure charts a "both/and" *via media*. Nevertheless, a functionally disposed and steadied soul will still not suffice for a human being to have certain knowledge, any more than open eyes and healthy visual power will be enough to see colors in a dark room. Besides upgrading our natural cognitive powers with infused habits, Divine ideas (the eternal reasons) must also act on the sensitized powers to move them to actual understanding.[10]

1.2.2 [Argument 2] Lack of Independence

This is the nerve of Bonaventure's second argument. Bonaventure reasons that since created things cannot *be* of themselves, they cannot *function* of

---

[7] Bonaventure, *DQX*, q.4, c. (p.23).   [8] Bonaventure, *DQX*, q.4, c. (pp.22–4).
[9] Bonaventure, *DQX*, q.5 c. (pp.29–30).
[10] Bonaventure, *DQX*, q.4 c and q.5 c. (pp.22–4 and 29–30).

themselves or be *intelligible* of themselves apart from Divine activity and cooperation. No creature can be or do anything by its purely natural powers apart from Divine aid. For Bonaventure, this follows from what it is to be a creature and so pertains essentially to any and every created function.[11]

Nevertheless, the kind of Divine cooperation varies with the excellence of the creatable nature. Starting at the bottom of the excellence hierarchy, Bonaventure identifies non-rational creation as a *vestige* of Godhead. Where non-rational creatures are concerned, all of their active and passive functional powers are directed towards (Aquinas might say, "immersed" in) Same-Level interactions. For example, fire includes active power to heat wood or water, which has the passive power to be heated. Digestive organs have active power to convert food into flesh, while food has passive power for the relevant substantial changes. Where vestiges are concerned, Divine cooperation does not (because it need not) go beyond creation, conservation, and general concurrence. With vestiges, Aristotelian Inward-Principle and Same-Level defaults hold.

By contrast, rational creatures made in God's *image* have God as their object; the knowledge and love of God is their end. Moreover, any act of judgment—e.g., that Beulah is a cow, that stealing is wrong, that the interior angles of Euclidean triangles sum to 180 degrees—makes essential reference to Divine ideas (eternal reasons) as regulative norms. Paradigm bovinity, justice, and triangle are the immutable realities that make necessary truths true, the standards against which the truth of such propositions is evaluated. And paradigm bovinity, justice, and triangle exist immutably in the Divine ideas. Because rational functions of understanding and willing "jump" levels, Divine cooperation with them goes beyond creation, conservation, and general concurrence. God also acts as a moving cause. And, just as for the soul to move the body, the soul must produce habits or dispositions in the body that make the body receptive to further causal inputs from the soul; so God produces influences or habits in the soul that make it sensitive to further causal inputs from the eternal light. When God acts as moving cause on the suitably disposed soul, God is not *in*tuited, or seen directly ("face-to-face"), but *con*tuited, so to speak, along with the created functional principles.[12]

For Bonaventure, there is more. Human beings created in God's image are meant to grow into God's *likeness*, where God-likeness involves

[11] Bonaventure, *DQX*, q.4, reply to con-arguments 3 and 14 (pp.24–5).
[12] Bonaventure, *DQX*, q.4 c, q.5 c and reply to con-argument 13 (pp.22–24, 29–31).

receiving the gift of indwelling Holy Spirit. Thus, God cooperates with created likenesses, not only as creator and conserver, not only via general concurrence and as mover, but also as infused gift and indwelling Spirit. Because human nature is made in God's image, its natural function aims at the knowledge and love of God and of knowing all things in God in the Truth of their essence (ultimately, at morning knowledge). The transition from image to likeness is a process whereby the soul becomes more deiform and so becomes a subject increasingly sensitive to God's action as a moving cause. Once again, no matter how present the object, not just anything is a subject that is apt to be affected by it. The subject has to have passive power to receive the cognitive inputs from an object of that sort. Divinely infused habits are passive disposing conditions that fit the soul to be an ever more suitable subject. Bonventure thinks that sensitivity to Divine inputs develops by degrees, which he schematizes as wings or stages in the *Itinerarium Mentis in Deum*, the journey of the mind into God.

1.3 The Activity of the Created Light

Arguments from Stability and Lack of Independence aim at the conclusion that Divine illumination is *necessary* for human beings to have certain knowledge of creatable quiddities. But Bonaventure's accounts could make us wonder, is Divine illumination also *sufficient*? Here Bonaventure charts another *via media*: where human knowledge in this present state is concerned, neither Divine illumination nor the activity of created natural powers is alone sufficient. *Ante-mortem* knowledge of creatable quiddities involves both/and.

When our souls become maximally disposed—maximally deiform and cleansed from all deformity of sin—the eternal reasons will act as the sole moving cause of our knowledge and we will see them directly. Our morning knowledge of them will be full and clear. But in our present fallen state, our souls are deformed by sin and lacking in maximal deiformity. Our souls are not sufficiently sensitized to the eternal reasons for them to serve as the total moving cause of our knowledge. We also need the activity of the created intellect and of likenesses of created objects produced in us by a cognitive psychological process beginning with sensation. The eternal reasons act together with the created intellect and such likenesses to produce the act of understanding. In their role as partial moving causes, the eternal reasons are only *con*tuited rather than directly and distinctly seen and so are not known with full clarity.[13]

1.4 Summary

Bonaventure's language in the *Disputed Questions* leaves many questions unanswered. How do created cognitive powers work? What do they achieve? In what does the concept formed from sense images fall short? If Bonaventure is clear that God must first sensitize the soul with infused habits and then act on the disposed soul as a moving cause, Bonaventure is less forthcoming about how such motive action of the Divine ideas improves our cognitive grasp of creatable quiddities. If contuition contrasts with direct vision of the Divine ideas, what exactly is it? Does Bonaventure think we are aware of the eternal reasons the way Aquinas believes the soul is aware of itself when it understands the quiddities of material things? Does the soul here below contuit the eternal reasons the way it sees the glory of God in nature without recognizing that it is God that it sees (as in the *Itinerarium*)? Does contuition of the eternal reasons make a contribution to improved understanding of creatable quiddities, or is it only the efficient causal contact with the immutable paradigm that produces that result?

2. Matthew of Aquasparta's Account of Divine Illumination

2.1 Framing False Dichotomy

In his *Disputed Questions on Cognition*, Matthew of Aquasparta charts his own view about certainty in human intellectual cognition as a *via media* between two extremes about where the intelligible content (the *ratio cognoscendi*) is to be found. Plato insists on transcendence: the whole *ratio cognoscendi* comes from the archetypal intelligible world, from the "ideal reasons" or Platonic ideas. They are the eternal light that manifests the truth about creatable quiddities. Aristotle insists on a sublunary location: the whole *ratio cognoscendi* is caused by and comes from things here below and is

---

[13] Bonaventure, *DQX*, q.4 c, con-arguments 1–2, 5–6, 15–17 and q.5 c (pp.22–4, 17–19, 29–30).

accessed via sense, memory, and experience, with the natural light of our agent intellect abstracting species from phantasms and making them to be understood in act. Inward-Principle and Same-Level defaults apply and no appeal to eternal and transcendent light is necessary.[14]

Matthew declares that Plato's position—that all understanding involves a cognition of things in their archetypes—would destroy the distinctions between morning knowledge and evening knowledge, between philosophical and prophetic knowledge, between cognition that comes by nature and cognition that comes by grace.[15] Matthew notes how influential doctors (such as Aquinas) follow Aristotle's insistence on Inward-Principle and Same-Level defaults and deny that any special Divine influence (Divine action over and above creation, conservation, and general concurrence) is involved. Matthew counters that Aristotle's position fails to do justice to the fact that rational creatures are made in God's image and so are a place where the eternal reasons indwell![16]

2.2 Purely Natural Cognitive Functioning

Focusing on the cradle-to-grave human condition in this present state, Matthew acknowledges that human cognition originates with sense experience.[17] But even *ante-mortem* the human soul—as an intellectual nature—is not immersed in the senses or bound to the body. It is not restricted to cognizing material quiddities, for the simple reason that we have *ante-mortem* cognition of our own souls and mental acts.[18] So far as the cognition of material quiddities is concerned, since material things are not themselves in the mind, knowledge of them is through species or likenesses.[19] Embracing Augustine's Causal Nobility Principle (that equivocal causes are nobler than their effects), Matthew reasons that because souls are nobler than bodies, the latter cannot act as an efficient cause on the former.[20] Rather, the intellect perceives changes in corporeal sense organs and configures itself accordingly—i.e., the agent intellect forms a species for itself and impresses

---

[14] Matthew of Aquasparta, *DQC*, q.2 (pp.231).
[15] Matthew of Aquasparta, *DQC*, q.2 (pp.233–4).
[16] Matthew of Aquasparta, *DQC*, q.2 (p.232).
[17] Matthew of Aquasparta, *DQC*, q.5 c (p.304).
[18] Matthew of Aquasparta, *DQC*, q.3 c and q.5 c (pp.263 and 304–7).
[19] Matthew of Aquasparta, *DQC*, q.5 c (pp.306–7).
[20] Matthew of Aquasparta, *DQC*, q.3 c (pp.257, 264, and 267).

it on the possible intellect.[21] In this process, Matthew explains, the species taken from the senses are a quasi-material cause; the agent intellect is a quasi-efficient secondary cause; and the species produced by the intellect is the quasi-formal cause.[22] He also refers to the intelligible species that is produced in the possible intellect as a *ratio cognoscendi*.[23]

2.3 The Need for Divine Illumination

Nevertheless, Matthew insists with Bonaventure that certain knowledge must be common, immutable, and infallible.[24] Intrinsic cognitive powers thus exercised do not suffice for certain knowledge without appropriate contact with the eternal exemplars. Where certain knowledge is desired, both created objects and created subjects are deficient.

Focusing first on the object, Matthew explains that truth is declarative; it is the *ratio cognoscendi* and the *ratio manifestandi* of intelligible content. But, Matthew asserts, the form or quiddity as it is found in creatures is not sufficient to manifest itself; it cannot by itself move the intellect. Aquinas' reason was that insofar as material quiddities exist in reality in particulars, they are not actually but only potentially intelligible. Matthew's reason may be (at least he explicitly mentions) the "Phantasm Problem": that because nothing falls under the senses but sensible qualities, either the phantasm will not represent the quiddity of the thing at all, or—as Matthew suggests— the species of the quiddity will be "clothed" by the species of the accidents the way the substance is "clothed" by the accidents. But what is thus clothed does not appear in all of its naked clarity![25] Matthew infers, that is why God provides the agent intellect, a cognitive power for abstracting the quiddities from sensibles by "purifying" them, perhaps by stripping off their individuators and/or the species of accidents.[26]

Nevertheless, Matthew contends, the agent intellect is not adequate for abstracting quiddities unless it is subordinated to and acts in conjunction with the eternal light.[27] Like Bonaventure, Matthew is motivated by Stability

---

[21] Matthew of Aquasparta, *DQC*, q.3 c, q.3 ad 16, and q.3 ad 20 (pp.264–265, 267, 271, and 272).
[22] Matthew of Aquasparta, *DQC*, q.3 ad 12 and q.3 ad 16, (pp.270–1).
[23] Matthew of Aquasparta, *DQC*, q.3 (p.266).
[24] Matthew of Aquasparta, *DQC*, q.2 (p.238).
[25] Matthew of Aquasparta, *DQC*, q.3, arg. 13 and ad 13 (pp.252 and 270).
[26] Matthew of Aquasparta, *DQC*, q.1, c and q.2, c; (pp.211 and 233).
[27] Matthew of Aquasparta, *DQC*, q. 2 c and q. 2 ad 5em (pp.233 and 241–2).

Problems: certain cognition is common, immutable, and infallible, while every created light is limited and mutable.[28] But exactly what does the eternal light do for the created light to overcome these obstacles?

Matthew emphasizes: God is not a *ratio cognoscendi*, because—as Matthew understands it—a *ratio cognoscendi* must inhere in the cognizing subject as a quasi-formal cause of the act of understanding. God, however, is not the kind of thing that can inhere in any subject.[29] *Ante-mortem* God does not act on the intellect as an object either, because in almost all cases face-to-face vision of God is reserved for the life to come.[30] Rather God acts together with the agent intellect as a moving cause.[31] Because what a cognizing subject can perceive depends on the receptivity of the subject, God produces "an influence"—presumably a created accidental quality—in the soul.[32] And with this assistance, the intellect that has abstracted the species can understand with certainty and without doubt.[33] To be sure, that created quality is as unstable as any creature, but God lends stability by acting to conserve both that influence and the abstracted species.[34] God is the efficient cause, but the influence is a formal *ratio* by which the intellect becomes more deiform.[35]

Matthew explains: normally, God does not act alone but only together with the species abstracted from created things, so that God is not the total and sole *ratio videndi*,[36] but rather "completes and consummates" the formal cause. Matthew does not clarify whether this is by causing the "influx" or disposing condition that increases the receptivity of the subject, or by doing something to improve upon the abstracted species, or both. What he does add is that created things are not necessary as a cause of our knowledge, because God could act alone to impress on us a species of things through which we understand their quiddities.[37]

---

[28] Matthew of Aquasparta, *DQC*, q.2 (p.238).
[29] Matthew of Aquasparta, *DQC*, q.2 and ad 16 (pp.244 and 271).
[30] Matthew of Aquasparta, *DQC*, q.2 c and ad 6 (pp.234 and 242).
[31] Matthew of Aquasparta, *DQC*, q.1 c and ad 7 (pp.215 and 217); q.2 c and q2 ad 5–6 (pp.241–2).
[32] Matthew of Aquasparta, *DQC*, q.2 ad 14 and 16–17 (p.244).
[33] Matthew of Aquasparta, *DQC*, q.2 ad 5 (pp.241–2).
[34] Matthew of Aquasparta, *DQC*, q.1 ad 1 and ad 12 (pp.216 and 219).
[35] Matthew of Aquasparta, *DQC*, q.1 ad 21 (p.221).
[36] Matthew of Aquasparta, *DQC*, q.2 c and ad 21–2 (pp.233 and 246).
[37] Matthew of Aquasparta, *DQC*, q.1 ad 12 (p.219).

2.4 The Objection from Natural Sufficiency

Matthew has read his Aristotle. He knows that appeal to special Divine action (over and above creation, conservation, and general concurrence) to account for human understanding of creatable quiddities violates Aristotle's Inward-Principle and Same-Level defaults. For Aristotelians, it is foundational: nature does nothing in vain; natures do not lack what is necessary for their natural functions.[38] Moreover, Matthew is sensitive to the "Miracles" Problem. Natural functions should receive natural explanations. Doesn't "special" Divine action imply interruptions in the natural order and threaten to put our scientific knowledge on the same footing as prophetic inspiration or miraculous intervention to change water into wine?

Matthew responds with a distinction. The term "natural" can be taken two ways: [i] for what is caused by the principles of the nature; [ii] for what is never lacking to the nature and what is inseparably concomitant with the nature.[39] The functions of non-rational natures or vestiges are natural in the first sense: inward and same-level functional powers suffice—together with Divine creation, conservation, and general concurrence—to account for their functional activities. The functions of rational natures—understanding and willing—are not natural in the first sense. This is not because rational natures are defective or less excellent than non-rational natures but rather the reverse: the fact that rational functions make contact with the Divine exemplars is a mark of their superiority. But such contact requires special Divine action (over and above creation, conservation, and general concurrence) to produce by efficient causality an infused quality in the creature's mind and to move our mind[40] so that it can cognize creatable quiddities with certainty and without doubt.[41] Functional independence is a good-making feature, but the very superiority of natural function that involves contact with the eternal reasons is a better-making feature, even though it makes functional independence impossible.

Nevertheless, Matthew maintains, if rational functioning is not natural in the first sense, it is natural in the second sense, because such Divine assistance is *regularly* available to created intellects that have exercised themselves in relevant ways. Divine action to infuse qualities and move the

---

[38] Matthew of Aquasparta, *DQC*, q.2 c and arg.13 (pp.225 and 231).
[39] Matthew of Aquasparta, *DQC*, q.2 ad 13 (pp.243–4).
[40] Matthew of Aquasparta, *DQC*, q.2 ad 3 and ad 4 (p.241).
[41] Matthew of Aquasparta, *DQC*, q.2 ad 5 (pp.241–2).

created intellects does go beyond creation, conservation, and general concurrence, but it does not interrupt business-as-usual. Rather Divine policy makes Divine illumination a given that can be counted on. Special Divine action is a condition of the possibility of business-as-usual where human understanding is concerned.[42]

In his *Disputed Questions on Cognition*, Matthew follows Bonaventure's analysis in many respects: in recognizing that the truth of creatable quiddities can be found at three levels; in insisting that *ante-mortem* certain knowledge requires special Divine action as a moving cause; and in holding that God acts as a moving cause to produce an influx in the created soul to facilitate understanding. Matthew does not speak of the creature's contuiting the Divine exemplars, but seems to keep special Divine action behind the scenes, as hidden from conscious view as the agent intellect's action to produce the species from the sense images. Matthew does not explicitly say whether special Divine action regularly does more than infuse a disposing quality. In particular, he does not elaborate on how or whether special causal contact with the Divine exemplars might alter or replace the species produced by the agent intellect. What he does divulge is his conviction that God could act alone *ante-mortem* to produce a species of creatable quiddities in our intellects.

3. Henry of Ghent on Divine Illumination

3.1 Henry's Early Account

When Henry of Ghent opens his *Summa Quaestionum Ordinariarum* with questions about the possibility of human knowledge, he tries to set issues in the widest possible epistemological frame. Reviewing the positions of Aristotle, Augustine, and the Academic skeptics, Henry sees partisans debating at cross-purposes, because they have different standards of certain knowledge in mind. Henry identifies four certainty-making features: [i] freedom from doubt and error, [ii] stability of knower and known, [iii] infallibility, and [iv] clarity. He also distinguishes knowledge in the broad sense from knowledge properly speaking, knowledge of what is the case

---

[42] Matthew of Aquasparta, *DQC*, q.2 ad 13 (pp.243–4).

(*id quod verum est*) from knowledge of the truth of things (quidditative knowledge that—for Henry—requires a grasp of the conformity of a thing with its exemplar).

3.1.1 Low-Grade Certainty

Where *knowledge in the broad sense* is concerned, the certainty we are interested in is [i] freedom from doubt and error. Henry affirms: we human beings can have a lot of knowledge in the broad sense by our purely natural powers. We can acquire it second-hand from the testimony of others (e.g., knowledge of cities we have never visited, knowledge of historical events before we were born).[43] We can also come by it first-hand from the testimony of our own senses and intellect. Henry has read his Aristotle. Henry knows how Aristotelian metaphysics sponsors a kind of natural reliabilism. Aristotelian natures "work" always-or-for-the-most-part, because it is on the basis of always-or-for-the-most-part regularities that powers are assigned. What goes for fire's power to heat up nearby combustibles also holds for human cognitive powers. Henry allows that unobstructed sensory powers deliver veridical perceptions.[44] Experience allows the intellect to identify conditions under which powers are apt to be obstructed (whether by sickness, or by distance, or by a distorting medium), and—where perceptions conflict—to follow those from the unobstructed power.[45]

More remarkably, in the *Summa Quaestionum Ordinariarum*, Henry also acknowledges the possibility of our having *knowledge properly speaking* by our purely natural powers—quidditative knowledge that meets the standard [i] of being free from doubt and error. Henry distinguishes two exemplars: the created exemplar which is a species based on sensations, and the uncreated exemplar which is in the mind of God. Doubt-and-error-free knowledge of conformity to the *created* exemplar, is what is possible for us by our purely natural powers. If the created exemplar is the species based on sense experience, Henry equivocates as to whether it is a particular determinate sense image of the sort we experience in dreams[46] or a "purified" and "abstracted" universal species.[47] His cognitive psychological story follows

---

[43] Henry of Ghent, *SQO*, article (henceforward, a.)1, q.1 (Leuven I.10–13 [fol.1vB]).
[44] Henry of Ghent, *SQO*, a.1, q.1 ad 2 (Leuven I.17–19 ff. [fol.2vF]).
[45] Henry of Ghent, *SQO*, a.1, q.1 (Leuven I.10–13 [(fol.1vB]). Steel agrees in his helpful article, "Henricus Gandavensis Platonicus," pp.17–39, esp. 30.
[46] Henry of Ghent, *SQO*, a.1, q.2 (Leuven I.31–46 [fol.5r–vE]).
[47] Henry of Ghent, *SQO*, a.1, q.2 (Leuven I.31–46 [fol.5vE–F]).

familiar Aristotelian lines: sensations are stored in memory; repetition produces a phantasm from which we abstract a universal species, produce a concept conformed to that exemplar, and make judgments.[48] When free from doubt and error, Henry affirms, such quidditative concepts and judgments constitute knowledge properly speaking. At first, Henry implies that we use such naturally acquired concepts not only in formulating judgments such as "Beulah is a cow" and "This is triangular," but also in coming to have certain knowledge of "Cows are animals" and "Animals are substances," which are first principles of speculative science. But then he expresses qualms about going that far.[49]

In any event, Henry's concession—that we *can* have knowledge properly speaking by our purely natural powers—is plagued by the Phantasm Problem, even where low-grade certainty is concerned. Since the proper objects of sensation are sensible qualities, sensible species will be likenesses of accidents only. How, then, can they lead us to a cognition of substance-quiddities?[50] Henry replies that we first understand on the basis of intelligible species of sensible things, but "through the investigation of natural reason" the mind "conceives through itself" things that are not sensible: viz., the quiddities of substance. He reasons by analogy: just as the psyche of sheep is so structured that perceiving the sensible qualities of a wolf triggers its natural instinct to flee, so human minds are so structured that perceiving and abstracting concepts of the sensible qualities of things provokes rational inquiry into their substance-natures.[51] Henry does not elaborate here on what sort of rational investigation is involved. Does he perhaps have in mind sifting observations through the Aristotelian method of difference?[52] Nor does he clarify whether and how the resultant concept of quiddity (as opposed to the first-mentioned universal concept of the sensible qualities) conforms to the created exemplar (i.e., to the phantasm or the universal concept of sensible qualities). Seemingly more relevant would be its incomplete and imperfect conformity to the uncreated exemplar, which does represent the substance or quiddity of things.[53]

---

[48] Henry of Ghent, *SQO*, a.1, q.2 (Leuven I.31–46 [fol.5r–vE]).
[49] Henry of Ghent, *SQO*, a.2, q.1 (Leuven I.200–6).
[50] Henry of Ghent, *SQO*, a.1, q.1 ad 7 (Leuven I.27–8).
[51] Henry of Ghent, *SQO*, a.1, q.1 ad 7 (Leuven I.27–8).
[52] Marrone, in his *Truth and Scientific Knowledge in the Thought of Henry of Ghent*, sees an emphasis on scientific investigation into the quiddity in Henry's middle works.
[53] Henry of Ghent, *SQO*, a.1, q.1 ad 7 (Leuven I.27–8).

3.1.2 Aiming Higher

If Aristotelian reliabilists might be satisfied with natural powers delivering knowledge that is free from doubt and error, ancient Academics and Augustinians were aiming higher for certainty that meets the tests of [ii] stability, [iii] infallibility, and [iv] clarity. It is this level of certainty, Henry argues, that cannot be had by our purely natural powers.[54] *Stability* is out of reach from both object- and subject-side. Henry declares, any exemplar abstracted from a mutable thing has some principle of mutability in itself. The created exemplar abstracted from phantasms received through sense experience from bodies is itself mutable. Subject-wise, the human soul is mutable, and that makes every exemplar received into it mutable as well.[55] Where knowledge that begins with sense images is concerned, *infallibility* is also unavailable, because experience shows that we have no infallible criterion for distinguishing the true from the false. Henry references the Academics' objection recited by Augustine: that in dreams, we mistake sense images for the things themselves.[56] Scotus protests that this is to confuse the sense images with the universal species abstracted from them. No one mistakes universal species or universal concepts for real concrete particulars![57] A more generous interpretation might understand Henry to be making a different point. Aristotelian scientific investigation begins with regular patterns of sensible qualities, and tries to burrow under these to find the quidditative root of these regularities. But dreams scramble such patterns. Academics press: where is the infallible criterion by means of which we can tell which patterns are to be found in nature, which clusters are really rooted in substantial form? For Henry, this last argument combines with the Phantasm Problem, to explain why our purely natural cognitive psychological processes cannot meet the *clarity*-standard. Quidditative concepts derived by the mediation of the senses are bound to be "imperfect, obscure," "nebulous," and "incomplete."[58]

For Henry, human beings have not been endowed with natural powers sufficient for stable, infallible, and clear cognition of creatable quiddities, whether at will or when acted upon by creatures. Divine illumination is required. But Henry's account of Divine illumination differs from his predecessors' in two significant ways. First, Henry does not follow Bonaventure

---

[54] Henry of Ghent, *SQO*, a.1, q.2 (Leuven I.45–6); a.2, q.1 (Leuven I.202–4).
[55] Henry of Ghent, *SQO*, a.1, q.2 (Leuven I.45–6).
[56] Henry of Ghent, *SQO*, a.1, q.2 (Leuven I.45–6).
[57] Scotus, *Ordinatio* I, d.3, p.1, q.4, n.251 (Vat III.153).
[58] Henry of Ghent, *SQO*, a.2, q.1 (Leuven I.200–4); a.1, q.2 and q. 3 (Leuven I.29–90).

and Matthew of Aquasparta, who insist that human minds need to be "sensitized" to God's motions by infused habits. Rather Henry seems to hold that human minds are by nature such that they can be brought to these higher degrees of certainty by Divine action.[59] Second, *pace* Matthew of Aquasparta, Henry denies that there is any psychological state producible in human beings by creatures alone upon which Divine illumination follows with law-like regularity. Divine illumination lies within God's voluntary control.[60] If much of the time, God sheds light on those who have made relevant cognitive efforts, other times—Henry implies—moral criteria might figure into God's calculations. A person might be deprived of Divine illumination because of some serious misdeed.[61] Conversely, God might have reason to reveal truths to the wicked, even the devil himself,[62] while hiding them from the good.[63]

Henry agrees with Bonaventure and Matthew of Aquasparta that *ante-mortem* the Divine exemplar comes to our aid, not by manifesting Itself as *the object* of our thought, but by acting as *a cause*. "Like is known by like," but the created exemplar furnishes the mind only with an imperfect and incomplete likeness of the thing, with the result that the concept the mind forms thereby is itself imperfect and incomplete. Henry explains that the Divine exemplar complements the created exemplar by acting together with it as a single cause of the cognition. Henry compares the effect of the Divine exemplar on our concept to that of a signet ring that leaves its impression in wax.[64] In *Summa Quaestionum Ordinariarum*, a.1, q.3, Henry speaks of created and Divine exemplars as two species. Nevertheless, if the created intelligible species informs the mind by inhering in it, the Divine "species" does not inhere but shapes thought by virtue of its indwelling presence to the mind.[65] Henry declares that the result of such collaboration is clear knowledge of the unadulterated truth of the thing.

---

[59] Henry of Ghent, *SQO*, a.1, q.2 (Leuven I.66–8).
[60] Henry of Ghent, *SQO*, a.1, q.2 and 4 (Leuven I.61f., 63, 98).
[61] Henry of Ghent, *SQO*, a.1, q.2 (Leuven I.68).
[62] Henry of Ghent, *SQO*, a.1, q.3 (Leuven I.72).
[63] Henry of Ghent, *SQO*, a.1, q.2 (Leuven I.63). For scholarly comment on Henry's emphasis on God's attention to moral criteria for Divine illumination, see Steel, "Henricus Gandavensis Platonicus," p. 37, and Macken, "La théorie de l'illumination divine dans la philosophie d'Henri de Gand," esp. pp.104–7.
[64] Henry of Ghent, *SQO*, a.1, q.2 and 3 (Leuven I.57, 85).
[65] Henry of Ghent, *SQO*, a.1, q.3 (Leuven XXI.86f.).

3.2 Later Reflections

For better or worse, Henry's own analysis of human cognitive psychology is unstable across the corpus of his writings. Among many later developments and elaborations, three bear on his view of what happens in Divine illumination.

3.2.1 Creatable Quiddities in *Esse Essentiae*

In his *Quodlibeta*, Henry forwards a distinctive explanation of how creatable quiddities have their eternal and immutable being in God. Henry is concerned to distinguish true beings—possibles including creatable natures such as bovinity or equinity—from fictitious beings—impossibles such as chimeras, goat-stags, and round squares. Henry wants to say that God has knowledge of the former but not of the latter, and that God has eternal knowledge of creatable quiddities whether or not they really exist. Yet, Henry believes that for a thought of F to count as knowledge of F, F must have some sort of being to which the thought corresponds. Henry concludes that there is some sort of absolute reality (*esse simpliciter*) that fictitious beings lack but true beings have whether or not they really exist[66]—call it *esse essentiae*[67] or quidditative *esse*.[68] Because correspondence of thought to a thing that has *esse essentiae* is what makes that thought count as knowledge, a thing's having *esse essentiae* must be prior not only to its existing in reality but also to its existence in the mind.[69]

Nevertheless, Henry cannot allow that creatable quiddities have this status independently of the Divine essence. On the contrary, he explains, the Divine intellect is the formal cause of creatable quiddities having *esse essentiae*. If eternity rules out any *temporal* succession in the Godhead, there is at least a sequence of natural or explanatory priorities. First, God knows Godself through the Divine essence. Because creatable quiddities are

---

[66] Quoted by Scotus, *Lectura* I, d.36, q.u, nn.4–5, 7–8, 18 (Vat XVII.462–3, 465).

[67] Henry of Ghent, *Quodlibeta* III, q.90 (fol.61r), where Henry speaks of the natures or essences of things having *esse* in three ways, to which there corresponds a three-fold understanding: real existence (*esse naturae in rebus*), existence in the mind (*esse rationis*), and *esse essentiae* which is prior to both.

[68] In *SQO*, a.43, q.2, Henry speaks of the nature of animal being considered according to a three-fold *esse*: quidditative *esse*, real existence (*esse naturale*), and existence in the mind (*esse rationis*). In *Quodlibeta* VII, q.1–2 (Leuven XI.18), he speaks of quiddity or essence as having only a double *esse*—one in reality in particulars and the other in the intellect—but a four-fold consideration.

[69] Henry of Ghent, *Quodlibeta* III, q.9 (fol.61v).

contained in the Divine essence insofar as they are at bottom ways of imperfectly imitating the Divine essence, God—by understanding the Divine essence in Itself—understands creatable quiddities *indistinctly*. Next, God conceives of the Divine essence as imitable in distinct ways and thereby produces creatable quiddities in *esse essentiae* and knows creatable quiddities *distinctly*. In some passages, Henry identifies the idea with the Divine essence under the aspect of imitability, but in others with the relation of imitability itself. Either way, the Divine intellect's reflection on the Divine essence as imitable in distinct ways, as it were eternally emanates distinct creatable quiddities in *esse essentiae*.[70] It takes a further (free and contingent) act of the Divine will to give those creatable quiddities real existence in extra-mental particulars. *The same essence* exists both ways. Henry joins Bonaventure and Matthew of Aquasparta in their insistence that cognitive access via really extant particulars alone will not deliver high-grade certainty; causal contact with the creatable quiddity in God is required.

One wishes that Henry had been still more explicit. He is probably not thinking that the requisite causal contact is with the Divine essence in Itself, because Divine illumination is supposed to clarify our concepts, while the Divine essence in Itself affords even God only indistinct knowledge of creatable quiddities. Ideas identified with relations of imitability would not do much better, because—while distinct—relations of imitability are merely beings of reason, and beings of reason cannot have any real causal impact. Seemingly, Henry's best answer would be that the requisite causal contact is with the creatable quiddities in their *esse essentiae*, a kind of being *simpliciter* that they have eternally and immutably but not independently of God.[71]

3.2.2 Understanding without Intelligible Species

If Henry's early discussion (in the first two articles of *Summa Quaestionum Ordinariarum*) seems on balance to imply that the agent intellect abstracts intelligible species from the phantasms, his later treatment in *Quodlibeta* V, q.14, backs off from any notion that intelligible species are involved in angelic or human cognition.[72] Charging that intelligible species are

---

[70] Henry of Ghent, *Quodlibeta* IX, q.2 (Leuven XIII.25–6).

[71] But Steel insists that for Henry the Divine essence is the exemplar and the creatable essences are the exemplata ("Henricus Gandavensis Platonicus," p.20).

[72] Macken understands Henry already to be leaving intelligible species behind in *Quodlibeta* IV, q.7–8 ("La théorie de l'illumination divine dans la philosophie d'Henri de Gand," 94). Likewise, Wolter refers readers to *Quodlibeta* IV, q.7, 8, 23; and V, q.4. In *Quodlibeta* IV, q.7, however, Henry seems more concerned to argue that intelligible species are not *necessary*, indeed, that they are superfluous for understanding what is immediately present to the created

theoretical entities posited to explain cognitive psychological phenomena, Henry demands to know, what theoretical work are intelligible species supposed to do? [i] They are not needed to supply the created intellect with active power to produce an act of understanding, because—as Augustine maintains—such power belongs to immaterial angels and souls of themselves.[73]

[ii] More surprisingly, Henry argues that intelligible species could not function to make the intelligible object present to the intellect. Adherents of intelligible species think that an extra representation is necessary, because phantasms represent things under the aspect of singularity, while the proper object of the intellect is universal. Henry counters that what a representation represents (i.e., the object of the representation) is a function of the *cause* of the representation. Signet rings produce seal-designs of the same shape. Effects are always to some degree like their causes. So the causes of representations affect the represented content. What Henry focuses on here is that if the cause contains the intelligible content *under the aspect of singularity*, the representation will represent the content only *under the aspect of singularity*. Since only singulars really exist, and only really extant things act, any real representations and their real causes will be singular. Hence any real representations will represent only *under the aspect of singularity*. But—Henry agrees—the object of understanding is universal. So positing intelligible species over and above phantasms and sensible species amounts to piling up more and more singular mental representations—which will do nothing to make *the universal* object present to the intellect.[74]

[iii] Neither, Henry argues, can intelligible species be formal principles of understanding and/or sufficient efficient causes of understanding. For angelic intellects are by nature able to understand all intelligibles, of which there are infinitely many (perhaps infinitely many natural kinds, but certainly infinitely many numbers). If to be able to think of intelligible object X required having an intelligible species of X, then angelic intellects would have to have infinitely many intelligible species simultaneously. If having an intelligible species of object X were sufficient for understanding X, then

---

intellect (the angelic essence or the soul and their acts); and that intelligible species would be counter-productive for understanding the Divine essence (Leuven VIII.32–42). But he seems to admit that the need for species is an imperfection in created intellects. Because they are finite, they do not eminently contain the essences of other things. This seems to imply that in this question Henry still thought created intellects would need species to understand material quiddities.

[73] Henry of Ghent, *Quodlibeta* V, q.14, fol.174vV.
[74] Henry of Ghent, *Quodlibeta* V, q.14, fol.174rZ.

angelic intellects would understand infinitely many simultaneously. Both of these are impossible for a finite being.[75]

If intelligible species are not fit for any cognitive psychological jobs, Henry concludes, it would be superfluous to posit them. Human and angelic understanding must be accounted for without them. In fact, his third argument would not hold against Aquinas, who doesn't think angels require a distinct intelligible species for each distinct intelligible object. On the contrary, the smarter the angel, the fewer the intelligible species it requires. Moreover, when Henry turns to explain human understanding, he seems to backtrack on the causal principle that underlies his second argument. He contends that the same singular representation—the same phantasm—can represent its content under the aspect of singularity when illumined by the light of the imagination and under the aspect of universality when illumined by the agent intellect. The phantasm abstracts from the presence of matter but does not abstract from particular conditions that are accidental to the form insofar as it exists in individual matter, and so cannot act on the intellect directly. The agent intellect is able to abstract the intelligible content from the phantasm, but it doesn't—*pace* Aquinas—produce any singular real representation in the possible intellect. That would be self-defeating, since such a singular real representation would represent only under the aspect of singularity. Instead, what the agent intellect does is make the abstracted intelligible content to have objective existence as the intentional object of an act of understanding in the possible intellect. Henry says that the possible intellect thereby looks on phantasms under the aspect of the universal.[76] Henry adds that intelligible species play no role in explaining our dispositions to understand what we do not actually understand at the moment. Rather knowledge-habits do that job.[77]

Eliminating intelligible species between the phantasm and the act of understanding might at first seem to make the Phantasm Problem worse. Without intelligible species, there is a double leap—between sensible accidents and quiddities, on the one hand, and between singular and universal, on the other—to be taken all at once. The intelligible species of sensible qualities mediated by making the move from singular to universal. Scientific research to arrive at a quidditative concept was a separate step. Henry's arguments in *Quodlibeta* V, q.14 reject any such advantage as merely

---

[75] Henry of Ghent, *Quodlibeta* V, q.14, fol.174vA–175rC, 175rE–175vE–F.
[76] Henry of Ghent, *Quodlibeta* V, q.14, fol.176vO–177rO.
[77] Henry of Ghent, *Quodlibeta* V, q.14, fol.175vF–176rM, 176vO–177rP, 177rR–177vR.

apparent because intelligible species would be singular representations and so would not help the agent intellect jump orders from singular to universal. Even so, one can see how the notion that all the agent intellect has to work with is determinate sense images, might encourage a Divine illuminationist view.

3.3 Double Agency!

In *Quodlibeta* IX, q.15, Henry confronts the suggestion that Augustine embraced Plato's theory of recollection according to which the soul pre-exists its incarnation and brings along with it habitual knowledge of intelligibles—habitual knowledge that is acquired through direct contact with the incorporeal truth itself and "excited" by sense experience of things in which those quiddities exist here below.[78] Henry denies that either Augustine or Plato held any such thing. On the contrary, neither believed in the mind-independent existence of universal quiddities, and both were proponents of Divine illumination.[79] Creatable quiddities exist in reality only in particulars, and knowledge of them is not brought along from a pre-existent state but acquired by the soul in this present state. While Henry refers the reader to his earlier discussions for details, he here makes the at least terminologically novel suggestion that God's role in human understanding is that of a second agent intellect. Just as the created agent intellect illumines the phantasms to abstract the universal content, so God illumines the mind to furnish it with genuine ("sincere," high-grade certain) knowledge of the truth of material forms that really exist only in mind-independent particulars. The important difference is that "the agent intellect that is God acts as the art that puts the form in the matter of the artifact"—in God's case, in the really extant particular—while "the agent intellect that is the soul-power" illumines the phantasms to expose the universal in the particular.[80]

---

[78] Henry of Ghent, *Quodlibeta* IX, q.15 (Leuven XIII.263).
[79] Henry of Ghent, *Quodlibeta* IX, q.15 (Leuven XIII.265-6). Steel agrees ("Henricus Gandavensis Platonicus," 23-4).
[80] Henry of Ghent, *Quodlibeta* IX, q.15 (Leuven XIII.265).

6
Outsourcing the Object: Divine Illumination II
Henry of Ghent and Scotus

1. *Dramatis Personae*

Historians love a story with conflictual plots and seismic shifts, peopled by leaders and followers, heroes and villains. Even historians of *philosophy* feel pressured to oblige. Textbooks, encyclopedia articles, and articles on medieval philosophy identify and pit nominalists against realists, voluntarists against naturalists, Augustinian traditionalists against boat-rocking Aristotelians. One dramatic episode features Duns Scotus the Aristotelian naturalist versus Henry of Ghent the last-gasp Augustinian champion of Divine illumination.[1] It must be confessed, the drama is quite lopsided in one way which is not uncommon in the history of philosophy. Scotus had a lot to say about Henry, and certainly respected him. But Henry had little or nothing to say about Scotus—understandably, for when Henry died in 1293 after a long life, Scotus was still transitioning, in his studies and teaching, from Aristotelian philosophy to theology, and had not yet moved from Oxford to the "most happening" university of the time, which was in Paris. That did not keep Henry from being party to a controversy with Scotus; philosophers whose views attract interest are often parties to controversies after their deaths. But Scotus was the one who kept this controversy going. What was the controversy?

---

[1] In correspondence, Professor Gordon Wilson rightly registers that Henry speaks of *illustratio*, not *illuminatio*. I have not been able to discern any difference in Henry's meaning, however, from authors like Bonaventure and Matthew of Aquasparta, who speak more often of *illuminatio*. Nevertheless, it should be kept in mind.

1.1 Narrowing the Issue

Christian Latin scholastics agreed: purely natural powers would not bring us to knowledge of articles of faith such as the Trinity, Incarnation, and eucharistic real presence. Special Divine action—over and above creation, conservation, and general concurrence—was involved in revelation.[2] What was at stake in this dispute was the adequacy of natural human cognitive powers to acquire knowledge of creatable quiddities.

Moreover, Christian Latin scholastics all expected to have improved knowledge of creatable quiddities in the life to come. There will be morning knowledge in which we see God and see all things in God, who indisputably has paradigm comprehension of creatable quiddities. Scotus held that already separate souls will have intellectual intuitive cognition of creatable quiddities and be able to abstract general concepts of them from the really present things themselves.

The dispute between Scotus and Henry over Divine illumination concerned our *ante-mortem* cognitive possibilities. Can we—in this cradle-to-grave life—have certain and infallible knowledge of the genuine truth of creatable quiddities by our purely natural powers, or is special Divine illumination required?

1.2 Sketch of the Disagreement

At a high level of abstraction, Henry appeals to special Divine illumination to answer the Academic skeptics. Scotus counters that—so far from evading—Henry's worries land him in that very Academic skepticism that Aristotle proleptically mocks and that he (Henry) was trying to avoid.[3] Closer to the ground, Henry and Scotus agree that human *ante-mortem* cognition begins with sense experience and continues with sensory memory and imagination; that human *ante-mortem* intellectual cognition proceeds by the agent intellect abstracting universal intelligible content from the phantasms and acting on the possible intellect which issues in a cognitive act.

---

[2] Henry of Ghent, *SQO*, a.1, q.2 c, q.5 (Leuven XXI.32, 126–7); *SQO*, article (henceforward, a.)22, 1.5 (fol.134vCD).
[3] Scotus, *Ordinatio* I, d.3, p.1, q.4, n.218 (Vat III.132).

Henry insists, however, that this cognitive process is not sufficient to provide us with certain and infallible knowledge of the genuine truth of creatable quiddities. The concept that results from what our unaided natural powers do and suffer is unclear, incomplete, and imperfect. Special Divine action is required to clarify and perfect our concepts. Scotus not only insists that no such special Divine action occurs *ante-mortem* but also appears to hold that—for the Aristotelian science that we do *ante-mortem*—none is required.

1.3 Elusive Precision

Still, if our focus is on our *ante-mortem* knowledge of creatable quiddities, we may wonder: what exactly is the source of the disagreement between Henry and Scotus? To get to the bottom of this question, we need to know why and where Henry thinks our *ante-mortem* natural cognitive processes are deficient, and precisely what God can and sometimes does do to make up for their inadequacy. The trouble is that when we probe for details, it turns out that Scotus and Henry agree more than is commonly advertised, and many of their differences are not salient explainers of their attitudes toward Divine illumination. In what follows, I will muddy the waters before tumbling to the obvious, all the while leaving many murky matters unresolved.

2. Shared Optimism

Scotus accuses Henry of first flirting with and then falling for Academic skepticism. But in fact Henry sets his epistemological reflections in the widest possible frame. If certain knowledge is what we are out for, Henry explains that certainty comes in degrees. He identifies four markers of certainty: freedom from doubt and error, stability, clarity, infallibility. Henry contrasts knowledge in the broad sense from knowledge properly speaking. He famously distinguishes non-complex knowledge of *id quod est verum*, from complex knowledge of its truth, which involves grasping the conformity of the thing (*id quod est verum*) to its exemplar.

Henry declares that we have lots of knowledge in the broad sense that meets the standard of freedom from doubt and error. With Augustine, Henry insists, it would be an insult to human intelligence to suggest that we do not.⁴ We have lots of second-hand knowledge—of plants, animals, and cities that we have never seen; of historical facts about what happened elsewhere and before we were born.⁵ Like Augustine, Henry affirms that our senses are generally reliable about their proper objects; that experience and reason allow us to develop criteria for discerning when they mislead us about extra-mental sensible things in our surround;⁶ that we have knowledge of our own mental acts; and that we have knowledge of *per se nota*.⁷

In his notorious critique of Henry, Scotus embraces freedom from doubt and error as his own criterion of certainty. Scotus' own list of the sorts of things we can know through our purely natural powers matches Henry's, virtually item for item.⁸ This is no wonder, because—so far as freedom from doubt and error are concerned—both Scotus and Henry want to embrace the implications of Aristotelian reliabilism, and both want to accommodate Augustine's insistence that we are certain about our own mental acts. Egged on by Aristotle, Scotus perhaps goes beyond Augustine in claiming that when we are awake, we can be certain that we are awake.⁹

Nevertheless, holding to the standard of freedom from doubt and error, Henry—at least at first—grants that we can even have certain knowledge properly speaking by our purely natural powers.¹⁰ At least at first,¹¹ Henry was inclined to say that our purely natural powers (our senses and imagination together with the agent intellect) produce the intelligible species or created exemplar. Relative to that exemplar we can conceive of natural kinds and form judgments about which particulars instantiate them, chart relations among properties and so explain connections between causes and

---

⁴ Henry of Ghent, *SQO*, a.1, q.1 c and q.2 c (Leuven XXI.15–18 and XXI.32–5).
⁵ Henry of Ghent, *SQO*, a.1, q.1 c (Leuven XXI.10–11).
⁶ Henry of Ghent, *SQO*, a.1, q.1 c, q.1 ad 2 and ad 3, and q.2 c (Leuven XXI.11–12, 22–3, and 35).
⁷ Henry of Ghent, *SQO*, a.1, q.1 ad 1 and q.5 c (Leuven XXI.19, 126–7); *SQO*, a.2, q.1 c (Leuven XXI.202–3).
⁸ Thus, Scotus contends that we have knowledge that is free from doubt and error of *per se notae*: *Ordinatio* I, d.3, p.1, q.4, nn.230–4, 250 (Vat III.138–40, 152–3); of experience-based inferences to causal connections: *Ordinatio* I, d.3, p.1, q.4, nn.235–7 (Vat III.141–4); of our own mental acts: *Ordinatio* I, d.3, p.1, q.4, nn.238–9 (Vat III.144–6); and of criteria for sorting mistaken versus reliable sensory inputs: *Ordinatio* I, d.3, p.1, q.4, nn.240–5 (Vat III.146–8).
⁹ Scotus, *Ordinatio* I, d.3, p.1, q.4, nn.238–9, 256–7 (Vat III.144–6, 155–6).
¹⁰ See Pickavé, "Henry of Ghent and Duns Scotus on Skepticism and the Possibility of Acquired Knowledge." Pickavé emphasizes Henry's disagreements with the skeptics and his relative epistemological optimism.
¹¹ In several places, Henry qualifies this concession with "if perhaps our natural powers allow us to do this": *SQO*, a.1, q.3 c, q.7 c, and q.7 ad 1 and ad 2 (Leuven XXI.85–6, 145–6, and 148); *SQO*, a.2, q.1 c (Leuven XXI.203). I shall return to these qualifications in section 6.

effects.[12] Isn't this just the sort of knowledge that Scotus seems to advertise as Aristotelian science? At least at first, it is only when we turn to the (for Henry) higher standards of stability, clarity, and infallibility that Henry sees our natural powers as letting us down where creatable quiddities are concerned.[13] The plot thickens, because Scotus never claims that our natural powers serve up knowledge of creatable quiddities that meets Henry's higher standards. Are the two men simply disputing at cross purposes, or does some more substantial disagreement underlie?

3. Converging Pessimisms

3.1 Academic Arguments

When Henry denies us certain and infallible knowledge of the genuine truth about creatable quiddities by our purely natural powers, he trots out three Academic arguments that move at a high level of metaphysical abstraction. Two contend that human natural knowledge will fall short of the stability standard. [1] Object-side, sensible things that produce the sensible species are themselves mutable and constantly changing. [2] Subject-side, the human soul is itself mutable. [3] A third argument maintains that the species produced are not infallible signs, because we could have the very same signs whether or not things were as the signs represent them to be. Augustine points to the experience of vivid dreams in which we sometimes mistake images for the mind-independent sensible things.[14]

Scotus snaps back: if [R1] object-side and [R2] subject-side mutability were the problem, there would be nothing God could do to fix it, because mutability pertains to sensible things and to our own souls by their very natures. [R3] As for the Ambivalent-Representation argument, Scotus scoffs: intelligible species are of universals, while only particulars really exist. Nobody confuses universals with sensible particulars.[15]

Such Scotistic ripostes border on polemical point-scoring, however. [RR2] Henry's subject-side worry is more nuanced. Yes, the soul is

---

[12] Henry of Ghent, *SQO*, a.1, q.2 c, q.7 c, and q.12 c (Leuven XXI.39–43, 147–8, and 188–9); *SQO*, a.3, q.4 c (Leuven XXI.258); *SQO*, a.24, q.3 c (fol.138vP–139rS).
[13] Henry of Ghent, *SQO*, a.1, q.2 c and q.7 c (Leuven XXI.43–6 and 148).
[14] Henry of Ghent, *SQO*, a.1, q.2 c (Leuven XXI.43–5); *SQO*, a.2, q.1 c, q.3 ad 2 and q.6 c (Leuven XXI.203, 217, 238–41).
[15] Scotus, *Ordinatio* I, d.3, p.1, q.4, nn.219–22, 251 (Vat III.133–5, 153).

essentially mutable, but it could be stabilized by something from the outside. Henry's argument is that only what is ontologically superior to the soul would have enough to it to stabilize the soul.[16] Neither sensible things nor the species and sense-images they produce can stabilize the soul because they are lower on the Great Chain of Being than the soul is (in Scotus' sometime terminology, have less intensive actuality than the soul does). Thus, God is precisely the One who could act on the soul to fix its attention and to keep its attention fixed.

[RR3] Likewise, Henry's various comments about what's wrong with phantasms encourage a more charitable reading of the Ambivalent Representation worry. Sensible accidents are experienced as always-or-for-the-most-part clusters. They come to us in a certain order or pattern. Once the agent intellect abstracts the simple concepts, Aristotelian science reasons from the data of regular conjunction to find its root cause in some natural power that brings this about. But—depending on the condition of the imagination—the imagination may scramble these images—so that, e.g., we imagine not only a horse but a goat-stag or chimera—and so may mislead us about which conjunctions have an underlying root in nature and which do not.[17]

3.2 Problems with Phantasms

The fact is that both philosophers recognize serious limits to how much information about creatable material quiddities we can get out of phantasms. In his crisp article "Scotus on Doing Metaphysics *in statu isto*,"[18] Giorgio Pini focuses what is the principal phantasm problem for Scotus: viz., that the proper and common objects of the senses are sensible qualities and quantities—in short, sensible accidents. Substances do not act on the senses directly but only by means of their accidents. But that means that what the agent intellect in the first instance abstracts from phantasms is universal accidents. Scotus eventually concludes that we can reason from these to an abstract concept of substance and further to constructed con-

---

[16] Henry of Ghent, *SQO*, a.1 and 2 c (Leuven XXI.44).
[17] Henry of Ghent, *SQO*, a.2, q.5 c (Leuven XXI.226–7).
[18] Pini, "Scotus on Doing Metaphysics *in Statu Isto*." See also "Scotus on Knowing and Naming Natural Kinds," and "Scotus and Avicenna on What It Is to Be a Thing," esp. pp.382–4. Pini's points are anticipated by Frank and Wolter in *Duns Scotus, Metaphysician*, ch.4, pp.134–83, esp. 134–8, 147–9, 174–5.

cepts of particular substance kinds, only because we can arrive via Aristotelian abstraction at a concept of being that is univocal to substances and accidents. It follows further that for Scotus, the *ante-mortem* functioning of our purely natural powers—the agent intellect abstracting from phantasms—can afford us no *simple* proper concepts of creatable material quiddities. All of the concepts we have of them are constructed: the nature is the root of the powers that underwrite such always-or-for-the-most-part conjunctions of accidents, different natures for different functional- and accident-clusters. As already noted, Scotus thinks this problem can and will be fixed after death, indeed, as soon as the soul is separated from the body. Then it will no longer have to get its information about created material quiddities indirectly, but will be able to abstract universal concepts from its own intuitive cognitions of those quiddities.[19]

Henry identifies almost the same difficulty with knowledge via phantasms. Henry forwards the following principle:

[P] X can cause a clear and perfect concept of a quiddity F only if [i] X has the nature F, and [ii] X acts through the nature F.

But a stone does not-[ii] act through the nature stone to cause a concept of stone; rather it acts through sensible accidents and sensible species. Therefore, a stone does not thereby cause a clear and perfect concept of stone-nature in the knower.[20] Note: Henry does not make the platonizing claim that not-[i] the spatio-temporal particular stone does not have the true nature of stone, but reasons on the basis of not-[ii] the stone does not act through the nature of stone in causing knowledge. Henry's conclusion is that a clear and perfect concept of the quiddity can be produced only by causal contact with the quiddity itself.

In his *Summa Quaestionum Ordinarium*, Henry meets the problem that phantasms are caused by and so directly representative only of accidents, by appealing to an analogy with the animal's *vis aestimativa*. Just as the sheep sense-perceives the wolf-accidents and the *vis aestimativa* enables it to dig under the phantasms to perceive danger; so when we sense-perceive and imagine the accidents, reason is triggered to dig under the phantasms to discover the quiddity.[21] Scotus thinks that the *vis aestimativa* is a mistaken

---

[19] Scotus, *Ordinatio* I, d.3, p.1, q.3, nn.185–7 (Vat III.112–14).
[20] Henry of Ghent, *SQO*, a.1, q.4 c (Leuven XXI.106–7).
[21] Henry of Ghent, *SQO*, a.1, q.1 c (Leuven XXI.28); *SQO*, a.24, q.2 (fol.138rI).

theoretical posit. He mocks Henry's metaphor of "digging under," contending that a sheep would run away from a sheep in wolves' clothing (wolf-accidents) as much as from a real wolf.[22]

Yet, both philosophers think that we "dig under" the phantasms in that we start from them and the concepts abstracted from them, and reason via *a priori* principles to constructed concepts of substance. The agent intellect abstracts the accident concepts. We give a name to the regular accident-cluster. We seek more experiences and apply the method of division to construct a concept to which we can give a definition. The dangling question for each and both is how we are able to do this, how we are able to get such results starting from phantasms. Scotus says a condition of the possibility of doing this is the univocity of being. But Henry thinks "being" applies only analogically to substance and accident as to God and creatures. I will return to this issue in section 6.

Scotus also illustrates how the move from phantasms to knowledge of quiddities is non-trivial. His example is that of someone who recognizes that the whole log is greater than part of the log, and the whole stone greater than part of the stone, but does not yet recognize that what makes these propositions true has nothing to do with log or stone, but only to do with the relation of whole and part. Here Scotus' remedy is further Aristotelian abstraction.[23]

Henry gives a different example: that sometimes what we abstract from phantasms doesn't enable us to tell fool's gold from real gold. Here the difficulty is just the one cited above—that clusters of accidents might mislead us. Not only would not every cluster clothe a nature (chimera and goat-stag accidents do not).[24] Sometimes a given cluster might go with more than one nature. We need more discriminating accident-clusters to distinguish them. Scotus would acknowledge: further experience, further application of the method of division would be required to sort this out. What Scotus denies is that any special Divine action is necessary. These further investigative moves are within the repertoire of our purely natural powers. That such mistakes occur, that not everyone gets this right, is not a function of special Divine favor, but of varying degrees of diligence and natural intelligence. Experience supports this conclusion. Why would Henry think otherwise?

---

[22] Scotus, *Ordinatio* I, d.3, p.1, q.2, n.62 (Vat III.43–4).
[23] Scotus, *Ordinatio* I, d.3, p.1, q.4, n.275 (Vat III.167–8).
[24] Henry of Ghent, *SQO*, a.2, q.3 ad 2 (Leuven XXI.217).

In fact, both philosophers think that constructed quidditative concepts can be arrived at starting with abstraction from phantasms. Both recognize that intelligence and perseverance are required for progress from phantasms to quidditative knowledge, so that—unlike the phantasms themselves—it is not common to all. *And* both recognize a limit to the quidditative knowledge that can be extracted from phantasms.

Invoking Averroes, Henry observes: "there is more to be known about quiddities of substances than that they are the causes of the accidents."[25] Scotus would agree that—roughly speaking—this is all that the constructed concepts arrived at via the methods of Aristotelian science give us. Scotus also agrees that there is more and better to be known. Once again, Scotus maintains that separate souls become acquainted with it via intuitive cognitions, on the basis of which they abstract universal concepts. Likewise, *post-mortem*, we will be able to cognize a triangle's having three…insofar as it is a participation of God and fits into the order of the universe which expresses God's perfection. Scotus declares that this will be a nobler way to cognize a triangle's having three…than through the definition of triangle. Likewise, to cognize "life ought to be lived with moderation" for the sake of attaining ultimate happiness which is to attain the Divine essence in itself, is to cognize this more perfectly than through some principle in the genus of morals such as "life is to be lived worthily."[26]

Thus Scotus recognizes that the perfection and completion of scientific knowledge would not be to know the definition of a quiddity and to have demonstrations of its other properties *propter quid* in the manner of Euclidean geometry. The perfection and completion of scientific knowledge would involve the universe, as a whole, knowing where this quiddity fits into the order of the universe as a whole—the essential orders of dependence and eminence, to know this all the way back to the first cause. Scotus believes that we are naturally suited to have but—by free and contingent Divine policy—will have to wait for these satisfactions.[27] The remaining question is, why does Henry think that some researchers get beyond working with our constructed concepts of creatable quiddities? Henry makes clear that he does not envision any *general* Divine policy according to which God produces clear and perfect concepts whenever thinkers have made

---

[25] Henry of Ghent, *SQO*, a.24, q.6 c (fol.142rvR).
[26] Scotus, *Ordinatio* I, d.3, p.1, q.4, n.277 (Vat III.170).
[27] Scotus, *Ordinatio* I, d.3, p.1, q.4, n.277 (Vat III.169).

advanced and persistent intellectual efforts.[28] But the real puzzle is, why think that in this life any one other than the human soul of Christ ever gets these clarified and perfected concepts at all?

4. Intelligible Species

If phantasm problems are not sufficient by themselves to explain why Henry did and Scotus did not believe in special Divine illumination to clarify and perfect our *ante-mortem* concepts of creatable quiddities, perhaps their differences arise over the next phase of the Aristotelian cognitive psychological process—viz., the abstraction of intelligible species.

4.1 Intelligible Species, Impressed or Expressive?

If phantasm problems have to do with their intentional content and their order, Henry came to problematize Aristotelian notions of intelligible species on the ground that *their presumed ontological status was at odds with their supposed functional role*. Standard Aristotelian accounts treated the intelligible species as an inherent form that the agent intellect abstracts and impresses on the possible intellect. In earlier passages, Henry appears to agree that intelligible species are necessary for human understanding, and to treat the intelligible species as an inherent form with two functions: to make the intelligible object present to the intellect; and to actualize the possible intellect, with the result that the possible intellect forms a concept.[29]

Evidently, several considerations brought him to change his mind. First, in *Quodlibet* IV, q.7, and V, q.14, Henry argues that no intelligible species is necessary for understanding objects that are themselves immediately present to the intellect—*ante-mortem* (Henry thinks) that includes the soul and what exists in the soul (e.g., soul acts); *post-mortem* the naked Divine essence.[30] Second, Henry came to think that no really inherent intelligible species could be involved in understanding extra-mental material objects either. Henry continues to acknowledge that sensible species are inherent in

---

[28] Henry of Ghent, *SQO*, a.1, q.2 c and q.4 c (Leuven XXI.60–3, 67–8, and 99).
[29] Henry of Ghent, *SQO*, a.1, q.3 c (Leuven XXI.84); *Quodl.* III, q.1 (fol.48rV).
[30] Henry of Ghent, *Quodl.* I, qq.12–13 (Leuven V.80); III, q.1 (fol.48rV); IV, q.7 (Leuven VIII.34–43).

and propagated through the medium and into the sense organs.[31] Henry counted such changes as natural and material accidental changes. But where the intellect is concerned, Henry began to tell a different story, because he became convinced that no such really inherent accident could represent universal intelligible contents. Henry reasons:

[i] Real accidents require real causes.
[ii] Effects are assimilated to their causes.
[iii] Only particulars really exist.
[iv] If intelligible species were really inherent accidents, then they would have particular causes and be particular effects.
[v] Therefore, they would be able to represent their effects only under the aspect of the particular.

Thus, if impressed intelligible species were supposed to account for object presence, they are unfit for purpose. No really inherent accident could do that job.

Henry concludes that the bearer of universal intelligible content abstracted by the agent intellect from the phantasms will have to have a different ontological status from that of really inherent accident. Accordingly, Henry distinguishes being in the soul as a really extant inherent accident from being in the soul objectively, as an object. Henry comes to hold that what the agent intellect abstracts is not an *impressed* intelligible species but an *expressive* species. The agent intellect abstracts the universal intelligible content and makes it to be in the intellect as an object that actualizes the intellect as a *ratio movendi* or *ratio cognoscendi*.[32]

Some commentators[33] say that Henry thus abolished intelligible species. In his magisterial article "Intelligible Species in the Mature Thought of Henry of Ghent,"[34] Michael E. Rombreiro argues that it would be better to say that Henry reconceptualized, that he came to treat intelligible species as expressive rather than impressed species. Rombreiro finds that Henry maps back this distinction between impressed and expressive species onto the

---

[31] Henry of Ghent, *Quodl.* V, q.14 (fol.176rLM); *SQO*, a.33, q.2 (Leuven XXVII.151); *SQO*, a.58, q.2 ad 3 (fol.129vE and 130rGH).
[32] Henry of Ghent, *Quodl.* III, q.21 and V, q.14 (fol.136vH and 176vO–177rO). Summarized by Scotus, *Ordinatio* I, d.3, p.3, q.1, n.340 (Vat III.205–6).
[33] For example, Macken, "La théorie de l'illumination divine dans la philosophie d'Henri de Gand"; Cross, *Duns Scotus's Theory of Cognition*, ch.4, pp.90–5.
[34] Rombreiro, "Intelligible Species in the Mature Thought of Henry of Ghent."

senses. The medium (air, water, etc.) receives only impressed sensible species. The external senses receive both impressed species and expressive species: by means of the impressed species of red, red exists in vision as in an object. The imagination does not receive further impressed species, but on the basis of those received by the external senses and stored in memory, it has phantasms that are not really extant inherent accidents but exist objectively in the imagination as an object. These objectively extant contents of the phantasm have a double aspect: shone on by the light of sensory powers, they represent particulars; by the light of the agent intellect, universals.

4.2 Scotus' Critique

In *Ordinatio* I, d.3, p.3, q.1, Scotus argues that what Henry calls impressed intelligible species *are* required for *ante-mortem* human understanding.

4.2.1 No Double-Aspect Representation

Negatively, Henry's account—that the content of the phantasm can represent particulars under the light of the imagination and universals under the light of the intellect—cannot hold, because it is impossible for one and the same species to represent particulars and to represent universals. Scotus subsumes the relation between the representation and what it represents under the essential order of dependence, and maintains that what is represented is naturally prior to the representation, as a measure of the representation. But just as over-determination is impossible in the order of efficient causality (there can't be two sufficient efficient causes of one and the same effect), so Scotus reasons, there can't be two measures of one and the same representation.[35]

4.2.2 Autonomous Access

Positively, Scotus here seems to say that it is essential to cognitive power that its object be present naturally prior to its cognitive act. But since *ante-mortem* we have no direct cognitive access to material quiddities, object presence must be secured by a species. Of course, Henry allows that where extra-mental material things are concerned, the soul receives sensible species.

[35] Scotus, *Ordinatio* I, d.3, p.3, q.1, nn.353–8, 381 (Vat III.211–16, 231–2).

Scotus insists, however, that it is a perfection in a cognitive power not to depend on some other power for the presence of its object. Object presence is mediated to the external (and internal) senses by sensible species. Because the intellect is a cognitive power superior to the senses, it must have its own species over and above any received into the senses or imagination. Therefore, the presence of intelligible objects is secured for the intellect by *intelligible* species. On Rombreiro's reading, however, middle-years Henry also posits intelligible species, only they are expressive species rather than impressed species.[36]

4.2.3 Real Accidents

Scotus contends: these species have to be *real and really inherent impressed species*. The reason is that they are produced by the agent intellect, and the agent intellect is a real cause. But real causes have real effects. Scotus concludes: the intelligible species must be a real effect! Since the intelligible species is not a substance, it must be a really extant inherent accident.[37]

4.3 Upshot?

Certainly, the Scotus of *Ordinatio* I, d.3, p.3, q.1, is at logger-heads with middle-years Henry over the ontological status of intelligible species. But so what? It is not that *Ordinatio*-Scotus rejects Henry's distinction between existing in the soul as an inherent accident and existing in the soul as an object. *Ordinatio*-Scotus repeatedly implies that when the intellect understands an object, that object has *esse intelligibile*, which Scotus counts as a diminished mode of existence. Thus, *Ordinatio*-Scotus and Henry appear to agree that abstraction from the phantasms results in the abstracted content existing in the soul as an object. Still more surprising, Giorgio Pini calls attention to an apograph to Scotus' *Lectura* discussion in which Scotus seems to say that God could cause my thought of F without causing me to have an intelligible species of F—which seems to imply that the intentional direction of human thought does not essentially depend on intelligible species after all.[38] Even if Scotus held to the necessity of impressed intelligible

---

[36] Scotus, *Ordinatio* I, d.3, p.3, q.1, nn.366–9 (Vat III.222–5).
[37] Scotus, *Ordinatio* I, d.3, p.3, q.1, nn.359–60 (Vat III.216–18).
[38] Pini, "Can God Cause My Thoughts? Scotus' Case against the Causal Account of Intentionality."

species and Henry rejected them, it is not clear why this difference should make a difference. It is what exists in the soul as an object that is allegedly unclear and imperfect. Scotus and Henry roughly agree on how our constructed concepts of creatable quiddities are what Henry calls "unclear" and "imperfect." This assessment seems not to depend on whether or not the quiddity's existing in the soul as an object is taken to be underwritten by an impressed intelligible species.

5. A Role for Divine Exemplars?

Exasperated readers/listeners may protest. Surely, the difference between Henry and Scotus is obvious: for Henry, the Divine exemplars play a role in human cognition, whereas for Scotus—apart from whatever way they figure in creation, conservation, and general concurrence—they do not! However refreshingly straightforward, this proposal also turns out to be false.

There are unsurprising areas of agreement. For there to *be* Divine exemplars of creatable quiddities, creatable quiddities have to be objects of God's thought. Both philosophers affirm that the perfection of Divine knowledge means that God necessarily has determinate, certain, and infallible cognition of everything knowable, and hence of creatable quiddities.[39] Both maintain that the Divine essence is the primary object of Divine cognition, while creatable quiddities are secondary objects. What encourages the just-mentioned hypothesis—that disagreements about Divine illumination are rooted in contrasting estimates of the Divine exemplars—is Scotus' notoriously vigorous critique of Henry's account of God's knowledge of creatable quiddities.

5.1 Henry of Ghent on *Esse Essentiae*

Henry holds that the Divine essence as infinite virtually contains all creatable essences. For Henry, creatable quiddities are at bottom imperfect ways of imitating the Divine essence. Accordingly, by knowing the Divine essence, God has implicit and indistinct knowledge of creatable quiddities. But indistinct knowledge is not enough for Divine perfection. Because only

---

[39] Scotus, *Ordinatio* I, d.3, p.1, q.4, n.262 (Vat III.160).

beings can be thought of, God can have distinct knowledge of creatable quiddities only if they are beings—indeed, beings distinct from one another. Henry explains that the Divine intellect necessarily produces creatable quiddities in *esse essentiae* and accordingly knows them as such. Henry understands *esse essentiae* to be a kind of *esse simpliciter* and not a kind of *esse secundum quid* (in this case, *esse* in relation to the intellect: being thought of). He reasons that if creatable essences were merely produced in *esse secundum quid*, then the object of God's knowledge would not be the quiddity *simpliciter* but rather the quiddity *qua* thought of.[40] Moreover, it is the fact that "horsehood" corresponds to a quiddity in *esse essentiae* while "goat-stag" does not, that accounts for why "horsehood" names an essence while "goat-stag" stands for nothing. Where the Islamic philosopher Avicenna (as discussed in Chapter 4) was read as holding that God acts as a natural cause necessarily emanating the first intelligence and its celestial sphere in real existence (Henry's *esse exsistentiae*), Henry sees the Divine essence as necessarily emanating creatable quiddities in *esse essentiae*. Henry is firm: *esse essentiae* (which creatable quiddities have from God as a natural cause) and *esse exsistentiae* as are two distinct kinds of *esse simpliciter*. Creatable quiddities have *esse essentiae* eternally and necessarily as objects of God's knowledge. Those that really exist come to have *esse exsistentiae* as a result of a free choice of the Divine will.

Like other illuminationists, Henry thinks that for humans to have certain and infallible knowledge of creatable quiddities, requires causal contact with those quiddities. In the early articles of *Summa Quaestionum Ordinariarum*, he under-explains how this works, except to say that the Divine exemplars are a *ratio cognoscendi* but *in statu isto* not the *object* of our clarified and perfected thoughts. Throughout his career, Henry insists that *ante-mortem* Divine illumination presupposes the agent intellect's action to produce a created exemplar.[41] It would be insulting to a created intellect to consign it to the role of obstacle-remover, preparing the way for a separate intellect to cause its thought.[42] Henry goes further to treat the Divine exemplar and the created agent intellect as *a single agent* acting to produce clarified and perfected conceptual content relative to what is had from the created agent intellect alone.[43] In *Quodlibet* IX, q.15, Henry will

---

[40] As summarized by Scotus, *Ordinatio* I, d.36, q.u, nn.30–1 (Vat VI.282–3).
[41] Henry of Ghent, *SQO*, a.1, q.2 and a.1, q.3 (Leuven XXI.56–7, 67, and 83).
[42] Henry of Ghent, *SQO*, a.1, q.4 (Leuven XXI.98, 103–4).
[43] Henry of Ghent, *SQO*, a.1, q.3 (Leuven XXI.84–5).

even speak of *two agent intellects*—one Divine and one human—involved in producing infallible cognition of creatable quiddities.[44] If we were to use Henry's later analysis of Divine cognition to flesh out his account of Divine illumination, it would seem that causal contact with the creatable quiddity cannot be merely a matter of contact with the Divine essence, even though the Divine essence virtually contains all creatable quiddities. The reason is that Divine illumination is supposed to *clarify* our concepts, while—on Henry's view—the Divine essence by itself gives the Divine intellect only indistinct cognition of creatable quiddities. It would seem that for distinct cognition of creatable quiddities, causal contact with the creatable quiddities in *esse essentiae*—or with the Divine intellect *qua* emanating or thinking creatable quiddities in *esse essentiae*—would be involved. Henry's thought is that because the creatable quiddities that have *esse essentiae* eternally, are the same ones that exist individuated in extra-mental particulars contingently and temporarily, causal contact with the former would improve our knowledge of the latter.[45]

5.2 Scotus Making Something of "Augustine's Words"

Scotus shares Henry's respect for Augustine's authority.

5.2.1 Common Ground

Like Henry, Scotus maintains that while the Divine intellect is one simple immutable act of thought, it is possible to distinguish natural priorities and posteriorities among the objects of God's thought: in the first instant of nature [n1], God understands the Divine essence; in the second instant of nature [n2], God understands creatable quiddities.[46] Like Henry, Scotus reasons: because only beings can be thought of, God's understanding of creatable quiddities necessarily requires creatable quiddities to have some sort of being. Because God's knowledge of creatable quiddities is naturally prior to their creation in real existence, God's knowledge necessarily requires creatable quiddities to have some sort of being other than *esse exsistentiae*.

---

[44] Henry of Ghent, *Quodlibet* IX, q.15 (Leuven XIII, 265).
[45] Marrone makes a great deal of this in his "Henry of Ghent's Epistemology." Compare his earlier book *Truth and Scientific Knowledge in the Thought of Henry of Ghent*.
[46] Scotus, *Ordinatio* I, d.3, p.1, q.4, n.262 and d.43, q.u, n.14 (Vat III.160 and VI.358–9).

5.2.2 Contrasting Problematics

Nevertheless, in making these claims, Henry and Scotus are focused on somewhat different problems. Henry's background worry is how to distinguish possibles (such as horse) from impossibles (such as goat-stag). His contention is that horsehood is knowable while goat-stag is not, because horsehood has a kind of *esse simpliciter* while goat-stag is *purum nihil*. Since only beings are knowable, Henry can explain why there is a Divine exemplar of horsehood but not of goat-stag in terms of that contrast. Henry hopes to do this without positing any eternal *entia simpliciter* independent of God, by insisting that it is the Divine intellect that necessarily and naturally produces them in *esse essentiae*.

By contrast, Scotus thinks the contrast between possibles and impossibles is easily explained in terms of the formal compossibility or incompossibility of their constitutive principles. Horsehood is possible because of the formal compossibility of its formal constitutive principles, while goat-stag is impossible because of the formal repugnance of its constitutive principles (presumably, the formal incompossibility of goat (the genus and differentia of goat) and stag (the genus and differentia of stag)).[47] As Allan B. Wolter pointed out long ago,[48] Scotus' main interest lies in finding a way to preserve the *aseity* of Divine knowledge. Typically, where human knowledge is concerned, objects are naturally prior to acts of cognizing them, as partial causes (*rationes movendi*) of those acts. If creatable quiddities had being independently—say, if God knew creatures because they were (as Aquinas says) present in their own determinate *esse*—then God's knowledge would be dependent on those objects. Since only beings can be thought of, and because God's thought of creatures is naturally prior to the action of the Divine will in producing them in real existence, *Ordinatio*-Scotus' solution to the aseity problem is to say that the Divine intellect *produces* its objects in being, a kind of being other than *esse exsistentiae*.[49]

5.2.3 Ontological Differences

What Scotus disagrees with Henry about is the sort of existence the Divine intellect necessarily confers on its objects. If Scotus thinks that the middle-years Henry assigns intelligible species a status that is too low (*esse objective*

---

[47] Scotus, *Ordinatio* I, d.43, q.u, nn.5–7, 16–17 (Vat VI.353–4, 359–60).
[48] In his article "Duns Scotus, John," reprinted in Wolter, *The Philosophical Theology of John Duns Scotus*, ch.1, pp.1–27; esp. 18.
[49] Scotus, *Ordinatio* I, d.3, p.1, q.4, n.268 (Vat III.163–4).

instead of real existence), Scotus now contends that Henry's doctrine of creatable quiddities in *esse essentiae* assigns them an ontological status that is too high (*esse simpliciter* as opposed to *esse secundum quid*, specifically *esse intelligibile*) and thereby threatens the doctrine of creation. Scotus charges: if the Divine intellect necessarily emanated creatable quiddities in *esse simpliciter*, then not only God but all creatable quiddities would be formally necessary.

It would be easy to find Scotus' argument underwhelming. After all, the separate intelligences that are members of Avicenna's Great Chain of Being are like God in existing *necessarily*, but that is not to make them dangerously Godlike, because they are *produced* necessarily and do not—like God—have the reason for their being in themselves. So in a way they are not *formally* necessary. Moreover, on Henry's account: God's essence is identical with God's *esse simpliciter*, but creatable quiddities are derivative; any *esse simpliciter* they have, they have from God.

Scotus counters that Henry's doctrine is still at odds with the Christian doctrine of creation, which makes the stronger claim that nothing other than God is necessarily an *ens simpliciter*.[50] If creatable quiddities necessarily and eternally had *esse simpliciter* from God, then quiddities other than God would not be creatable *de nihilo*. The Divine volition to produce them in *esse exsistentiae* would merely add a kind of *esse simpliciter* which already had another kind of *esse simpliciter*. Likewise, because Divine knowledge is *necessarily* perfect, God would not be able to annihilate creatable quiddities either. God would only be able to deprive them of one kind of *esse simpliciter* (namely, *esse exsistentiae*) while leaving them with another that—while derivative—cannot be taken from them (namely, *esse essentiae*).[51]

Indeed, Scotus wonders what *esse exsistentiae* could add? At times, Henry talks of *esse* just being a relation to the Divine essence. Scotus asks how two necessary and immutable *entia simpliciter* (namely, the Divine essence, and creatable quiddities in *esse essentiae*) could come to be newly related except externally (e.g., if for the first time I think of them as related).[52]

How can Scotus defend the aseity of Divine knowledge of creatable quiddities, while avoiding pernicious consequences for the doctrine of creation? In a nutshell, *Ordinatio*-Scotus' reply is that the Divine intellect does not necessarily produce its objects in *esse simpliciter* but in *esse intelligibile*, a

---

[50] Scotus, *Ordinatio* I, d.36, q.u, nn.19–20 (Vat VI.278–9).
[51] Scotus, *Ordinatio* I, d.36, q.u, nn.14, 16–18 (Vat VI.276–8).
[52] Scotus, *Ordinatio* I, d.36, q.u, nn.15–16 (Vat VI.276–7).

diminished mode of being, a kind of *esse secundum quid*![53] Scotus contends: Henry is just wrong to infer from the fact that an object has a diminished mode of being (e.g., mind-dependent *esse intelligibile*) that the object of thought would be the object *qua* having that diminished mode of being. In a non-complex act of apprehension, the intelligible content has *esse intelligibile*. But its existence in *esse intelligibile* is not part of the content, but what makes the content into an object.[54] Thus, in the second instant of nature, the Divine intellect necessarily acts as a natural cause to produce creatable quiddities in *esse intelligibile*, God gives them their intelligibility and thereby *gives them standing as objects capable of moving created intellects to an act of understanding*.[55]

Scotus is explicit about what the Divine intellect does and does not give creatable quiddities. The Divine essence produces creatable quiddities in the *being* required by the tag "only beings can be thought of." Their *intelligibility* is a function of the formal compossibility or repugnance of their constitutive principles. So Scotus says that God is the source of their esse *possibile* and their esse *intelligibile* "*principiative*," as their causal source. But the constitutive formal principles are *formally* the source of their *esse possibile* and their *esse intelligibile*.[56] In other words, the Divine intellect does not "mess with the content" but rather gives it being as an object of thought. Scotus makes this clear with a contrary-to-necessary-fact conditional: if *per impossibile* the formal principles existed without God, they would still be compossible or repugnant or genus-differentia or genus-propria complements.[57] Scotus concludes that creatable quiddities have *necessary and immutable existence* in the Divine intellect. But because this *esse* does not make them *entia simpliciter*, and because eternity is a characteristic of being, creatable quiddities are only *eternal secundum quid*.[58]

5.2.4 Essential and Causal Dependence

The desire to preserve the aseity of God's knowledge is what drives *Ordinatio*-Scotus to declare that God produces the secondary objects of Divine thought. But does he also join Henry in positing a causal connection

---

[53] Scotus, *Ordinatio* I, d.36, q.u, n.44 (Vat VI.288–9).
[54] Scotus, *Ordinatio* I, d.36, q.u, nn.32–5 (Vat VI.283–5).
[55] Scotus, *Ordinatio* I, d.3, p.1, q.4, nn.266–7 (Vat III.162–3).
[56] Scotus, *Ordinatio* I, d.43, q.u, nn.16–17 (Vat VI.359–60).
[57] Scotus, *Ordinatio* I, d.43, q.u, n.5 (Vat VI.353–4).
[58] Scotus, *Ordinatio* I, d.3, p.1, q.4, n.265 (Vat III.162).

between the Divine exemplars and human thought? Surprisingly, the answer is "yes."

To begin with, Scotus asserts that the Divine intellect produces creatable quiddities in *esse intelligibile* as "their first and primary producer," evidently as a condition of the possibility of the creatable quiddity's being understood by anything else.[59] When we think, our agent intellect produces a thing in *esse intellgibile* as well, thereby making it an object of our own thought.[60] Even if there were no exercise of efficient causal power between God's thought and ours, this would qualify as one of Scotus' "non-evident" essential connections: the efficient causal power of the human agent intellect is so ordered that it cannot produce anything in *esse intelligibile* unless the Divine intellect exercises its natural efficient causal power to produce those objects in *esse intelligibile*.[61]

Nevertheless, Scotus does not stop there, but goes on to identify multiple causal connections between Divine and human thought. He begins by focusing on the objects of thought, first and foremost, with his above claim that the Divine intellect acts as a naturally necessary cause in producing creatable quiddities in *esse intelligibile*.[62] Scotus then recognizes that creatable quiddities contain within themselves many necessary truths, such that when apprehended and compounded, the non-complex cognitions of the terms are the sufficient proximate causes of their truth (the propositions are true by *virtue* of their terms). Moreover, Scotus claims, when apprehended and compounded, such terms act by natural necessity to cause an act of apprehending their conformity and so of recognizing their truth.[63]

Scotus next turns to analyze God's *causal* role in relation to the truth of these propositions. Scotus wants to say that as the proximate productive cause of the terms of such propositions, God is also *a remote cause* of the truth of the necessary propositions they contain: "as the prior cause" the Divine intellect "seems to cooperate with those intelligibles for their natural effect."[64] Since Divine intellect is a naturally necessary productive cause of the terms in *esse intelligibile*, Scotus is inclined to say that the Divine

---

[59] Scotus, *Ordinatio* I, d.36, q.u, n.28 (Vat VI.281–2).
[60] Scotus, *Ordinatio* I, d.36, q.u, n.29 (Vat VI.282).
[61] Scotus lays out this notion of non-obvious essential order in *De Primo Principio* 1.8–1.14. See also my "Essential Orders and Sacramental Causality" and ch.3, pp.51–79 in my *Some Later Medieval Theories of the Eucharist*.
[62] Scotus, *Ordinatio* I, d.3, p.1, q.4, n.268 (Vat III.163–4).
[63] Scotus, *Ordinatio* I, d.3, p.1, q.4, n.268 (Vat III.263–4).
[64] Scotus, *Ordinatio* I, d.3, p.1, q.4, n.268 (Vat III.263–4).

intellect is *a naturally necessary cause of the truth of those necessary propositions as well*.

Those intelligibles—when apprehended and compounded—have a second natural effect, however: namely, they cause *an act of apprehending* the truth of such propositions. Is God a naturally necessary remote cause of this effect as well? With this second natural effect, there is a complication. The propositions won't exist unless humans formulate them. But it is not the case that when humans cognize the terms of such propositions, they automatically formulate the propositions by natural necessity. Such a created act of formulating the proposition will be a really existent creature, and God acts only voluntarily and so *not* by natural necessity in producing things in real existence.[65]

Scotus concludes that Divine cooperation with the intelligibles and the created intellect in formulating the proposition will be voluntary. This means that God *does play a causal role, indeed, not one but three causal roles in our knowledge of per se notae* contained within the simply creatable quiddities: the Divine intellect acts by natural necessity as a proximate cause of the terms and as a remote cause of the *truth* of the proposition, while the Divine will acts voluntarily and contingently as a concurrent cause for the production of the act of formulating the proposition.[66] Nevertheless, Scotus insists, God acts together with the terms for this effect "by general influence" (general concurrence); "no special illumination is required."[67] Where Divine exemplars are concerned, it looks as if the salient difference between Henry and *Ordinatio*-Scotus is not whether there *is* a causal connection between them and human knowledge, but rather which causal connection and whether it happens as a matter of general Divine policy rather than an exceptional intervention.

5.2.5 Real Causes, Real Products?

Unfortunately, this account of Divine exemplars seems inconsistent with Scotus' arguments for impressed intelligible species (see section 4.2.3). Scotus insisted against middle-to-late Henry that the agent intellect is a real cause and abstraction is a real production, which must have a real product.

---

[65] Scotus, *Ordinatio* I, d.3, p.1, q.4, n.269 (Vat III.164–5).
[66] So I do not think it is quite right when Robert Pasnau insists that the Divine light does not act on us but only on the objects of our thought. See Pasnau, "Cognition," esp. pp.303–4.
[67] Scotus, *Ordinatio* I, d.3, p.1, q.4, n.269 (Vat III.164–5).

Scotus concluded that the abstracted intelligible species must be really extant impressed species that inhere in the possible intellect as in a subject. How, then can the Divine essence, which is a real cause, be said to be *productive* of creatable quiddities, if they are not *entia simpliciter* but only *entia secundum quid*?[68] Conversely, if Scotus can say that the Divine essence can be said to produce products that are only *entia secundum quid*, why can't Henry say that the agent intellect produces only expressive species in a diminished mode of existence? Put otherwise, even if the Causal Nobility Principle stands in the way of saying that unreal causes have real effects, why can't real causes sometimes act to produce real effects and other times to produce objects in an *esse* other than *esse exsistentiae*?

In the face of this unwelcome dilemma, Scotus chooses to hold onto the axiom that real causes have *entia simpliciter* as effects, and moves to identify something real in the effect. Scotus proposes: the real element is the Divine act of understanding, which can be "quasi-principiated" not so far as the real being of the thing (*res*) that it is (= the Divine essence) is concerned, but insofar as it is *of* secondary objects. Scotus suggests: we can say that the Divine essence is a univocal *ratio movendi* quasi-moving itself to being an act of understanding of the Divine essence, and an equivocal *ratio movendi* quasi-moving itself to understanding secondary objects or creatable quiddities. The creatable quiddities are neither the primary objects nor the *rationes movendi* of the Divine act of understanding. They are not necessary for the act of understanding to exist, but they are required for the Divine act of understanding to be an act of understanding creatable quiddities as well as an act of understanding itself.[69]

Yet, if this maneuveur is open to Scotus, to save real production by real causes of *entia secundum quid*, why not allow Henry to say that the agent intellect produces expressive species in *esse obiective*. He can say that what is principiated is the act of understanding in the possible intellect. Perhaps he can even say that the agent intellect acts together with the expressive species as the *ratio movendi* of the possible intellect's act of understanding. Likewise, he can say that the Divine exemplar (most saliently the creatable quiddity in *esse essentiae*) acts together with the agent intellect to form one cause in the production of a clarified and perfected concept in *esse objective*?

---

[68] Scotus, *Ordinatio* I, d.36, q.7, n.37 (Vat VI.285–6).
[69] Scotus, *Ordinatio* I, d.36, q.7, n.44 (Vat VI.288).

5.3 Summary Comparison and Contrast

So both Henry and Scotus think that the Divine exemplars play a causal role in our knowledge of creatable quiddities. They agree that creatable quiddities would not *be* intelligible apart from the action of the Divine intellect. They agree that creatable quiddities contain within them *per se notae*, and that when apprehended and compounded, the creatable quiddities cause the truth of the formulated proposition, and that the Divine intellect as the proximate cause of creatable quiddities in a mode of being other than *esse exsistentiae* is a remote cause and naturally necessary cause of the conformity of the proposition to the terms. They agree that the Divine will acts by general concurrence in the production of our really extant acts of intellect—the act of apprehending the quiddities, and the act of formulating the proposition. Both hold that the causality involves not only the Divine intellect but also the Divine will and the creatable quiddities in a mode of being other than *esse exsistentiae*. They agree that real causes can produce things in *esse secundum quid*, but that *esse objective/intelligibile* is "reduced" to some *ens simpliciter* (viz., to the intellect), where the intellect is not formally the *esse* of what is said to be *secundum quid* (say, the nature of stone), but is its principiative source. "The *esse secundum quid* of X is reduced to the *esse simpliciter* of Y" entails "X would not exist *secundum quid* if Y were not an *ens simpliciter*."[70]

What they disagree about is not whether the Divine exemplars play any causal role in our cognition, but about whether there is any *ante-mortem special Divine illumination* to clarify and perfect our concepts of creatable quiddities. Scotus appears to hold that human production of objects in *esse intelligibile* is essentially and even causally dependent on the Divine intellect's prior production of those objects in *esse intelligibile*. But there is nothing to suggest that Scotus would join Henry in having us believe that X *qua* having *esse intelligibile* in the Divine intellect has any causal impact on X's having *esse intelligibile* in our intellects. From Scotus' point of view, the only connection would be a round about one involving general Divine concurrence.

---

[70] Scotus, *Ordinatio* I, d.36, q.7, n.46 (Vat VI.289).

5.4 Textual Complication

Some commentators[71] take Scotus at his word: real causes engage in real productions that issue in real effects. They conclude that Scotus' production-language in relation to the Divine intellect, should not be taken seriously. The Divine and human acts of intellect do not really produce anything in *esse intelligibile* or some diminished mode of existence. They point to parallel treatments of Divine knowledge in *Reportata Parisiensia*, where he backs away from such talk. They take such passages as evidence that Scotus had a reductive understanding of the intentional direction of cognitive acts, one that does not involve any "spooky" modes of existence. This debate is too big to referee here.

For present purposes, though, I feel justified in skirting it. Whatever Scotus may have come to think later, it is the *Ordinatio*-Scotus who attacks Henry's theory of special Divine illumination. I would like to know how the *Ordinatio*-Scotus put it all together, and why he felt it was so urgent to demolish Henry's line.

6. Analogy versus Univocity

Frank and Wolter think they know the difference that makes the difference: Henry is an Augustinian at heart, and Divine illumination is the integral core of his epistemological scheme. Whatever Scotus may say about the limits of phantasms, the ontological status of intelligible species, and the causal roles of Divine exemplars, Scotus' framework remains fundamentally Aristotelian with Augustinian add-ons. With Henry it is just the reverse.[72]

6.1 Exemplars and Priorities

Who can deny it? Despite changes of mind and maddening details, Henry's overall epistemology *is* organized around Augustinian themes. Henry insists

---

[71] For example, Cross, *Duns Scotus's Theory of Cognition*, ch.10, 182–99.
[72] Frank and Wolter, *Duns Scotus, Metaphysician*, ch.4, 134–83.

with Augustine that we see all things in the light of the first truth.[73] God is the first object of our intellect.[74] If *in statu isto* human cognition is occasioned by sensation and is in various ways "from creatures," Henry insists that it is not the case that the cradle-to-grave human intellect derives all of its intelligible contents from sensibles. Not only special, but general[75] Divine illumination is required. Henry takes from Augustinian Platonism the axiom that

[A1]   the perfect is [a] metaphysically and [b] epistemologically prior to the imperfect.[76]

For him, intellectual cognition of creatures—whether the non-complex cognition of *id quod verum est*, or the complex cognition of their truth—requires some sort—at least implicit—of measuring of the creature up against its paradigm. But according to Henry's cognitive psychology, this happens in different ways.

6.1.1 Non-Complex Cognition and Analogy

At the level of non-complex cognition, to conceive of a creature as a being (or as true, one, good, beautiful in the transcendental sense), one has to recognize it as a being (or as true, one, good, beautiful). But recognizing it as a being presupposes a prior cognition of perfect being or being itself.[77,78] Thus, Henry posits that no matter what intelligible species we first abstract from phantasms, we get our first concepts of indeterminate being, true, good, etc., at the same time.[79] But being, good, true…cannot pertain to the perfect and the imperfect *univocally*, because the paradigm and the participant do not—like two horses—share the same form or common nature, so that they are related by similarity. Rather paradigm and participant have nothing real in common (no common metaphysical constituent), but are related only by imitation.[80] For Henry, no common reality means no com-

---

[73] Henry of Ghent, *SQO*, a.24, q.8 c ("omne quod intelligitur, in prima veritate intellegitur"), and q. 9 (fol.145vS and 146vY).
[74] Henry of Ghent, *SQO*, a.24, q.7 c (fol.144rH).
[75] Henry of Ghent, *SQO*, a.24, q.2 c (fol.138rI).
[76] Henry of Ghent, *SQO*, a.24, q.8 c (fol.145rvP).
[77] For a remarkably clear and helpful discussion of this topic, see Teske, "Henry of Ghent and the Analogy of Being," ch.11, 247–63.
[78] Henry of Ghent, *SQO*, a.21, q. 2 c (fol.124vP); a.24, q.7 c (fol.144rH and 144vI–K).
[79] Henry of Ghent, *SQO*, a.24, q. 7 c (fol.145rN); a.1, q.5 c, q.11 c, and q.12 c (Leuven XXI.126–7, 181, and 189–90).
[80] Henry of Ghent, *SQO*, a.21, q. 2 c (fol.124rFG, K and 126rE).

mon intelligible content. Henry concludes that while our first concepts of indeterminate being, good...appear simple, they are not. Instead, what appears to be a single concept of indeterminate being is really the mind's confusion of two "closely related" but distinct concepts. The first concept of negatively indeterminate being is of being itself which in its simplicity is not apt to be further determined. This is a concept of God under the aspect of his most general attributes. The other is a concept of privatively indeterminate being, of universal being that *is* apt to be further determined.[81] The confusion of these two concepts which we receive is what Henry counts as an analogical concept of being—one that applies analogically to God and creatures.

Henry clarifies: among other things, the intellect's natural function is to understand creatures. The intellect cannot perform this function without first concepts. Henry repeatedly says that humans receive first concepts *ex puris naturalibus* when sensation prompts and they begin to understand. Henry concludes that acquiring first concepts does not require effort or investigation.[82] Avicenna attributes the causation of first concepts to the separate agent intellect. Henry knows better: God is their *ratio cognoscendi*.[83] But there is more: God is their *object*. The concept of negatively indeterminate being is a non-complex concept of God under his most general attributes. Because the concept is non-complex, and because God is simple (so that God's essence is identical with God's *esse*),[84] the concept is a simple confused cognition of God's quiddity and God's *esse*.[85] Corollary to this is that God's *esse* and quiddity are co-understood whenever a creature is conceived of as a being or as *id quod verum est*.[86]

Henry concludes: humans have a simple concept of God's *esse*/quiddity *ex puris naturalibus*.[87] Once again, their natural functioning requires it, because it is a condition of the possibility of the intellect's conceiving of anything as a being. But because the intellect conceives of God under the most general attributes and the concept of negatively indeterminate being is usually confused with the concept of privatively indeterminate being, it is possible (indeed usual) for us to have such cognitive access to God's quiddity

---

[81] Henry of Ghent, SQO, a.21, q. 2 and a.24, q.7 (fol.124vP–124rPQ and 144rH).
[82] Henry of Ghent, *SQO*, a.24, q.2 c (fol.138rH–M).
[83] Henry of Ghent, *SQO*, a.24, q.7 (fol.145rN–O).
[84] Henry of Ghent, *SQO*, a.21, q.4 c and a.23 (fol.127vS and 136vX).
[85] Henry of Ghent, *SQO*, a.22, q.3 c (fol.132rC).
[86] Henry of Ghent, *SQO*, a.22, q.2 c (fol.130vQ).
[87] Henry of Ghent, *SQO*, a.24, q.2 c (fol.137vH).

without recognizing that we do. Hence, having the confused analogical concept is not enough by itself to put us in a position to see that God's *esse* is included in God's quiddity or to recognize "God exists" as a *per se notum*. That would require a determinate conception of the quiddity, which the first concepts do not provide.[88]

Even though we begin by conflating the concept of negatively indeterminate being with privatively indeterminate being, we can also come to distinguish them and in the process come to know that God exists, not by reasoning—through the way of causality and/or the way of eminence—but by a distinctive kind of abstraction. Here Henry brings together Augustine's *De Trinitate* VIII with Avicenna's claim that God's existence can be known "from universal propositions."[89] There are two types of abstraction: "Aristotelian" abstraction from particular to universal: e.g., from Socrates and Callias to homo; and "Augustinian" abstraction from participated F to subsistent F.[90] As Giorgio Pini notes, Aristotelian abstraction is just an operation of generalization.[91] It does not add new content, but rather subtracts from it. As Frank and Wolter say, Aristotelian abstraction moves from concepts of more content and less extension toward concepts with less content and greater extension.[92] The concept of privatively indeterminate being is a simple concept with minimal content and maximal extension.

As for "Augustinian" abstraction, Henry quotes *De Trinitate* VIII: "see this good, that good; take away 'this' and 'that', and if you can, see the Good Itself."[93] Augustine's language suggests that abstraction is a matter of subtraction: "take away 'this', take away 'that.'" But in fact what Augustine envisions is a process neither of addition nor of subtraction but a shift of attention from participated F to paradigm F. Henry has emphasized that participated F and paradigm F have nothing real in common. And Henry maintains that univocity requires having something real in common (such as the univocal predication of "horse" of Silver and Lightning). Since the content "negatively indeterminate being" cannot be derived from "privatively indeterminate being" by Aristotelian abstraction, and since the perfect is epistemologically prior to the imperfect, it must be acquired from

---

[88] Henry of Ghent, *SQO*, a.22, q.2 c, a.22. q.6 c, and a.24, q.3 c (fol.130vQR-131rS; 135vL; and 139vX).
[89] Henry of Ghent, SQO, a.22, q.5 (fol.134vD).
[90] Henry of Ghent, SQO, a.22, q.5 (fol.134vE).
[91] Pini, "Scotus on Doing Metaphysics *in statu isto*," p.36.
[92] Frank and Wolter, *Duns Scotus, Metaphysician*, ch.4, p.143.
[93] Henry of Ghent, *SQO*, a.22, q.5 c (fol.134vE).

elsewhere. For Henry, however, the content is given *ex puris naturalibus* in our first concepts. The concept of indeterminate being appears to be one concept, but is in fact two. So Augustinian abstraction involves a shift in attention to the concept of negatively indeterminate being itself, which we had in the first place. Moreover, if you can make that cognitive shift, you can know being itself and are acquainted with God's *esse* without reasoning and without having determinate knowledge of God's quiddity of the sort that would allow you to recognize "God exists" as a *per se nota*.[94]

In sum, because the perfect is metaphysically and epistemologically prior to the imperfect, God's essence/quiddity under the aspect of its most general attributes is understood prior to any creature's being understood.[95] God is the *first* object of cognition. Moreover, God's essence/quiddity/*esse* under the aspect of its most general attributes is co-understood whenever a creature is understood or conceived of as being, true, good...This happens *ex puris naturalibus* with *general* Divine illumination assisting (*assistente divina illustratione generali*)[96] without any study or investigation on our part, whether we notice it or not.[97] We can notice with effort and distinguish the two concepts that our mind conflates into the analogical concept. Where this first concept is concerned, God is *both a ratio cognoscendi*[98] and *an object*[99] but under the aspect of his most general attributes. Moreover, as the *first* object, cognition of which under its most general attributes is a condition of the possibility of understanding anything else, God is a *ratio cognoscendi* of everything else that is understood.[100]

6.1.2 Special Illumination and the Truth of Creatable Quiddities

Classifying Henry as an "illuminationist" encourages us to lump Henrican general and special illumination together. But that would ignore significant differences between them. First, Henry does not endorse [A1] the epistemological priority of the perfect where our *ante-mortem* knowledge of creatable quiddities is concerned. On the contrary, he consistently maintains that *ante-mortem* abstracting the created exemplar is presupposed for special Divine illumination. What is true is that both general and special

---

[94] For a very helpful analysis of Henry's argument, see Teske, "Henry's Metaphysical Argument for the Existence of God," ch.3, pp.65–91.
[95] Henry of Ghent, *SQO*, a.22, q.6 c (fol.135vL).
[96] Henry of Ghent, *SQO*, a.24, q.2 c (fol.138rI).
[97] Henry of Ghent, *SQO*, a.22, q.2 c and a.24, q.9 c (fol.130vR and 146vY).
[98] Henry of Ghent, *SQO*, a.22, q.6 c (fol.135vI).
[99] Henry of Ghent, *SQO*, a.24, q.7 c (fol.144vK).
[100] Henry of Ghent, *SQO*, a.24, q.8 c and q.9 c (fol.145vS and 146vY).

illumination involve implicit comparison of the creature with its exemplar. Second, whereas so-called first concepts are had *ex puris naturalibus* without study or effort, *ante-mortem* knowledge of the truth of creatable quiddities does require study and effort which leads to the agent intellect's abstracting the created exemplar from the phantasms (whether an impressed intelligible species really inhering in the possible intellect, or an expressive species in objective existence—in the soul, as an object of thought). Third, because creatable quiddities are more determinate contents than privatively indeterminate being, perfect and complete cognition of their truth requires cognitive contact with the Divine essence under a more determinate aspect—not merely with the Divine essence under the aspect of its most general attributes, but with the Divine essence under the aspect of artist's exemplar. The Divine quiddity under the aspect of the artist's exemplar acts together with the agent intellect to clarify and perfect the intelligible content of the concept naturally acquired. Fourth, whereas the Divine essence under the aspect of its most general attributes is both *ratio cognoscendi* and object of our cognition, the Divine essence under this more determinate aspect is not an object but only its *ratio cognoscendi*.[101] Fifth, whereas general Divine illumination happens *ex puris naturalibus*, special Divine illumination is neither natural (because voluntary) nor a matter of general Divine policy (because there are no creaturely conditions upon which special Divine illumination is regularly consequent).[102]

6.2 Scotus' Transcendental Deduction of Univocity

Frank and Wolter do not mind, because they are convinced that it is Henry's theory of general illumination that exposes his core disagreements with Scotus. For they see Henry's theory of analogy as his solution to the Phantasm Problem to which Aristotelian cognitive psychology gives rise (see section 3.2). If the following four theses—

[T1] In this present state, all of our conceptual content derives from phantasms;

[T2] in this present state, only sensible accidents contribute to sense-images;

---

[101] Henry of Ghent, *SQO*, a.24, q.8 c (fol.145vP).
[102] Henry of Ghent, *SQO*, a.24, q.8 c (fol.145vP).

[T3] univocity requires something real in common;

[T4] neither [a] God nor [b] substance has anything real in common with sensible accidents

—are all true, then we will not be able to form any concepts of God or substance in this present state. In effect, Henry holds on to [T3] and [T4] but rejects [T1] and [T2]. His theory of general illumination forwards God as a natural *ratio cognoscendi* that acts directly to cause a concept of God under God's most general attributes. Curiously, Henry does affirm [T4b] that substance and accidents have nothing real in common,[103] he does not say how we come by our *ante-mortem* concept of substance. Does he think that privatively indeterminate being is itself an analogical concept that conflates concepts of subsistent and inherent being? Does our need for such a concept explain Henry's worry about whether Divine illumination (in this case general) might be needed to produce a created exemplar in the first place?

Roughly speaking, Scotus insists on taking the opposite tack, conceding [T4] but holding on to [T1] and [T2] (suitably adjusted for his sometime admission of intuitive cognitions of our own soul-acts) and rejecting [T3]. Scotus contends that in this present state, all of our conceptual content derives from what is naturally capable of moving our intellect: namely, the object, the object shining in the phantasm, and the agent intellect.[104] Because what impresses the species of the less universal can impress the species of the more universal, the agent intellect in abstracting concepts begins with the *species specialissima* and proceeds with further abstractions up the Porphyrian tree.[105] Whether in this present state or the next, God is not a natural cause that moves our intellect to conceive of the Divine essence.[106] Rather God will be a voluntary cause of beatific vision. In this present state, neither substance nor its essential parts (matter and substantial form) are natural causes that move our intellect either.[107] If they were, we would be able to recognize when the bread-substance was no longer present in eucharistic consecration.[108] Rather [T3] in this present state, the natural movers are the sensible accidents. So if it were not possible for the agent intellect to abstract, from the phantasms they cause, transcendental

---

[103] Henry of Ghent, *SQO*, a.21, q.2 c (fol.124rF and 124vL).
[104] Scotus, *Ordinatio* I, d.3, p.1, q.1–2, n.35 (Vat III.21-4).
[105] Scotus, *Ordinatio* I, d.3, p.1, q.1–2, nn.35, 61, 63 (Vat III.22, 42, 44–5).
[106] Scotus, *Ordinatio* I, d.3, p.1, q.3, nn.126, 139 (Vat III.79, 86–7).
[107] Scotus, *Ordinatio* I, d.3, p.1, q.3, nn.139, 145–6 (Vat III.87, 90–1).
[108] Scotus, *Ordinatio* I, d.3, p.1, q.3, n.140 (Vat III.87–8).

concepts that apply univocally to God and creatures, to substance and accident, we would not be able to conceive of God or substance by any quidditative concept.[109] But God and substance are *per se* intelligible to us, even in this present state.[110] Univocity is a condition of the possibility of our having such concepts *ante-mortem*. Scotus's corollary conclusion is that not-[T4]: univocity in concepts that is sufficient to avoid the fallacy of four terms is detachable from having anything real in common.[111] For Scotus, our *ante-mortem* concepts of God are derivative, so that not-[A1] the perfect is not epistemologically prior to the imperfect. Where our *ante-mortem* concepts of creatable quiddities are concerned, the issue between Henry and Scotus is not so much whether the Divine exemplars play any causal role, but rather whether they add anything to our conceptual content over and above what we get from natural objects and phantasms.

7. Summary

It is time to sum up. Why do Henry and Scotus disagree about Divine illumination when there are wide areas of agreement between them? [i] Henry and Scotus agree that we have knowledge that is free from doubt and error about many things. [ii] Henry appears to agree that natural cognition can produce a created exemplar without Divine help, although in several passages he qualifies this with an "if perhaps." [iii] Henry and Scotus are troubled by roughly the same Phantasm Problem: how can we get a concept of substance out of images of sensible accidents? [iv] Even if they disagree about whether intelligible species are impressed as really extant inherent accidents or are expressive existing in the intellect as objects of thought, Henry and Scotus concur that objects of thought have *esse obiective* or *esse intelligibile*.

[v] Henry and Scotus agree that human thought essentially and causally depends on the Divine exemplar, but they are not of the same mind as to which causal roles the Divine exemplar plays. For Henry, the Divine exemplar

---

[109] Scotus, Ordinatio I, d.3, p.1, q.1–2, n.61 (Vat III.42).
[110] Scotus, Ordinatio I, d.3, p.1, q.3, n.129 (Vat III.80–1).
[111] Thus, Scotus gives us a logical conception of univocity. See Ordinatio I, d.3, p.1, q.1–2, n.26 (Vat III.18). Once again, see Pini, "Scotus on Doing Metaphysics *in statu isto*." For trenchant discussions of Scotus on univocity, see Dumont, "The Univocity of the Concept of Being in the Fourteenth Century: John Duns Scotus and William of Alnwick," and "De Ente of Petrus Thomae"; and Pini, "Univocity in Scotus's Quaestiones super Metaphysicam: The Solution to a Riddle."

is the *ratio cognoscendi* but not the object in special Divine illumination. For Scotus, the Divine intellect is a naturally necessary immediate cause that produces creatable quiddities in *esse intelligibile*, and a naturally necessary remote cause of the truths contained within them. Divine production of intelligibles is a condition of the possibility of our producing them in *esse intelligibile*, so that Divine production of these intelligibles is something on which our thought non-obviously essentially depends. The Divine will is a concurrent voluntary cause of our acts of compounding and apprehending the propositions that formulate such truths. But no special Divine action is involved.

Both Henry and Scotus agree that abstraction from phantasms affords no simple concepts of creatable quiddities. With effort and investigation, we construct concepts of the form "the being that roots the powers that produce this always-or-for-the-most-part cluster of accidents." Since such descriptions presuppose a quidditative concept of being that applies to substances, Scotus concludes that one must be abstractable from the phantasms. Henry denies this.

So when all is said and done, the salient disagreement seems to be this. Scotus insists that *ante-mortem* all of our conceptual content is derivable by abstraction from phantasms, while Henry holds that God plays an efficient causal role in furnishing further contents: our "first" concepts of indeterminate being, good, true, one, beautiful; presumably our concept of subsistent being; and whatever content additions are involved in taking us beyond constructed concepts to clear and perfect concepts of creatable quiddities.

7
Scotus and His Predecessors on the Metaphysics of Habits

1. Aristotelian Method

Aristotelian method begins with observed always-or-for-the-most-part functional regularities and infers powers to explain the regularities. Where should these powers be located: in the functioning thing, or outside it? In something here below, or in something transcendent (such as the heavens on separate intelligences)? One Aristotelian default is to locate salient functional powers in the functioning substance. Moreover, Aristotelian observation notes how powers always-or-for-the-most-part travel together and coordinate to produce a functional focus and how this collaboration lasts for a characteristic length of time. Aristotelian method posits a substantial form to explain why and how such powers travel and work together in a substance of such and such duration. Aristotelian substances are functional integrities that are underwritten by primitive metaphysical unity. Aristotelian substances are one *per se*.

Aristotelian method burrows under functional regularities to identify the substantial natures of things. But Aristotelian method can be reapplied. When new functional patterns emerge, when an individual substance starts to do things (such as speak Chinese) or behave in ways (easily controlling her/his temper, for example) that the individual couldn't manage before, Aristotelian method looks to explain this by reaching for the same range of options. Either there are changes in something external and transcendent (say, in the configuration of the heavenly bodies or in Divine policies), changes in something external and proximate, or changes in the functioning substance itself. Habits are explanatory factors posited in the functioner to explain functional regularities over and above and/or different from those explained by its being a member of a given substance kind. Positing habits in the functioner fits with the anti-platonic Aristotelian bias that locates salient positive explanatory factors in the functioner itself.

Christian theology goes beyond common experience to identify two further contexts of functional variation. Sacramental participation confers on wayfarers (*viatores*) special helps that reverse functional damage consequent upon Adam's fall and begin to fit them for new functions in the life to come (*in patria*). Moreover, the medieval theologians that we are discussing thought that after judgment-day, the whole cosmos will function differently. The motion of the heavens will cease. Generation and corruption will come to an end. Human souls and bodies will function then otherwise than they do now. Aristotelian method got reapplied. Aristotelian bias toward the internal encouraged many of Scotus' predecessors to explain such supernatural functional differences in terms of habits and dispositions infused into the functioners. Scotus disagrees, and his reasons expose fundamental metaphysical differences with his predecessors and contemporaries.

2. Aquinas' Appeals to Habits

To appreciate the distinctiveness of Scotus' approach, it helps to begin with Aquinas as a point of contrast. When Aquinas sets out to explain habits, his attention is on *natural ends* and *norms*. Habits are ordered to natures, and natures are ordered to internal or proximate ends which are characteristic functional acts or something else for the sake of which it produces such functions.[1] Habits are to be normed as suitable or unsuitable, good or bad depending on whether they aid and abet or obstruct a thing from engaging in its nature-perfecting function and pursuing its end.[2] The connection of habits with powers is indirect: habits are ordered to natures and the functional acts that are their proximate ends; habits are related to powers because it is powers that are the immediate principles that produce the functional acts.[3]

2.1 Habits as Perfecting Natural Functioning

In Aquinas' metaphysics, *potentia* has to be rendered determinate. In some cases, nature suffices to render power fully determinate with respect to one

---

[1] Aquinas, *Summa Theologica* I–II, q.49, article (henceforward, a.)3 c; q.50, a.1 c and a.2 c; q.51, a.4 c.
[2] Aquinas, *Summa Theologica* I–II, q.49, a.4 c; q.55, a.2 c and ad 1um; q.56, a.3 c and a.6 c.
[3] Aquinas, *Summa Theologica* I–II, q.50, a.2 ad 3um; q.51, a.4 c; q.56, a.1 c.

effect (e.g., the fire for heating; the stars for circulating). When a heatable is nearby, fire-power acts to its limit always or for the most part to produce its natural effect. Likewise, nature sufficiently determines the heavens to their eternal circular motion.[4] In other cases, however, natures under-determine the coordination of natural powers, which can be exercised in many different ways. Here rational agency is paradigm: the end may be happiness, but practical reasoning suggests many ways to reach it.[5] Where nature under-determines, habits are forms added to the power to make it more determinate by inclining the agent to one pattern of functional options as opposed to others.[6]

Aquinas explains, human beings are metaphysically complex. Besides vegetative powers, we have sensory cognition and sensory appetites, speculative as well as practical reason, and rational appetite or will. Human nature does not "build in" as factory equipment powers that determine human beings to one pattern of action. Rather, human beings are voluntary agents, "lords" of our acts, who—through deliberation—self-determine how and whether to coordinate the exercise of these powers on a given occasion. Habits of practical reason and sensory and intellectual appetites incline and so make it easier to exercise these powers in certain ways.[7] Such habits are qualities, functional principles which make their subject to be in first act, where the actual function is second act.[8] If Aristotelian scientific explanation moves from observed always-or-for-the-most-part functional patterns to powers, substantial forms, and habits as explanatory posits, ethics recommends acquiring good habits the better to promote reliably suitable functional patterns—that is, patterns conformed to right reason.

2.2 Habits as Supernatural Ordering

If habits complete the ordering of rational agents to their natural end and perfecting function, Aquinas appeals to more and different habits to order rational agents to their supernatural end in the first place. Human *nature* is ordered to God as to first cause and common good. Intellectual and moral

---

[4] Aquinas, *Summa Theologica* I–II, q.49, a.4 c; q.50, a.5 ad 1um; q.51, a.1 c; q.55, a.1 c.
[5] Aquinas, *Summa Theologica* I–II, q.49, a.4 c; a.50, a.2 c; q.50, a.3 ad 1um; q.56, a.6 c.
[6] Aquinas, *Summa Theologica* I–II, q.49, a.4 c; q.50, a.1 c; q.50, a.3 ad 1um; q.50, a.4 ad 1um; q.54, a.1 c; q.55, a.1 c; q.55, a.4 c.
[7] Aquinas, *Summa Theologica* I–II, q.50, a.3 c and ad 3um; q.50, a.5 c and ad 1um; q.51, a.3 c.
[8] Aquinas, *Summa Theologica* I–II, q.49, a.3 ad 1um; q.55, a.2 c.

virtues order human functioning toward the goal of happiness proportioned to human nature. Divinely infused habits—the theological virtues of faith, hope, and charity, and the spiritual gifts—order human beings to their supernatural end—to God as friend and companion—and to beatific vision and enjoyment, to a happiness that exceeds human nature.[9] If the natural light of reason makes human intellectual power determinate with respect to understanding the quiddities of material things by abstraction from phantasms, the infused *lumen gloriae* perfects human intellectual power by extending its scope and *modus operandi* to intuitive cognition of the Divine essence.[10] Likewise, the habit of charity is needed to widen the scope of our love, to enable us to love neighbor as self and God above all and for God's own sake.[11] If natural inclination consequent upon natural form readies the individual to act by natural instinct, and moral virtues acquired by repeated acts make the individual more apt to be moved by the dictates of right reason, so infused spiritual gifts make the individual more receptive to being moved by God and ready it to act by the Holy Spirit's instinct.[12]

3. Scotus on Habits

When Scotus thinks about habits, he is more focused on *material* and *efficient causality*. For Scotus, habits pertain primarily to powers, and they affect how the power produces and/or how or how readily the receiver receives.[13]

3.1 Habits and Material Causality

Many of Scotus' predecessors, including Aquinas, assume that the human soul and the human body are able to receive a wide range of supernatural habits and other qualities that make the human body and/or soul able to receive acts that they weren't able to receive before, and to enable them to do many things they weren't able to do before. Scotus does think that

---

[9] Aquinas, *Summa Theologica* I–II, q.62, a.1 c and ad 3um; q.62, a.3 c.
[10] Aquinas, *Sent.* IV, d.49, q.2, a.6.
[11] Aquinas, *Summa Theologica* I–II, q.56, a.6 c; see also q.50, a.6 c.
[12] Aquinas, *Summa Theologica* I–II, q.68, a.1 c and ad 3um; q.68, a.2 c; q.68, a.4.
[13] Scotus, *Ordinatio* III, d.33, q.u, nn.24–5 (Vat X.153–4); *Op. Ox.* IV, d.49, q.1–2, n.11 (Wad X.335–6).

passive disposing conditions can make it easier for subjects to receive, just as the right degree of warming makes the wax able to take and hold the impression of the signet ring. But Scotus thinks that the "fresh habits and infused qualities" move has been over-used in explaining supernatural functional patterns both *ante-mortem* and in the life to come.

First, Scotus digs in where material causality is concerned. Aquinas held that the ultimate material cause, prime matter, is of itself utterly indeterminate, pure potency (*potentia tantum*), getting all of its actuality from form. In not a few passages, Aquinas flirts with the commentators' position that the possible intellect is like prime matter in being a *tabula rasa*, pure potency (evidently for understanding) that gets all of its actual determination from received form.[14] Nature gives the primary determination, the *sine qua non* of there being anything actual. Substantial form is that through which a thing gets its *esse*. But his idea of natural under-determination in human agency opens him to the idea that new forms could be added, not only to give further functional determination to the functions that nature makes possible and aims toward but also to order powers including intellect and will to functions that they did not naturally possess.

By contrast, Scotus begins with the conviction that material causes are naturally prior to what they constitute (en-matter) and hence naturally prior to their union with form.[15] This means that there is something to the material cause, prior in the order of explanation to its union with form, and hence that it is not in itself a *tabula rasa* so far as actuality is concerned. It doesn't get all of what it is—all of its determination—from what unites with or inheres in it (i.e., from substantial and accidental forms). Scotus and Ockham happily conclude that prime matter is not pure potentiality, but rather is actually something on its own—something actual that is in potency to receive further actuality by uniting with or receiving inherent forms.[16]

What is true about prime matter is true all the more so for substances and substance fragments (for Scotus, souls and bodies). Important for present purposes, it is also true for essential powers. There is quite a lot to them naturally prior to their receiving forms that inhere in them. Aquinas himself likes to say, "what is received is received after the manner of the receiver."

---

[14] For example, see Aquinas, *Summa Theologica* I–II, q.50, a.6 c.
[15] See Scotus, *De Primo Principio*, c.II, nn.4, 6, 14 (Wad III.216–17, 219).
[16] Scotus, *Op. Ox.* II, d.12, q.1, nn.10–15; d.12, q.2, nn.3–5 (Wad VI.2.670–3 and 682–3). Indeed, in these questions, Scotus maintains that it is metaphysically possible for matter to exist apart from any and every form, at least by Divine power. Cf. Scotus, *QM* VII, q.5, n.19 and q.6, nn.2, 15–16 (OPH IV.136, 141, and 144).

Scotus emphasizes that what the material cause is already sets limits on what it can unite with or receive and so on what other forms and features it can acquire.

3.1.1 Clarifying Distinctions

Scotus goes out of his way to make Aristotelian common-places explicit. Where substances here below are concerned, there are some qualities to which they are *naturally inclined* (e.g., water to cold), and some that they have the passive capacity to receive but that are *contrary to their natural inclination* (e.g., water to heat), some with respect to which they are *neutral* (have no natural inclination for it or against it—e.g., the surface of a wall to black versus white)[17] and others with respect to which they are *formally repugnant* (e.g., a stone to wisdom).[18] Drawing on then-contemporary discussions, Scotus distinguishes *formal* versus *virtual repugnance*. F-ness and G-ness are formally repugnant if and only if it is impossible for F-ness and G-ness to characterize the same thing in the same respect simultaneously. But F-ness and G-ness are virtually repugnant if and only if the effect of F-ness is formally repugnant to G-ness and/or the effect of G-ness is formally repugnant to F-ness.[19]

Given these distinctions, Scotus draws the obvious morals regarding how God could go about remodeling the world in the post-judgment-day state. First, God could infuse into a subject *neutral qualities* that are not naturally producible, to give bodies and souls new features in the life to come. Second, God could *violently* infuse qualities contrary to the natural inclinations of bodies and souls, and could—*pace* Aristotle—preserve them in bodies and souls *perpetually*.[20] Third, God could violently obstruct the causal tendencies of *mutually repugnant* qualities so that the qualities themselves could both exist in the same subject without their effects, and could do that perpetually. Fourth, God couldn't infuse or preserve qualities that are *formally repugnant* to their receiving subject,[21] because that is not really something to do.

---

[17] Scotus, *Ordinatio*, Prol., p.1, q.u, n.5 (Vat I.36–7); *Op. Ox.* IV, d.43, q.4, n.3 (Wad X.67–8).
[18] Scotus, *Op. Ox.* Iv, d.49, q.12, n.3 (Wad X.573).
[19] Scotus, *Op. Ox.* IV, d.49, q.12, n.3 (Wad X.573).
[20] Scotus, *Op. Ox.* IV, d.49, q.13, n.14 (Wad X.592).
[21] Scotus, *Ordinatio* III, d.27, q.u (Vat X.66–7); *Op. Ox.* IV, d.49, q.13, n.14 (Wad X.592).

3.1.2 Infused Habits and Dispositions, Unfit for Purpose?

Scotus joins theological consensus that human history is divided into distinct states—before the fall, after the fall but before grace, after the fall but under grace, post-judgment-day—which are governed by different Divine policies. God's policies for governing the universe in general and humankind in particular are freely and contingently chosen and different for different states.[22] Nevertheless, Divine power does not include power to make contradictories true, or power to make something exist in a subject that is formally repugnant to it.

Moreover, Scotus emphasizes: *what is essential to a thing does not change from state to state*. What is essential to things in our present state will remain essential in the life to come. But [1] it is essential to human souls to perfect only a certain kind of mixed body,[23] and [2] it is essential to such mixed bodies to have a given chemical constitution which makes them dense. Moreover, [3] it is essential to contrary qualities (e.g., heat versus cold, wetness versus dryness, heaviness versus lightness) to be contraries. No change in circumstance could alter the fact that heat and cold are formally repugnant.[24] Likewise, [4] the essential receptivity of a subject—its natural aptitude to receive—cannot be taken away.[25] Scotus emphasizes: what is essential to the receiving subject is naturally prior to its receiving accidents or uniting with substantial forms, and what the subject is essentially sets limits on what it can receive. Scotus thinks that *in reaching for the "infused habit or quality" explanation, his predecessors have often treated as neutral what is in fact formally repugnant to the receiving subject*. What they put forward as *super*natural is—to Scotus' mind—*contrary* to nature!

3.1.2.1 *The Glorified Body's Dowery*

In the life to come, the bodies of the elect are said to be *impassible*. But Scotus denies that this could happen either through augmenting the soul's dominion over the body or by infusing dispositions either to make it more obedient to the soul or resistant to corruption. Scotus maintains that both soul and body will be essentially the same in the world to come as they are now. If the soul's union with the body as (dominant) substantial form in the composite does not take away the body's essential vulnerability to

---

[22] For example, see Scotus, *Op. Ox.* IV, d.49, q.12, n.6 and q.13, n.11 (Wad X.574 and 587).
[23] Scotus, *Op. Ox.* III, d.16, q.2, nn.4, 6 (Wad VII.1.364, 366); IV, d.49, q.13, n.5 (Wad X.579–80).
[24] Scotus, *Op. Ox.* IV, d.49, q.13, n.2 and q.16, n.6 (Wad X.578 and 613).
[25] Scotus, *Op. Ox.* IV, d.49, q.13, n.3 (Wad X.578).

corruption now, it will not do so then either.[26] If the soul's dominion over the body is understood in terms of efficient causal power, Scotus replies that God does not and really cannot make the soul omnipotent with respect to bodies (because it is formally repugnant to the soul to be that). Angels essentially have only limited power over corporeal nature. *A fortiori*, souls are not a kind of thing that could have power to keep their bodies from being corrupted by the action of contrary qualities.[27] Nor—Scotus argues—could impassibility be conferred by infusing dispositions. For what qualities would they be? Not the sort that belong to naturally incorruptible heavenly bodies, because such qualities are formally repugnant to the sort of mixed body that the human body essentially is. Not elemental qualities or qualities proper to mixed bodies, because those qualities do not prevent but rather give occasion for corrupting interaction.[28] Similarly, God could not make the glorified body *subtle* (capable of existing in the same place at the same time as another body) by taking away the body's density or infusing it with lightness; for it is essential to the human soul that it can perfect only high-density heavy bodies.[29] Enhancing the soul's power over the body won't work either, because creatures aren't the kind of thing that could make one body acquire a place without making another lose that place.[30] As to *brightness*, the essential density of the human body means that it is formally repugnant to the human body to be transparent.[31] And human souls are not the kind of thing that could receive power to make the body's brightness selectively visible to some nearby sighted perceivers and not others.[32]

The Aristotelian bias toward explainers internal to the functioner is defeasible. In these cases, Scotus thinks, no such internal explainer is metaphysically possible. The explanation is external, in terms of Divine power obstructing the interaction of contraries and selectively blocking the causal action of brightness on nearby visual powers as well as the causal tendencies of bodies to fill the places at which they are located. If glorified bodies move wherever and however their possessors want them to (say, if St. Peter flies through the air), this is because the Divine will has a *post-mortem* policy of moving the bodies of the elect however they want them to be moved.

---

[26] Scotus, *Op. Ox.* IV, d.49, q.13, nn.3 and 6 (Wad X.579–80).
[27] Scotus, *Op. Ox.* III, d.16, q.2, n.15 (Wad VII.1.374); IV, d.49, q.13, nn.6 and 11 (Wad X.580, 588).
[28] Scotus, *Op. Ox.* IV, d.49, q.13, n.7 (Wad X.583).
[29] Scotus, *Op. Ox.* IV, d.49, q.14, n.10 and q.16, n.20 (Wad X.601 and 621).
[30] Scotus, *Op. Ox.* IV, d.14, q.16, n.6 (Wad X.613).
[31] Scotus, *Op. Ox.* IV, d.49, q.15, nn.3 and 14 (Wad X.608).
[32] Scotus, *Op. Ox.* IV, d.49, q.15, n.5 (Wad X.609).

3.1.2.2 Soul-Powers and Their Scope
Scotus maintains that *powers are defined by their adequate object, where adequate objects are generically conceived and subsume each and every object over which the power could range.*[33]

Intellectual Power.[34] Because color is the adequate object of vision, only what falls under the genus color can be a *per se* object of visual power. No animal can *see* sound! But Scotus reads Aquinas as holding that it is essential to human nature to have an intellect whose object is the quiddities of material things.[35] (This is an important reason why our concepts apply only analogically to immaterial things such as God and the angels.) Scotus argues that if this were so, it would be *essential* to our intellectual power that only material things and their quiddities fall under its scope.[36] What makes this the case is the comparison between the power and its objects. But powers are the proximate subject (material causes) of habits. The essence of a material cause cannot be changed by the introduction of habits or any other qualities, however they are acquired, whether naturally, violently, or supernaturally. Inherent accidents are too late in the order of explanation to affect what is the power's adequate object (i.e., they are naturally posterior to the power's being the very power it is) and so too late to amplify its range.[37]

If intuitive cognition of the Divine essence essentially falls outside the scope of the intellectual power(s) that we have, and if not even God can expand the adequate object of any given power, then—to enable us to see God—God would have to change the power we have into a different power or to give us another power in addition. Generation and corruption naturally change a material object of one kind into a material object of another kind—in ancient science, water into air or air into water; menstrual matter into a cow-fetus and a cow into a cadaver. But Scotus doesn't think it is metaphysically possible for intellectual power of one kind to be turned into intellectual power of another kind. It is unclear whether Scotus was repelled by the impossibility or by the perceived superfluity of positing two intellectual cognitive powers in the same soul.

---

[33] Scotus, *Ordinatio*, Prol., p.1, q.u, nn.1 and 24 (Vat I.1–2, 15) and III, d.27, n.30 (Vat X.58–59); *Quodlibet* XIV, sec. 14 (Wad XII.376).
[34] Wolter took up this case in his seminal paper delivered to the ACPA in 1949: "Duns Scotus on the Natural Desire for the Supernatural."
[35] Scotus, *Ordinatio* I, d.3, p.1, q.3, nn.110–12 (Vat III.69–70).
[36] Scotus, *Ordinatio* I, d.3, p.1, q.3, nn.113 and 117 (Vat III.70, 72).
[37] Scotus, *Ordinatio*, Prol., p.1, q.u, nn.1, 24 (Vat I.1–2, 15) and I, d.3, p.1, q.3, n.114 (Vat III.71–72); *Op. Ox.* IV, d.49, q.11, n.12 (Wad X.561); *Quodlibet* XIV, sec. 14 (Wad XII.376).

Scotus himself reasons as follows: A power is defined by its adequate object. Therefore, what its adequate object is is essential to the power. Whatever falls under the power's scope must be subsumable by the adequate object. Therefore, if the Divine essence will be an object of our understanding in the life to come, it must fall under the adequate object of our intellectual power now. Therefore, the adequate object of our intellect cannot be the quiddities of material things. Rather, the adequate object of our intellect is being in general.[38]

This argument depends on a shared theological premiss[39]—that elect human beings will see God in the life to come—and it leads to a complication in the application of Aristotelian method. Aristotelian method and always-or-for-the-most-part experience would posit in human beings intellectual power to understand the quiddities of material things by abstraction from phantasms. But theology recognizes two sources of always-or-for-the-most-part regularities: powers in creatures and always-or-for-the-most-part uniform Divine policies. Beatific vision in the life to come requires that human intellectual power essentially have wide-scope everywhere and always. Always-or-for-the-most-part restriction to understanding by abstraction from phantasms in this life is to be explained by Divine policy for the present state: one that always-or-for-the-most-part obstructs the natural interaction between immaterial beings and the human intellect.

The possible intellect is the passive receiver of acts of understanding. Many understood created intellects to be entirely passive in receiving the beatific vision. What we have been discussing so far is whether its essential receptive capacity can be expanded by infused habits or qualities. But Scotus contends that normally and naturally the subject of understanding is active in producing its act as well as passive in receiving it. Normally and naturally, the human possible intellect is an efficient partial cause of its intellectual act. Scotus agrees that beatific vision is supernatural, not only in the sense that no package of created causes suffice to produce it but also in the sense that God acts not as a natural but a voluntary cause in producing it. The question arises, is the human possible intellect somehow active (say, as a partial efficient cause) or merely passive in beatific vision? Scotus does not decide the

---

[38] Scotus, *Ordinatio*, Prol., p.1, q.u, n.1, 60 (Vat I.1-2, 37-8) and I, d.3, p.1, q.3, n.117 (Vat III.72-3); *Op. Ox.* IV, d.49, q.11, n.8 (Wad X.553); *Quodlibet* XIV, 14 (Wad XII.376).
[39] Scotus, *Ordinatio* I, d.3, p.1, q.3, nn.113, 124 (Vat III.70, 76).

question, but he reasserts his conviction that essential powers have fixed scope. If created intellects will exercise any active power in beatific vision, then that power pertains to them in this life as well, although all but a few saints will lack *ante-mortem* opportunity to exercise it.[40]

Will-Power. What goes for the scope of intellectual power goes for will-power as well. In *Quodlibet* IV, q.11, Henry of Ghent argues that an infused habit of charity is necessary to make altruism possible. Henry reasons that, generally speaking, nature is determined to one, so that its natural appetite is focused on its own *esse*. He infers that intellectual nature is determined to loving itself more than anything else, God and neighbor included. Henry concludes that a supernatural habit of charity is needed to enable the creature to love God above all and to love neighbor as self.[41]

Scotus' views about material causality and what is essential to powers tell us that if the will were essentially a natural appetite for its own *esse*, then no infused habit could expand its scope the way Henry envisions. That loving God above all and loving the common good at the expense of one's own individual good, are essentially included in the will's scope is—Scotus suggests—provable on philosophical grounds. First, the will is normed by right reason. No true norm deems a power deficient for not doing what falls outside its scope. But right reason dictates that God is to be loved above all. Likewise, right reason dictates that in certain circumstances (think of the burghers of Callais) leaders of bodies politic ought to sacrifice their own lives for the good of the whole, quite apart from any hope of future reward.[42] Pagans behave altruistically but lack infused charity which comes to believers only as a result of sacramental participation. For Scotus, what fixes the will's scope is not any infused or acquired habit, but the will's native and essential *affectiones*: both the *affectio commodi* (inclination to seek one's own advantage) and the *affectio iustitiae* (inclination to do what right reason dictates) are essential to will-power.[43] If the former insures that the agent's own advantage falls under the will's scope, the latter guarantees that other *bona honesta* also fall within its scope as well.

---

[40] Scotus, *Op. Ox.* IV, d.49, q.11, n.12 (Wad X.561).
[41] Henry of Ghent, *Quodlibet* IV, q.11 (Leuven VIII.88–100); summarized by Scotus in *Ordinatio* III, d.27, q.u, nn.35–6 (Vat X.62–3).
[42] Scotus, *Ordinatio* III, d.27, q.u, nn.47–53 (Vat X.69–72); cf. III, d.27, q.u, n.14 (Vat X.52).
[43] Scotus, *Ordinatio* III, d.27, q.u, nn.47, 54 (Vat X.69, 72).

3.2 Efficient Causal Power?

If infused charity does not and cannot account for the will's altruistic scope, what function does it play? Where habits of the will are concerned, Scotus has two worries about saying that habits add efficient causal power.

3.2.1 Habits vs Powers

First, *if habits add efficient causal power, what keeps them from simply being powers in their own right?* Henry of Ghent brought this issue to Scotus' attention when he contrasted the metaphysical roles of acquired and infused habits. Henry agrees that acquired habits *presuppose* the being (*esse*) of the nature along with the formal functional principles that it essentially includes and/or that are naturally consequent upon it. Socrates' having a command of Euclidean geometry (an intellectual habit) presupposes that Socrates is a human being with intellect among his natural powers. Job's patience (a oral virtue) presupposes that he is a human being with intellect and will and sensory appetites. By contrast, Henry declares, infused habits do not presuppose but *constitute* the soul in supernatural being (*esse*) and redound to the soul's powers to make their acts candidates for merit. Henry insists that the formal functional principle of supernatural action is not the will *qua* modified by infused habits (say, infused charity). Rather the supernatural habit itself is *the* principle of supernatural action. Infused habits confer both supernatural being (*esse*) and supernatural functioning.[44]

Henry's way of explaining the idea that infused habits (the theological virtues) elevate human beings "above" human nature, seems to turn the infused habit into a power in its own right. But if infused charity *is* the power to produce the act, and if infused charity acts on its own so that active will-power is not involved in the production of the act, then the infused habit cannot be said to perfect will-power any more than heat perfects wood. When the heat in the wood acts on its own to heat up and set fire to surrounding objects, the ignited wood may be said to *share* in the act, insofar as it is the receiving subject of the heat. But the wood is not a *per se* cause of the heating, because the wood itself does nothing to produce the

---

[44] Henry of Ghent, *Quodlibet* IV, q.10 (Leuven VIII.81–7); summarized by Scotus in *Lectura* I, d.17, p.1, q.u, nn.32–7 (Vat XVII.194) and II, d.26, q.u, nn.7–8 (Vat XIX.266); *Ordinatio* I, d.17, p.1, q.1–2, n.21 (Vat V.146).

heat. So also, the infused habit and the will on Henry's account. Scotus protests, on the contrary, *the metaphysical role of habits is to perfect powers.*[45]

Scotus isn't much happier with Godfrey of Fontaines' explanation. To be sure, Godfrey corrects Henry: acquired and infused habits both presuppose the nature of the thing and the formal functional principles or powers that are naturally consequent on it. Godfrey insists that both the power and the infused habit make efficient causal contributions. But when it comes to explaining how the power is related to the habit, Godfrey "divides and conquers": the power produces the substance of the act, while the habit causes its intensity. Power and habit are, as it were, two efficient causes with two different effects. Put them together and the power informed by the habit is the formal active principle of the intense act.[46]

Scotus' first objection is metaphysical: the intensity of the act is not distinct from the substance of the act in any way that would allow for the two causes two divide and conquer. What causes the substance of the act, causes its intensity: the infinite will, an act of infinite intensity; finite wills, acts of finite intensity.[47]

Scotus' second caution reflects his own estimate of will-power. He insists that it would be wrong to think that there is any degree of will-act for which an infused habit is needed as a co-cause. Rather *will-power as such ranges over acts of any and all finite degrees up to and including a will-act of infinite degree.* Inhering habits might perfect finite will-power by acting together with it to produce acts of higher intensity, but this would not be by expanding the domain of acts for which it is the power.[48]

3.2.2 Habits and Will in Competition?

This latter observation brings Scotus to his second worry about assigning efficient causal power to habits: namely, that *such power might seem to be in competition with will-power in the production of a will-act and so undermine the freedom of the will.* Scotus toys with but in the end rejects the idea that infused charity does not add efficient causal power but rather is a passive

---

[45] Scotus, *Lectura* I, d.17, p.1, q.u, nn.47 and 49 (Vat XVII.198); *Ordinatio* I, d.17, p.1, q.1–2, n.23 (Vat V.147).
[46] Godfrey of Fontaines, *Quodlibet* XI, q.4 (PB V.22–4); Scotus *Lectura* I, d.17, p.1, q.u, n.51 (Vat XVII.199); *Ordinatio* I, d.17, p.1, q.1–2, n.27 (Vat V.149–50).
[47] Scotus, *Lectura* I, d.17, p.1, q.u, n.52 (Vat XVII.199); *Ordinatio* I, d.17, p.1, q.1–2, n.28 (Vat V.150).
[48] Scotus, *Lectura* I, d.17, p.1, q.u, nn.54–5 (Vat XVII.200); *Ordinatio* I, d.17, p.1, q.1–2, n.31 (Vat V.151–2).

disposing condition that makes the will more receptive to such a will-act.[49] In the end, however, Scotus seems to agree with everyone else that acquired habits are efficient partial causes—incliners but not determiners. And he reluctantly bites the bullet to say the same of infused charity.[50] Scotus explains that *what the infused habit does is to give the act more intensity than the same power would be able to produce alone* <u>with the same effort</u>. Nevertheless, he does not think that natural reasoning from observation would ever entitle us to conclude to the existence of infused charity, because—for any finite intensity—the will could produce an act of that intensity on its own with more effort.[51]

4. Grace on Top of Nature?

In this chapter, I have passed over questions about acquired habits as explainers of ordinary functional variations as when—through practice—one learns to speak a foreign language or—through accustomed acts—becomes more virtuous or vicious. Instead, I have concentrated on the theological cases of altered functional patterns, because I wanted to explore my hunch that Scotus' views about material causality help explain disagreements with his predecessors and contemporaries about the kind of metaphysical work habits can do.

Once again, Aquinas uses the metaphor of the indeterminate being made determinate. *Potentia* is indeterminate. *Potentia* is made determinate by inhering forms. Prime matter is *potentia tantum* (only potentiality). Substantial form is that through which a thing has *esse* and is placed in a determinate genus and species. Substantial form gives definition to what was otherwise indeterminate. Accidental forms provide further definition. Rational natures under-determine functional coordination and so are ripe for further determination by acquired habits.

I suggest that this metaphor of indeterminacy in the subject combines with the conviction that rational natures under-determine function, to make it seem that there is no reason to stop here. Grace can build on top of nature. Theological virtues order the soul to its supernatural end. To hear Aquinas and Henry of Ghent talk, human nature serves as a kind of

---

[49] Scotus, *Ordinatio* I, d.17, p.1, q.2, nn.47–50, 87–91 (Vat V.157–9, 181–4).
[50] Scotus, *Ordinatio* I, d.17, p.1, q.1–2, n.151 (Vat V.211) and III, d.27, q.u, n.75 (Vat X.81).
[51] Scotus, *Ordinatio* III, d.27, q.7, nn.63, 66 (Vat X.77, 78).

substrate, with its substantial form and naturally consequent powers. But on top of these, formal functional principles can be infused that functionally re-orient the individual to a different end—not to God as first cause and common good, but to God as source of individual happiness and companionship; not to obey the dictates of right reason, but to follow the norms laid down by Divine commands. New functional patterns are underwritten by new formal functional principles within the functioner—which observes the Aristotelian bias toward internal explainers.

To be sure, the infused formal functional principles are all accidents. Moreover, they are not proper accidents, naturally consequent upon the individual's substantial form. Rather, infused formal functional principles are rooted in a "super-nature," the Divine essence that is above and beyond any and all creatables. Infused functional principles emanate, not by natural necessity, but voluntarily from God. Certainly, the Divine essence does not become the creature's nature by inhering in it as a formal cause. Nevertheless, just as substantial form and proper accidents give the individual functional focus on its natural end, so infused habits and dispositions re-orient the individual toward a different and higher end. The infused formal functional principles re-do or at least radically tweak what Aristotelian nature and naturally consequent powers already did. And so, without changing the metaphysical identity of the substance individual, infused functional principles function as a kind of immanent "super-nature." This picture may seem the more natural because we already speak of acquired habits as making various behaviors (say, truth-telling to Socrates and murdering to Hitler) "second nature."

What drives Scotus' position is not the indetermination but the natural priority of receiving subjects and how what they determinately are already fixes what they can receive. What subjects—including prime matter, individual substances, substance fragments (body and soul), and powers—are essentially is the same in every state of human nature—whether in Paradise, in this world after the fall, or in the life to come. If we will receive something in the life to come (say, beatific vision in the intellect or brightness in the body), we must by nature have the passive capacity to receive it all along. Apart from the fact that naked divinity is its object, what makes beatific vision supernatural has to do, not with formal causality (our alleged need for infused habits), but with efficient causality. God alone is sufficient to make the Divine essence present to a created intellect, and God does so super-naturally because by a voluntary act! Moreover, nothing can be the receiving subject of formal functional principles that are formally repugnant to its nature. The natures of souls and bodies show that internal formal functional principles could not account for the functional variations revealed for the life to come. Aristotelian method dictates: where internal explanations are not possible due to formal repugnance, locate the explainer in something external. Because infused habits will not do, Scotus outsources to the free and contingent policies of God.

8
Genuine Agency, Somehow Shared?
The Holy Spirit and Other Gifts

1. Presenting Problems

Medieval philosophical theology is firm: the world as we know it results from the exercise of genuine agency, both Divine and human. Genuine Divine agency creates and sustains, is the source of the being and the well-being of everything else. But creatures also exercise genuine agency. The reason is that creatures come in Aristotelian natural kinds. Aristotle argued against Plato that the nature of a substance individual X had to exist *in* X and not separately from X (the way the Platonic form was supposed to exist separately from Socrates). Every substance nature includes and/or gives rise to formal functional principles that explain the individual substance's functions. Thus, an action A belongs to a subject X, only if a formal functional principle of A-ing exists in X.

As simple, the Divine essence is identical with Its formal functional principles of thinking and willing. Creatable natures either include formal functional principles in their substantial form, or emanate necessary accidents that are formal functional principles to act and be acted upon in certain ways. However great the created functional powers may be, they can do nothing without Divine concurrence. In general concurrence, God is the first cause who acts by understanding and willing, while the creature (say, fire) is a secondary cause that acts through its own form (which is the formal active principle included in or necessarily consequent upon its nature) together with God to produce the effect.

For present purposes, three points are important. First, medieval Aristotelians did not view this as a competitive situation. In general concurrence, genuine Divine agency does not compete with genuine created agency. Rather, they insisted, genuine Divine agency and genuine created agency play different roles and collaborate to produce the effect.[1] Second, God creates, sustains, and concurs with any created agent whatever—cows and stones as much as humans and angels,[2] Lucifer as much as Gabriel, Judas as much as Peter and Paul.[3] Nothing other than God could be or do anything apart from genuine Divine agency. Third, Augustinian Trinitarian theology insisted that—whatever may be true within the Godhead—Divine persons express "one action, one will *ad extra*." Because all three persons of the Trinity share numerically the same Divine essence, and the essential formal functional principles of understanding and willing are identical with the Divine essence, they share numerically the same thoughts and numerically the same volitions regarding creatures. The acts of creating, sustaining, and concurring belong no more to one Divine person than to another.

By contrast, in his controversy with Pelagius, Augustine did put genuine Divine agency and genuine human agency into competition. Pelagius evidently restricted God's role in salvation to the grace of creating human beings with free will and giving the law to reveal Divine commands. Human beings were free to obey and win heaven or disobey and go to hell. Augustine countered that God should get more credit. Augustine's strategy was to enlarge the role of genuine Divine agency by shrinking the role of genuine created agency. Human nature—he contended—had been damaged by the fall, so that we suffer under ignorance (of Divine norms) and difficulty (in willing what we believe to be right). At first he affirmed, then later denied that it was within our power to have faith that believes and asks God's help. In the middle of his controversy with Pelagius, Augustine declared that legal conformity to Divine commands is of no value unless it proceeds from a whole-hearted love of God—something not within our power to produce. Toward the end of the debate, Augustine insisted that our wills are more in God's power than in our own. Augustine's more extreme statements and subsequent—perhaps even more radical—interpretations, called into question whether God's plan of salvation left any room for genuine merely human agency at all. Call this **the "Genuine Agency Problem."**

Medievals inherited this problem frame. Their goal was a solution that made room for both genuine Divine and genuine human agency. They fixed on a promising premise: if we are to be worthy of Divine acceptance and

---

[1] Their confident assessment was problematized in the modern classical period by Malebranche. For a contemporary evaluation, see Freddoso's "Medieval Aristotelianism and the Case against Secondary Causation in Nature," 74–118.
[2] Lombard, *Sententiae* I, d.17, c.5, sec. 4, 147.
[3] Lombard, *Sententiae* I, d.17, c.5, sec. 4, 147.

able to perform meritorious acts, God must make us holy. They thought of two ways that God might do this: namely, through what God does as an efficient cause, and/or through a special kind of presence by which God indwells the elect and so turns them into sacred space.

The bible speaks of both. On the one hand, the elect enjoy a distinctive participation in Divine action: "God is at work in you, both to will and to work for his good pleasure" (Philippians 2:13). Again, St. Paul declares, "I worked...though it was not I, but the grace of God which is with me" (I Corinthians 15:10); or, more comprehensively, "it is no longer I who live, but Christ who lives in me" (Galatians 2:20). On the other hand, the Paraclete, indeed the whole Trinity will indwell believers in Jesus (John 14:23-4) with the result that they become God's temples (I Cor 3:16-17, 6:19); Christ indwells believers' hearts by faith (Ephesians 3:17). The bible also talks of "missions" and "gifts": the Father will send the Counsellor (John 16:7; cf. Ephesians 1:17); and "The love of God has been poured into our hearts by the Holy Spirit Who has been given to us" (Romans 5:5).

In itself, indwelling seemed not to be an efficient-causal connection and so looked like a way for God to make humans holy without compromising their genuine agency. But biblical language raised two further problems. First, biblical indwelling must be something different from Divine omnipresence,[4] because Godhead is metaphysically present to each and every creature—non-rational as well as rational, reprobate as well as predestinate—while God indwells only rational creatures and only some of them at that! How can selective indwelling be metaphysically possible for an omnipresent, necessarily concurrent Creator and Sustainer? What can this relation be? Call this **the "Special Connection Problem."**

Second, not only do bible verses imply that God is specially connected to some creatures and not others; they seem to divide the Trinity by implying that one Divine person indwells as opposed to the others: *Christ* indwells believers' hearts by faith; *the Holy Spirit* has been given to us. How is it metaphysically possible for one Divine person to be involved in created being and doing when the other Divine persons are not? Call this **the "Divided Trinity Problem."**

Peter Lombard's *Sentences* launch 13th- and 14th-century treatments of these problems. His answer to the Special Connection Problem made the Divided Trinity and Genuine Agency Problems seem more acute.

---

[4] Lombard, *Sententiae* I, d.17, c.5, sec. 4, 147. See Aquinas, *Summa Theologica* I, q.8, article (henceforward, a.)2 c, a.3 c, and a.4 c.

Bonaventure, Aquinas, and Scotus are most focused on the Genuine Agency Problem and use their solutions to it as a basis for dealing with the other two.

2. Lombard's Problem: The Gift of the Holy Spirit?

2.1 Construing the Authorities

In his *Sentences*, Peter Lombard squarely confronts Romans 5:5—"the love of God has been poured into our hearts through the Holy Spirit that has been given to us"—and raises the question, "is this gift the Holy Spirit Itself or some other" merely created "gift that the Holy Spirit gives?" Eminent authorities seem to disagree: Ambrose and Augustine say, "the Holy Spirit Itself," while Bede insists, not the Holy Spirit Itself, but a gift of grace.[5] In Book I, distinction 17, Lombard sides with Ambrose and Augustine and forwards two theses:

[T1]   the Holy Spirit is the love of the Father and the Son by which they love one another and us;

[T2]   "the Holy Spirit is [a] the love or charity by which we love God and neighbor"—[b] "the charity...that makes us love God and neighbor."[6]

Lombard insists, the Holy Spirit is not given to us so that we might *exist*, but so that we might be *holy*.[7] Through that gift, not only the Holy Spirit but the whole Trinity indwells us.[8]

In Lombard's circle, [T1] was uncontroversial, but [T2] was startling and provocative. Lombard declares, the Holy Spirit is *no mere cause* of that charity by which we love God and neighbor. The Holy Spirit *is* the charity by which we love God and neighbor.[9] Lombard is emphatic: the charity by which the Father and the Son love each other, and the charity by which we love God and neighbor are not two charities or two loves, but one![10]

---

[5] Lombard, *Sententiae* I, d.14, c.2, secs. 1 and 4, 128.
[6] Lombard, *Sententiae* I, d.17, c.1, sec. 2, 142, 144–6.
[7] Lombard, *Sententiae* I, d. 18, c.4, sec. 3, 157.
[8] Lombard, *Sententiae* I, d.17, c.4, sec. 2, 145–6.
[9] Lombard, *Sententiae* I, d.17, c.3, 144.
[10] Lombard, *Sententiae* I, d.17, c.6, sec. 4, 149–50.

2.2 No Genuine Agency?

Immediately, the Genuine Agency Problem raises its head. The Father and the Son are not supposed to be the only lovers in this picture. We, too, are supposed to be lovers of God and neighbor. If *we* act to love God and neighbor, then there must be some motion or affection in our own souls by which we are moved and affected to love God. But the Holy Spirit is not a motion or action in our soul. To say so would be to confuse the Creator with the creature![11] Again, the ignorance and difficulty into which we have fallen require repair in the form of faith, hope, and charity. These are in us through the Holy Spirit, as gifts of the Holy Spirit. But the Holy Spirit is not said to be the faith by which we believe or the hope by which we hope. So why suppose that the Holy Spirit is the charity by which we love?[12]

Lombard's reply acknowledges that the *acts* of believing, hoping, and loving are *in* the soul as in a receiving subject. (This is a minimum condition of genuine human agency.) Nevertheless, it is the Holy Spirit Who works acts of believing, hoping, and loving in the soul. But the Holy Spirit does so in different ways. Whereas the Holy Spirit produces acts of faith and hope in us by means of virtues of faith and hope infused into us, the Holy Spirit works acts of love by Itself alone and not by means of any virtue—infused or otherwise—in us.[13] The Holy Spirit is *not the act* by which we love God and neighbor. But whereas habits in the soul make the soul's actions more prompt, delightful, and expeditious, Lombard wants to say that—when it comes to producing acts in us of loving God and neighbor—the charity that the Holy Spirit *is* takes the place of any infused habit that the objectors suppose the soul to have and so—according to (T2b)—"makes us love God and neighbor."

2.3 Divided Trinity, Special Connections

If the Holy Spirit Itself is the gift, what does it mean to say that a Divine person is *given*? Juggling scriptural proof-texts to distinguish being sent from being given, Lombard explains that the Holy Spirit is *eternally* given insofar as it proceeds from the Father and the Son: the Holy Spirit is the love

---

[11] Lombard, *Sententiae* I, d.17, c.6, sec. 6, 150–1.
[12] Lombard, *Sententiae* I, d.17, c.6, sec. 5, 150 and c.8, 151.
[13] Lombard, *Sententiae* I, d.17, c.8–9, 151–2.

they give to each other. But the *temporal* donation of the Holy Spirit to creatures is something wrought by the whole Trinity. Thus, the Holy Spirit can be said to give Itself to us, just as much as the Father and the Son give the Holy Spirit to us (one action, one will *ad extra*).[14] Likewise, it is necessary to distinguish eternal from temporal missions. The Son and the Holy Spirit are eternally sent, insofar as each proceeds from a Divine person: the Son is begotten by the Father, while the Holy Spirit proceeds from the Father and the Son. Within the Godhead, only two—the Father and the Son—are eternal senders, and only two—the Son and the Holy Spirit—are eternally sent.

Lombard stipulates, only those Divine persons can be said to be temporally sent that are also eternally sent. Each of the Son and the Holy Spirit is temporally sent into creatures, both visibly and invisibly. The Son is sent visibly in the Incarnation when He assumes a human nature, but invisibly "when He transfers Himself into the souls of the pious in such a way as to be perceived or known by them."[15] The Holy Spirit is sent invisibly when It is the charity by which we love God and neighbor and when it illumines the minds of the faithful.[16] The Holy Spirit is sent visibly when attention is called to Its invisible mission by a visible sign such as the descending dove at Jesus' baptism or the tongues of flame at Pentecost.[17] Lombard underscores a difference between the visible mission of the Son and that of the Holy Spirit: viz., the Son is united with a human nature in hypostatic union and so becomes human, but the Holy Spirit is not united with the dove or dove-appearance in such a way as to become a dove or dove-appearance. Neither is the Son hypostatically united with the saints to whom He is invisibly sent the way the Word is made flesh in Mary's womb and becomes human.[18]

3. Additional Hypostatic Unions?

3.1 Attempted Clarification

Lombard's treatment is bold and suggestive, but it is not metaphysically precise. In his *Commentary on the Sentences*, Bonaventure mentions an

---

[14] Lombard, *Sententiae* I, d.15, c.1, secs. 2–4, 131–2.
[15] Lombard, *Sententiae* I, d.15, c.7, 135–6; d.16, c.1, sec. 1, 138.
[16] Lombard, *Sententiae* I, d.16, c.1, sec.1, 138.
[17] Lombard, *Sententiae* I, d.16, c.1, secs. 1–2, 138.
[18] Lombard, *Sententiae* I, d.16, c.1, secs. 2–5, 138–40.

"ancient" interpretation that understands Lombard to be positing a relation of hypostatic union between the Holy Spirit and the human wills of the elect who receive this gift. Just as the whole Trinity brings it about that the Son alone is united to the flesh formed in Mary's womb, so the whole Trinity brings it about that the Holy Spirit alone is united to the created will. To be sure, there are disanalogies. Theological consensus has it that God the Son has assumed one and only one human nature: the Incarnation of the Son is *unique*. But—on this hypothesis—the Holy Spirit would be hypostatically united to many created wills at once, indeed to the wills of all who at any given time are acceptable to God. Moreover, theological consensus had it that once God the Son assumes His human nature, He will never lay it aside: the Incarnation of the Word is *permanent*. Natures do not change with respect to their essential constitution: what it is to be human is eternally the same. By contrast, created will-power is essentially "convertible." It would be unseemly for the Holy Spirit to remain hypostatically united to a created will if that created will turned against God. So Its hypostatic union to created wills would be temporary and episodic.[19]

Hypostatic union would seem to solve the Special Connection and Divided Trinity Problems: hypostatic union is the special connection not shared by all three persons, but all three Divine persons act together to send one Divine person into personal union with a creature. Hypostatic union seems to promise a way out of the Genuine Agency Problem as well. For X to be a genuine *agent*-subject with respect to A-ing, it is not enough for X to be the receiving subject of A-ing. In addition, the formal principle of A-ing has to exist in and be operative in X when X becomes the receiving subject of A-ing. [T2b] (that the Holy Spirit is the charity that makes us love God and neighbor) seems problematic because it seems to imply that our souls are merely receiving subjects of acts of loving God and neighbor, because the charity which is their formal functional principle (the active principle that makes those acts of love exist in us) exists in something else—viz., the Holy Spirit Itself! But hypostatic union means that the person in whom the two natures are united acts (and/or suffers) through formal functional principles in both of its natures. God the Son acts through His Divine nature to sustain and govern the cosmos and through His human nature to take a walk, to touch blind men and bleeding women, to break bread and eat fish. Because both natures are *His* natures, statements such as "This man created

---

[19] Bonaventure, *Sent.* I, d.17, p.1, a.u, q.1 (Quaracchi I.294).

the heavens and the earth" and "God suffered and died on the cross" turn out true. Likewise, if the Holy Spirit were to assume the created will, the Holy Spirit would be acting through Its own created will-power to produce acts of loving God and neighbor. The Holy Spirit would be the person that produces the act, but that would not mean that the created will was not genuinely active, because the Holy Spirit would be understood to produce those acts by exercising Its own created will-power.

3.2 The Hypostatic-Union Hypothesis: Queries and Quandaries

This appeal to hypostatic union is ingenious, resourceful, and shows an instinct for theoretical economy. Hypostatic union is an explanatory posit already added to the array of available metaphysical connections to explain the Incarnation of God the Son. Why not use it again to explain the special connection between the Holy Spirit and those to whom It has been sent as a gift? Why not explain the Holy Spirit's indwelling St. Paul's heart in terms of the Holy Spirit's becoming hypostatically united to St. Paul's will? Let us call that hypothesis, specifically about the indwelling of the Holy Spirit, *the hypostatic-union hypothesis*. Certainly, there are some difficulties to be thought through.

First, it is a striking disanalogy that in the Incarnation, God the Son assumes the *whole* human nature, complete with body and soul, with all of its active and passive causal powers. But the present hypostatic-union hypothesis has the Holy Spirit assuming, not the whole human nature, but the human will, one of the soul's powers. Medievals disagreed about the relation between the intellectual soul and its essential powers. Some (e.g., Aquinas) argued that the soul's essential powers were necessary accidents that emanated from the substantial form,[20] while others (e.g., Scotus,[21] and Ockham[22]) maintained that intellect and will were really the same as the intellectual soul itself. Either way, for the Holy Spirit to assume a human will, would be for it to assume a *part* of a human nature.

Perhaps adherents of the hypostatic-union hypothesis would not have found this disanalogy defeating. After all, they were already committed to the notion that when Jesus died, His human body and soul ceased to be

---

[20] Aquinas, *Summa Theologica* I, q.54, a.3, c; q.77, a.1, c.
[21] Scotus, *Op. Ox.* II, d.16, q.7, nn.15–19 (Wad VI.2.770–3).
[22] Ockham, *Quaest. in II Sent.*, q.20 (*OTh* V.435–40).

united to each other, but each and both remained separately united to God the Son.[23] In the interval between death and resurrection, God the Son was separately united to parts of a human nature. Why would it be worse to say that the Holy Spirit assumes only the human will (whether a necessary accident or the intellectual soul) in the first place?

Second, the Genuine Agency Problem is not focused on whether the Holy Spirit can cause or even be the remote agent-subject of a human act of will, but on whether and how that act of love can belong to the human being (e.g., to St. Paul) at the same time. On the hypostatic-union hypothesis, that would be the case only if the same individual will-power could belong both to the Holy Spirit and to St. Paul at one and the same time. If it did, then the special connection between the Holy Spirit and St. Paul would consist in the fact that the same individual will-power is hypostatically united to the Holy Spirit *and* is either St. Paul's soul or a necessary accident emanating from and inhering in St. Paul's soul. The result would be that numerically the same soul power—by virtue of two different metaphysical relations of union—could belong to two persons at once. If human will-power is a necessary accident, then it is united to the substance of St. Paul by virtue of being an accident that inheres in his soul. If human will-power is really the same as the intellectual soul, then it is united to St. Paul by virtue of being really the same as the soul that is an essential part of the individual human being that St. Paul is.

If the will did belong to two supposits, each of the supposits could be denominated from its acts (e.g., the Holy Spirit could be said to will and St. Paul could be said to will). But much depends on how the Holy Spirit uses that created will to produce those acts. If, by [T2b], the Holy Spirit *makes* the human will love God and neighbor, that suggests that the Holy Spirit uses Its Divine will to cause an act of loving God and neighbor in Its human will. Such activity could still count as self-determination for the Holy Spirit, because *ex hypothesi* both wills belong to It: Its Divine will would be controlling Its human will, the way a human being exercises self-control by using will-power to curb sensory appetites. But even if the Holy Spirit acted freely in Its human will-act, how could St. Paul also be said to will freely? Whether or not the Holy Spirit is hypostatically united to St. Paul's will would make no difference: if the Divine will is the total efficient cause of the human will-act, the resultant act of loving God and neighbor would not be

---

[23] See Scotus, *Ordinatio* III, d.2, q.2, n.95 (Vat IX.159); III, d.16, q.1–2, n.39 (Vat IX.549–50). Likewise, Ockham, *Quaest. in III Sent.*, q.1 (*OTh* VI.21-3); *Quodlibeta* II, q.10 (*OTh* IX.160).

free for St. Paul, and the Genuine Agency Problem would not have been solved after all.

If the Holy Spirit did not go beyond general concurrence, however, if the human will-acts of loving God and neighbor were relevantly produced by the active power of the human will itself, then both the Holy Spirit and St. Paul would be denominated from the human will's active power and from its freely produced acts. That way, both agents could be said to act freely, and the Genuine Agency Problem would be solved. This is because the Holy Spirit's co-action by virtue of "co-owning" St. Paul's will would not by itself include any extra efficient causal input.

Third, some—Scotus, for one—would have challenged the notion that numerically the same individual nature or part-nature could belong to an individual creature and to a Divine person at one and the same time. For Scotus the default is that an individual substance nature self-supposits: it *is* its own supposit. That is, it does not depend on another as its subject, but subsists in itself. Individual substance natures have a natural aptitude to self-supposit, but they do not necessarily self-supposit. By Divine power, they can be assumed by a really distinct other—i.e., an "alien" supposit—on which they would depend as their subjects. Self-supposits are independent (i.e., do not depend on another as on a subject), while alien-supposited natures are dependent. Scotus concludes that it would not be metaphysically possible for numerically the same individual nature to be self-supposited and alien-supposited at one and the same time. If what goes for wholes goes for parts, then no human soul could be part of a self-suppositing nature (e.g., St. Paul's) and be "alien" supposited by a Divine person (e.g., the Holy Spirit) at one and the same time.[24]

Had he considered it, Ockham might have given a different answer. Not only does he concede the metaphysical possibility that numerically the same human nature be assumed by all three Divine persons at once; he allows that—by Divine power—numerically the same intellectual soul could be united as the dominant substantial form of three human beings (e.g., Sts. Peter, James, and John) at once.[25] Since, for Ockham, will-power is really the same as the intellectual soul, the three human beings would share numerically the same will-power and be denominated by numerically the same

---

[24] For a discussion of Scotus' understanding of self-suppositing, alien-suppositing, and hypostatic union, see my "What's Metaphysically Special about Supposits?", 15–52. See also my *Christ and Horrors: The Coherence of Christology*, ch.5, pp. 123–8.

[25] Ockham, *Quaest.*, q.6, a.vii (*OTh* VIII.239–40).

will-acts. Analogously, Ockham might claim that numerically the same intellectual soul could be simultaneously united to make something one *per se* with an individual human composite and assumed by a Divine person. Ockham would have insisted that, strictly speaking, only individual substance natures can be supposited, and that even broadly speaking only individual substance natures and/or their parts can be assumed. The Holy Spirit could not, strictly or broadly speaking, *assume* a quality. But Ockham might not deny that there was some other analogous way of being united with a quality (as opposed to a substance or a substance-part) by which the Holy Spirit could own it.[26]

3.3 Infused Habits After All?

Having brought up the hypostatic-union hypothesis in the first place, Bonaventure simply dismisses it. Lombard cannot consistently hold it, while denying any infused habit of charity in the soul. Bonaventure explains that the capacity for hypostatic union is supernatural. That means that no creatable nature includes within it any natural passive capacity to be so united, because *natural* capacities can be actualized by merely natural causes. Therefore, if any creature is capable of hypostatic union, it must be made such by a supernatural infused habit that expands its passive capacities beyond what is natural and disposes it for hypostatic union.[27] Thus, Bonaventure concludes against Lombard, hypostatic union would presuppose infused charity in the soul.[28]

Bonaventure himself does not believe that Lombard held the hypostatic-union hypothesis, however. Rather, Lombard recognized that "that by which we love God" can be understood three ways. The whole Trinity is an *efficient cause* by which we love God and neighbor. The Holy Spirit, who is that love by which Father and Son love each other and us, is the *exemplar cause* of our love for God and neighbor. And an affection or motion in our soul (i.e., the act) is the *formal cause* of our love for God and neighbor.[29]

---

[26] For Ockham's treatment of self-suppositing, alien-suppositing, and hypostatic union, see my "Relations, Subsistence, and Inherence, or Was Ockham a Nestorian in Christology?" "The Metaphysics of the Incarnation in Some Fourteenth Century Franciscans," and "What's Metaphysically Special about Supposits?" See also Cross's detailed analyses in *The Metaphysics of the Incarnation: Thomas Aquinas to Duns Scotus*.
[27] Bonaventure, *Sent.* I, d.17, p.1, a.u, q.1 (Quaracchi I.294).
[28] Bonaventure, *Sent.* I, d.17, p.1, a.u, q.1 (Quaracchi I.294).
[29] Bonaventure, *Sent.* I, d.17, p.1, a.u, q.1 (Quaracchi I.294).

Bonaventure's own verdict is that these claims are true so far as they go and imply no division of the Trinity or confusion of a creature's action with the creator's action.[30] Any defects lie not in what they affirm, but in what they leave out. The Genuine Agency Problem weighs with Bonaventure. The charity by which we love God must be a virtue in us, because not only does God cooperate with us, but *"we cooperate with God. We are his helpers."* Because our wills are "convertible" in the sense of being powers for opposite actions, they need a regulator to dispose them to will what God wills them to will. Divine omnipresence does not suffice. The created will has to receive some influence from Divine presence. What enables us to cooperate with God is an infused habit of charity, which is a likeness of Divine love (= the Holy Spirit) and disposes the will to will what is good and godly.[31] A habit of infused charity is needed to perfect the soul by distinguishing it from others (marking those who are accepted by God from those who are not), by ordering and disposing it for eternal life.[32]

Looking forward to the life to come, Bonaventure endorses the tag that "like is known by like." Deiformity is required for beatific vision and enjoyment. To fit fallen humans for heaven requires nothing less than the re-creation or the re-formation of them. But re-formation requires a form, in particular an informing habit that restructures the soul toward greater Godlikeness.[33]

4. Aquinas: Infused Qualities as Foundations of Special Connections

4.1 The Necessity of Infused Habits

Aquinas agrees with Bonaventure: the Holy Spirit is given to us to make us holy. To make us holy, is to perfect us. But Divine omnipresence and concurrence will not be enough to perfect *us*. What perfects a creature is an inherent form,[34] and God is not and cannot be an inherent form.[35] Aquinas

---

[30] Bonaventure, *Sent.* I, d.17, p.1, a.u, q.1 (Quaracchi I.295–6).
[31] Bonaventure, *Sent.* I, d.17, p.1, a.u, q.1 (Quaracchi I.295).
[32] Bonaventure, *Sent.* I, d.17, p.1, a.u, q.1 (Quaracchi I.294).
[33] Bonaventure, *Sent.* I, d.17, p.1, a.u, q.1 (Quaracchi I.295).
[34] Aquinas, *Sent.* I, d.17, q.1, a.1 ad 1um; *De Caritate*, a.1 ad 13em.
[35] Aquinas, *Sent.* I, d.17, q.1, a.1.c; *De Caritate*, a.1 ad 8, 13, 14, 18; *Summa Theologica* I, q.3, a.8, c and ad 2um.

gives detailed development to the views he shares with Bonaventure. Like Bonaventure, Aquinas' elaboration of the contention that *perfecting forms in us are needed* can be subsumed under the rubric of *three sorts of cause*.

4.1.1 First: Final Causality

For Aquinas, creation actualizes a creatable nature's potency for actual being (*esse*). The nature's inward principles of motion serve to define and to orient the creature to its natural end. Natural active and natural passive powers are matched: there is no natural passive power that cannot be actualized by a natural active power, and natural active powers can actualize only *natural* passive powers. Voluntary agents are further perfected for voluntary actions—so that they can not only perform them but do so promptly and delightfully—by habits of which the corresponding acts are an efficient cause.[36] For example, acts of choosing coffee engender a coffee-choosing habit; choices to act in the face of danger, the virtue of courage. Habits do not causally determine the will (they are at most partial causes of the will's act), but they make it easier for the will to act in accordance with them.

"Re-creation" endows the creature, not with natural, but with supernatural being (*esse*) and orders it to its supernatural end. None of human nature's inward principles of motion orders it to beatific vision and enjoyment of the Divine essence, or to loving God as a source of intimate companionship and happiness, as opposed to loving God as the first cause of the natural order. Aquinas emphasizes, human nature furnishes us with no passive powers to receive acts of beatific vision and enjoyment. Neither is there to be found anywhere in creation the natural active power to produce them in us.[37] What we need is the addition of supernatural inward principles of motion: supernatural passive powers to receive supernatural acts, and supernatural active powers to cooperate in producing them. If habits are what perfect a voluntary agent, and active and passive causal tendencies are what internally order a thing to its end, supernatural infused habits are required. Once again, Aquinas emphasizes: human nature includes neither the passive power to receive such supernatural habits (they are not "educible from the potency of the matter"), nor active power to cooperate in producing them. It is Divine power that infuses them,[38] and when it does so, it thereby raises us up to "super-nature," endows us with supernatural being (*esse*) and orders us to our supernatural end.

---

[36] Aquinas, *Sent.* I, d.17, q.1, a.3 c. [37] Aquinas, *Sent.* I, d.17, q.1, a.3 c.
[38] Aquinas, *Sent.* I, d.17, q.2, a.5 ad 3um.

4.1.2 Second: Exemplar Causality

To be suited for our supernatural end, we must be made more "deiform," more godlike. In Aquinas' mind, the supernaturally infused habits not only dispose us to greater functional similarity, they do so by virtue of being godlikenesses themselves. Not only the soul but also the soul's powers must be elevated. Because Aquinas understands the soul to emanate its essential powers as really distinct necessary accidents, he reckons that the supernaturally infused perfecting habits must be many, including graced-making grace in the soul, the theological virtues—faith, hope, and charity—in the soul's powers, and infused wisdom in the intellect. Graced-making grace is the foundation. Sometimes he says that it likens the soul to the Divine essence and so disposes the soul to beatific vision and enjoyment,[39] but other times to God the Son's personal property of filiation thereby fitting us to be adoptive daughters and sons.[40] Infused wisdom, which enlightens the intellect and prompts love, likens us to the Divine Word.[41] Infused charity likens us to the Holy Spirit Who is the love by which Father and Son love one another.[42]

4.1.3 Third: Efficient Causality

On Aquinas' reading, Lombard would not have been tempted by the—to Aquinas' mind—ridiculous notion that *the act* of love that we experience is the Holy Spirit Itself! What makes Lombard's view untenable is the Genuine Agency Problem. On Aquinas' reading of [T2b], Lombard holds that the Holy Spirit is *the* efficient cause of our act of loving God and neighbor,[43] so that the only formal active principle involved in producing the act is located in the Holy Spirit. The created will would be a merely receiving subject of that act. Aquinas draws out the untoward consequences in **four arguments**:

First, unless the act of love proceeds from a formal active principle within us, the act will not be voluntary. By definition, both natural and voluntary actions proceed from inward principles of motion. External causes can act alone to produce motions or changes in both rational and non-rational creatures. But not even God can make such motions or changes count as

---

[39] Aquinas, *Summa Theologica* I, q.43, a.5, ad 2um and ad 3um.
[40] Aquinas, *Sent.* I, d.16, q.3 c.
[41] Aquinas, *Summa Theologica* I, q.43, a.5 ad 2um and ad 3um; see also *Sent.* I, d.15, q.4, a.1 c; d.15, q.5, a.1, qc.2.
[42] Aquinas, *Summa Theologica* I, q.43, a.5 ad 2um and ad 3um; see also *Sent.* I, d.15, q.4.c; d.15, q.5, a.1, qc.2; d.17, q.1 c and ad 2um.
[43] Aquinas, *Sent.* I, d.17, q.1, a.1 c; *De Caritate*, a.1, c.

natural or voluntary, respectively, because omnipotence does not include the pseudo-power to make contradictories true simultaneously. When the archer shoots the arrow upwards, the arrow's upward motion is violent, not natural. When something external is the total efficient cause of a rational creature's act, the act is not voluntary but coerced.[44]

Second, on Lombard's view, no merely human being would act according to its own form in loving God and neighbor. But agents that do not act according to their own form, but only insofar as they are moved by another, are only *instrumental* agents (e.g., like the saw moved by the carpenter). If the human will were only an instrumental agent of the Holy Spirit, then it would not be within the power of the human being whether or not to love God and neighbor (any more than it is within the power of the saw whether or not actually to cut this piece of wood). If the act were not voluntary, it would not be meritorious either.

Third, habits are what enable a power to act promptly and delightfully. But on Lombard's view, there is no habit of charity in the human will to incline it to love God and neighbor. Aquinas concludes that if Lombard were right, the human will would be unable to perform such acts promptly and delightfully.[45]

Fourth, being meritorious is a perfection of an act. But function (*operatio*) pertains to the supposit. So far as necessity and contingency and perfection are concerned, the function follows the conditions of the proximate cause (in this case, the human being) and not the first cause (God). Hence, there is no perfection in an action unless there is perfection in the proximate functional power from which it proceeds. Functional power is perfected by a habit. Aquinas infers that there is no perfection in an action unless there is a habit infused into the functional power of the agent-supposit from which it proceeds. Just as the political virtues (e.g., justice) make their possessor good and in consequence render her/his acts good, so the habit of charity perfects the will of the human being to make him/her the object of Divine favor and in consequence makes his/her free acts in accordance with right reason and/or Divine commands meritorious. If—as Lombard maintains—there were no habit of charity perfecting the human will, no human acts would be meritorious.[46]

Aquinas' own conclusion is that we must be able to perform the act of loving God and neighbor *through our own form*. Since none of our natural

---

[44] Aquinas, *De Caritate*, a.1 c. [45] Aquinas, *De Caritate*, a.1 c.
[46] Aquinas, *Sent.* I, d.17, q.1, a.1 c.

forms is the formal active principle through which such an act can be produced, what we need is a supernaturally infused habit of charity to serve as the formal principle of an act of love. God is the *efficient* cause, but the supernaturally infused habit of charity is the *formal* cause of the human being's being graced.[47] The habit received into the agent-supposit's functional power actualizes its potency to be in a state of first act with respect to charity or meritorious action. The habit is a partial efficient cause of the agent-supposit's moving from first to second act with respect to charity or meritorious action.[48] Presumably, since Aquinas thinks the act of loving God and neighbor is voluntary, created will-power is also a partial efficient cause. Where, then, does the Holy Spirit come in? Aquinas' answer is significant: "the Holy Spirit, Who is uncreated charity, is in the human being that has created charity, moving the soul to an act of love, the way God moves all things to the actions to which they are inclined by their own forms."[49] In other words, the Holy Spirit acts—along with the Father and the Son—by general concurrence!

To the objection that it denigrates Divine power to suggest that it has to act through the intermediary of a habit of charity in producing an act of love in the creature, Aquinas protests that exactly the opposite is the case. The habit of charity is a formal cause of meritorious action. But it is a sign that an agent is stronger rather than weaker that it can produce formal active principles in other things, all the stronger the more perfect the produced formal active principles are. Thus, it would be impressive if God were to act alone to produce all of the effects here below. But it is even more impressive that Divine power has acted to introduce formal active principles into creatures and collaborated with them to produce said effects.[50]

4.2 Special Connections

For Aquinas, supernaturally infused habits are required to make the elect holy. But Divine indwelling and missions still play a role. Aquinas advances two accounts of special connections, both of which make the latter to depend upon the former.

---

[47] Aquinas, *Sent.* I, d.17, q.1, a.1 ad 5um.
[48] Aquinas, *Sent.* I, d.17, q.1, a.1 ad 1um and 3um and 6um; I, d.17, q.1, a.2 ad 3um.
[49] Aquinas, *De Caritate*, a.1 c.   [50] Aquinas, *De Caritate*, a.1 ad 13–14em.

4.2.1 First: The "Metaphysical" Account

It tackles both the Special Connection and Divided Trinity Problems at once. Aquinas is clear. The whole Trinity is the efficient cause of these infused habits: "one action, one will *ad extra*" holds where creation and preservation are concerned. But while—according to Aquinas—the Trinity are in everything by essence, presence, and power,[51] the further special connections of indwelling and mission arise because these particular infused habits ground primitive non-mutual relations between the creature into whom they have been infused and Godhead as a whole or one Divine person in particular.[52] Since not every created effect is the foundation of such relations, indwelling and mission constitute "special connections" of God to some creatures rather than others and of the creature to one Divine person as opposed to the others. On this account, the infused habits are prior in the order of explanation to the special connections (the relations of indwelling and mission).[53]

In general, Aquinas reaches for the category of non-mutual relations when he tries to explain how an eternal, absolutely simple, and immutable God can be newly related to temporary and transient creatures.[54] God becomes the creator of X, when the creature X comes into existence, but nothing real (no *res*) in God is said to change thereby. Aquinas' analysis is that the relations creator/creature are non-mutual: the created thing is the foundation of a real relation of created dependence. Because God is the term of that real relation of created dependence (i.e., X depends on God), God is said to bear a relation of reason to the creature (i.e., God is the creator of X). Again, when God the Son assumes a particular human nature into hypostatic union, nothing real (no *res*) changes in God the Son. Rather the human nature is the foundation of a real relation of being assumed, a relation of which God the Son is the term. And because of this, God the Son is said to bear a relation of reason to the assumed human nature (i.e., God assumes it). Likewise here: neither Godhead nor any Divine person undergoes any real change (any change of *res*) when It indwells or is sent to a creature. Rather the supernatural habit newly infused into the creature (e.g., graced-making grace into St. Paul's soul, wisdom into his intellect, charity

---

[51] Aquinas, *Summa Theologica* I, q.8, a.3 c.
[52] Aquinas, *Sent.* I, d.14, q.1, a.1 ad 2um; d.14, q.1, a.2 c and ad 1um and ad 3um; d.14, q.2, a.1, qc.1 c and ad 2um.
[53] Aquinas, *Sent.* I, d.14, q.2, a.2 c and ad 2um.
[54] For a detailed treatment of Aquinas on relations, see Henninger, *Relations: Medieval Theories 1250–1325*.

into his will) is the foundation of a primitive real relation of being indwelt or being that to whom someone is sent. Insofar as the Trinity/the Divine person is the term of such a relation, it bears a relation of reason to that creature (e.g., God indwells St. Paul, the Holy Spirit is sent to St. Paul).

Thus, when Aquinas appeals to the category of non-mutual relations, and posits special primitive relations to connect Godhead with some creatures and creatures with one Divine person and not another, he is re-using old strategies already deployed in his analyses of creation and assumption relations. All the same, indwelling and mission (and their co-relations) are *not the same* primitive relations as assuming (and being assumed). Like Bonaventure, Aquinas is clear that the Holy Spirit does not join Itself in hypostatic union to the creature's will.[55] By contrast with the hypostatic-union hypothesis, Aquinas sees indwelling and mission as additional primitive relations, different from the assumption relation.

Not every creature can be the foundation of a real relation of *being indwelt* or of *being the one to whom a Divine person is specially sent*; only supernatural habits that God alone has the active power to produce in souls, can. Moreover, not every supernatural habit grounds such relations. Aquinas identifies graced-making grace infused into the soul as the foundation of a real relation of being indwelt, of which the whole Trinity is the term. That is, when St. Paul's soul is infused with graced-making grace, the whole Trinity indwell or make their home with him. Again, God the Son is sent in the flesh to teach us many things. But it is infused wisdom or knowledge of God that makes the soul one to whom God the Son is specially sent. That is, when St. Paul's mind is infused with knowledge of God, God the Son is sent to him and indwells "the inner man." Likewise, supernaturally infused charity grounds the real relation of being one to whom the Holy Spirit has been specially sent and given. That is, when St. Paul's will is infused with the supernatural habit of charity, the Holy Spirit is specially sent and given to him. Since these habits would be not only "above and beyond" but contrary to the essential principles of non-rational creatures, Aquinas infers that Godhead and individual Divine persons can have these special connections to rational creatures only.[56]

What makes it the case that the infusion of these habits (as opposed to others) gives rise to real relations of being indwelt and being sent to? Aquinas may think that graced-making grace, infused wisdom or

---

[55] Aquinas, *Sent.* I, d.17, q.1, a.1 c.
[56] Aquinas, *Sent.* I, d.15, q.4, a.1 ad 3um.

knowledge of God, and infused charity fill these roles because they are special godlikenesses: graced-making grace, of Godhead; infused knowledge or wisdom, of the Son's personal property as Word; infused charity, of the Holy Spirit's personal property as the love between the Father and the Son.[57] If so, Aquinas could explain that it is simply the nature of these infused habits—when posited—to ground such real relations, just as it is the nature of whiteness—when two white things are posited—to ground mutual real relations of similarity. Even so, this rationale is incomplete, because, for a creature, to be is to be somehow godlike. The question rises again: what is so distinctive about these godlikenesses—viz., the infused habits of graced-making grace, supernatural wisdom or knowledge of God, and charity—that they ground special connections, when other godlikenesses do not? Perhaps in the end Aquinas will have to say that this is primitive, a necessary consequence of what these special habits (by contrast with those habits) are.

The real relation of dependence on God as Creator necessarily stays with a creature throughout its existence. The real relations of being indwelt by the Trinity or of being one to whom a Divine person is sent, pertain to a creature only when it acquires and so long as it has the infused habits. They are lost by mortal sin and restored by penance and absolution. In some moods, Aquinas would say that these real relations stay with a human being from the beginning and throughout its supernatural being (*esse*). Moreover, both infused wisdom and infused charity come in degrees, and so *ante-mortem* can be augmented. Aquinas connects the sending of the Son and Holy Spirit into a creature, with a new condition in that creature—viz., its fresh reception of infused habits.[58] Will it be right to speak of a new mission of the Son or the Holy Spirit every time infused wisdom or infused charity is augmented? Aquinas' answer is negative. It will be right to speak of a new mission of the Son or the Holy Spirit into a creature only where the increase is such as to enable or issue in some new function: e.g., prophecy, miracle-working, or the ability to turn all temptation aside.[59] In the blessed in heaven, there is no augmentation, but there are still new revelations by which the recipient is able to know God in a new way and so to love God under a different aspect.[60]

---

[57] Aquinas, *Sent.* I, d.15, q.4, a.1 c; d.15, q.5, a.1, qc.2. *Summa Theologica* I, q.43, a.5 ad 2um and ad 3um.
[58] Aquinas, *Sent.* I, d.15, q.1, a.1 c; d.15, q.3, a.1 c and ad 3um; d.15, q.4, a.2 c.
[59] Aquinas, *Sent.* I, d.15, q.1, a.2.
[60] Aquinas, *Sent.* I, d.15, q.5, a.1, qc.3 c and ad 1um.

Here, Aquinas follows rough theological consensus, but fails to give metaphysical satisfaction. Metaphysically, relations depend on their foundations. Indeed, for Aquinas, real relations are really the same as their foundations. Even if R1 and R2 are relations of the same species, they will be numerically distinct if their foundations F1 and F2 are really distinct. Metaphysically, the question should be, does augmenting the degree of infused wisdom or charity change the identity of the foundation in such a way as to require a numerically distinct relation of mission or indwelling?

4.2.2 Second: The Intentional Access Account

In *Summa Theologica* I, q.43, a.3, Aquinas distinguishes God's general omnipresence in creatures from "a special way" in which God exists in rational creatures as the intentional object of their knowledge and love. When God exists in the knower as what is known and in the lover as what is loved, God is said "not only to exist in but to dwell in rational creatures as in His temple." Such indwelling is nevertheless grounded on infused habits. Here Aquinas identifies graced-making grace as what confers on rational creatures "the power of enjoying"—of knowing and loving—"the Divine persons";[61] likewise, infused wisdom as what enlightens the intellect, and infused charity as what inflames affection. Infused wisdom grounds the sending of the Son, and infused charity the sending of the Holy Spirit.[62]

Here Aquinas' focus is on our ultimate end, which is beatific vision and enjoyment of Godhead. Creatures bear many relations to God by metaphysical necessity, and will do so for eternity. But in describing the union for which we are supernaturally destined, Aquinas' attention is not on these, but on cognitive and affective access. Aquinas holds that the natural capacities of the human mind equip it only to understand the quiddities of material things. His own view is that we have no natural capacity for intuitive awareness of immaterial beings with the possible exception of our own souls and mental acts. Even though God is omnipresent, our natural cognitive limitations keep the Divine essence behind the veil. Likewise, if nature builds in appetitive inclinations to love God above all as the source and end of natural good,[63] it includes none to love God above all *as an* object of

---

[61] Aquinas, *Summa Theologica* I, q.43, a.3 c.
[62] Aquinas, *Summa Theologica* I, q.43, a.5 ad 2um and ad 3um.
[63] Aquinas, *Summa Theologica* I–II, q.109, a.3, c and ad 1um.

happiness or social companionship.[64] The union for which we are headed is not the metaphysical relation of hypostatic union, but the union of intuitive vision and enjoyment of the Godhead. The metaphysical changes required to make this possible are precisely the supernaturally infused habits which expand our cognitive scope and affective range. The goal is an indwelling and mutual abiding, which consists in overflowing delight in the experienced presence of the Beloved, a shared joy in knowing and being known.

Aquinas leaves this account sketchy. After all, he has identified the infused forms that re-create and restructure the soul as *habits*, not acts. Aquinas joins many in holding that—apart from the human soul of Christ and a few saints—the elect do not enter into beatific vision and enjoyment before death. If the special way that God is in rational creatures is as an intentional object of acts, it would seem that Divine indwelling in the elect as in His temple is an eschatological hope to be realized only beyond the grave. Perhaps, however, Aquinas thinks that Divine indwelling begins with infused habits that target beatific vision and enjoyment. Alternatively, he could say that Divine indwelling comes with acts of love of God above all as an object of happiness and social companionship—will-acts that are based on cognitive acts that fall short of beatific vision. If so, those who use their infused wisdom and infused charity to perform such acts might get an anticipatory version of the mutual abiding for which the elect are destined in the life to come.

Seemingly, Aquinas identifies the "special way" in which things exist in (or indwell) rational creatures quite generically in terms of their being the intentional object of acts of knowledge and/or love. Such an understanding will certainly allow for God to exist in us *ante-mortem*. Unfortunately, the criterion is so permissive as to allow anything and everything else we think of and love to indwell us, too.

Aquinas' metaphysical account and his intentional access account are logically independent of one another, but they are also logically compatible. Although he does not say so explicitly, he may intend the intentional access account to supplement the metaphysical account. One difference between my knowledge and love of the chocolate ice cream I am eating and my knowledge and love of God, is that my habit of loving chocolate ice cream does not bear a real relation of being-indwelt-by to chocolate ice cream the

---

[64] Aquinas, *Summa Theologica* I–II, q.109, a.3 ad 1um.

way my infused habit of charity is supposed to bear a real relation of being-indwelt-by to the Holy Spirit.

5. Scotus on the Role and Relevance of Infused Habits

Bonaventure and Aquinas emphasize: the correct counter to Pelagius is not that the Holy Spirit *is* our love-act, or is the total efficient cause of it, but that God perfects the soul with inward functional principles, which they identify with infused habits. Scotus accepts theological consensus that supernaturally infused habits are needed to make us holy, or, more precisely, to make us worthy of Divine acceptance and our acts meritorious. But Scotus seeks further clarification on two questions. Exactly what role (compatible with genuine human agency) could such habits play? And we think of virtues as habits, but can there be habits or formal active principles of moral goodness and merit, in particular? Scotus reviews four answers to the first question, rejecting two while finding the other two defensible.

5.1 Henry of Ghent: Supernatural Causes for Supernatural Effects!

In his *Quodlibet* IV, q.10, Henry of Ghent distinguishes acquired from infused habits. Acquired virtues presuppose the being (*esse*) of the nature along with the functional principles that it essentially includes and/or that are essentially consequent upon it. What acquired virtues do is to perfect that nature and its functional principles. The nature is the functional principle of the act. Acquired virtue only affects *the way* the act is done (e.g., promptly and delightfully, expeditiously). By contrast, supernatural virtues do not presuppose but constitute the soul in supernatural being (*esse*) and redound to the soul's powers to make their acts meritorious. Henry concludes that supernatural virtue is *the* principle of supernatural action. The theological virtues thus confer both supernatural being (*esse*) and supernatural functioning.[65]

---

[65] Henry of Ghent, *Quodlibet* IV, q.10 (Leuven VIII.82–7); summarized in Scotus, *Lectura* I, d.17, p.1, q.u, nn.32–7 (Vat XVII.194) and II, d.26, q.u, nn.7–8 (Vat XIX.194); *Ordinatio* I, d.17, p.1, q.2, n.21 (Vat V.146).

5.2 Scotus' Critique of Henry's Opinion

Scotus counters that it is the metaphysical role of habits to perfect powers. But a power is the principle by which—simply and primarily—a thing is able to act. In declaring the supernatural habit the *only* active principle in the production of the meritorious act, Henry turns the habit into the power itself![66] If the supernaturally infused habit of charity *is* the power to produce the act, then it no more perfects created will-power in which it inheres than heat (which is itself the power to produce heat) perfects the wood in which it inheres. Heat is not a necessary accident of wood (the way—Aquinas would say—it is a necessary accident of fire), but is only produced in the wood by an external cause. Consequently, when the heat acts on its own to produce heat in surrounding objects, the act may be said to be "shared" with the wood insofar as the wood is the receiving subject in which the heat inheres. But the heating-action does not pertain to the wood properly speaking because the wood *qua* wood does nothing to produce heat.

Scotus raises the standards for genuine agency. In order for X to count as the agent-subject of A-ing, not only is it not enough for the *act* of A-ing to exist in X as in a subject; it is not enough for a *habit* that is an active principle of A-ing to exist in X as in a subject. It is further required either [a] that the habit in question be a natural perfection of X (the way heat is a natural perfection of fire) or [b] that some active principle included in or naturally consequent upon the nature of X be active in the production of A. Supernaturally infused habits are *ex hypothesi* not natural perfections of human beings. Consequently, if infused charity in St. Paul were the sole active principle producing in St. Paul an act of loving God and neighbor, that act would only be shared with St. Paul the way heating-action is shared with the wood. St. Paul would not be its agent-subject properly speaking.[67]

Scotus drives this point home with the further observation that if—among the formal active principles existing in St. Paul—supernaturally infused charity were the only active principle involved in the production of the love-act, then supernaturally infused charity could produce that act even if it existed on its own, separate from any and every subject, the way the Islamic philosopher Avicenna admits that heat could produce heat even

---

[66] Scotus, *Lectura* I, d.17, p.1, q.u, n.46 (Vat XVII.197–8); *Ordinatio* I, d.17, p.1, q.2, n.22 (Vat V.147).

[67] Scotus, *Lectura* I, d.17, p.1, q.u, nn.47 and 49 (Vat XVII.198); *Ordinatio* I, d.17, p.1, q.2, n.23 (Vat. V.147).

if it existed separately from fire or wood.[68] Moreover, habits are natural causes that—barring obstructions—act to the limit of their powers. If charity were the sole active principle in the production of the love-act, the love-act would be produced naturally and so would not be free,[69] nor would it be imputable to St. Paul, because it would not be within his power to control whether or not the habit produced the act.[70]

Conversely, if supernaturally infused charity did give the will supernatural being (*esse*) and action (*agere*), then that charity would so dominate the will that it could never sin mortally, so long as the charity existed in it.[71]

5.3 Godfrey of Fontaines: Two Causes, Two Effects?

The moral of Scotus' critique of Henry is that the love-act will not be free and imputable to St. Paul unless—whatever other active principles may be at work—his will-power is one of those active principles and his will-power retains control over whether to act or not. Godfrey of Fontaines agrees with this conclusion. In *Quodlibet* XI, q.4, he maintains—*contra* Henry—that acquired and infused virtues are related to acts the same way: the act has its substance from the power and its intensity from the habit. For Godfrey, the labor of love-act production is divided between two causes—will-power and supernaturally infused charity—that produce quasi-two different effects: the substance of the act and the intensity of the act, respectively. The power informed by the habit is the formal active principle of the intense act.[72]

5.4 Scotus' Rejection of Godfrey's Position

Godfrey justifies invoking two causes by distinguishing quasi-two effects. Scotus finds Godfrey's position philosophically confused, because the intensity of an act is not distinct from the substance of an act in any way

---

[68] Scotus, *Ordinatio* I, d.17, p.1, q.u, n.23 (Vat V.147–8).
[69] Scotus, *Lectura* I, d.17, p.1, q.u, nn.48–9 (Vat XVII.198); *Ordinatio* I, d.17, p.1, q.2, n.24 (Vat V.148).
[70] Scotus, *Ordinatio* I, d.17, p.1, q.2, n.26 (Vat V.149).
[71] Scotus, *Lectura* I, d.17, p.1, q.u, n.50 (Vat XVII.199); *Ordinatio* I, d.17, p.1, q.2, n.25 (Vat V.149).
[72] Godfrey of Fontaines, *Quodlibet* XI, q.4 (PB V.22–4). Scotus, *Lectura* I, d.17, p.1, q.u, n.51 (Vat XVII.199); *Ordinatio* I, d.17, p.1, q.2, n.27 (Vat V.149–50).

that would allow the two causes to divide and conquer.[73] What causes the substance, causes the intensity: the infinite will, an act of infinite intensity; finite wills, acts of finite intensity. Nor is there any degree of intensity in a will-act that so lies outside the scope of will-power as a species as to require a supernaturally infused habit as a co-cause. Will-power as such ranges over acts of any and all finite degrees up to and including a will-act of infinite degree. Inhering habits might perfect finite will-power to enable it to cause acts of higher intensity. But Godfrey misdivides the labor when he says that the habit causes the intensity and will-power the substance.[74] If he were right, while the habit was infused, all of the will's acts would have the same intensity, because the habit—as a natural cause—would always act to the limit of its power![75]

Henry of Ghent and Godfrey of Fontaines both recognize the supernaturally infused habit of charity as an *active* principle in the production of the love-act. Scotus judges both accounts untenable, Henry's because it assigns created will-power no active role, and Godfrey's because it gives the supernaturally infused habit the wrong role. Scotus recognizes two other positions, both of which he deems defensible and which differ over whether the habit is an active or a merely passive disposing principle in love-act production.[76]

5.5 Partial Causes of a Single Effect?

Accepting what is good and rejecting what is allegedly mistaken in Godfrey, the third approach holds that will-power and the infused habit of charity are two partial causes that make essentially one total cause of a single effect (the love-act). These two partial causes are of different orders (unlike the two sailors dragging the ship). Neither depends on the other for its causality (just as mother and father, the intellect and its object each have their causal powers independently of the other). A given finite will-power could act alone to produce a less perfect love-act, but the infused charity perfects that

---

[73] Scotus, *Lectura* I, d.17, p.1, q.u, n.52 (Vat XVII.199); *Ordinatio* I, d.17, p.1, q.2, n.28 (Vat V.150).
[74] Scotus, *Lectura* I, d.17, p.1, q.u, nn.54–5 (Vat XVII.200); *Ordinatio* I, d.17, p.1, q.2, n.31 (Vat V.151–2).
[75] Scotus, *Lectura* I, d.17, p.1, q.u, n.53 (Vat XVII.200); *Ordinatio* I, d.17, p.1, q.2, nn.29–30 (Vat V.150–1).
[76] Scotus, *Ordinatio* I, d.17, p.1, q.2, n.53 (Vat V.160).

finite will-power so that together they produce a more perfect love-act. Of the two, will-power is the principal cause—it is that by which the agent can have a will-act—and the habit is the secondary or perfecting cause—it is that by which the agent can have a more perfect act than its will can produce all by itself.[77] Nevertheless, there is no degree of a created will-act that requires a supra-natural cause; any and all degrees fall within the scope of will-power as such.[78] By contrast, the habit, no matter what its degree, would not be sufficient to produce the will-act.[79]

5.6 Infused Habits as Passive Dispositions?

If Aquinas and Bonaventure read Lombard to say that the Holy Spirit alone is the efficient cause of the love-act, and if Henry of Ghent holds that the infused habit does all of the work, the fourth approach seizes the other extreme to say that efficient causality belongs to created will-power, while the infused habit is not an active principle at all, but only a passive disposing principle that inclines the power to its function. Scotus cites the following methodological principles in its favor:

[P1] causality should not be attributed unless it is evident in the nature of things;

[P2] perfect causality should not be denied to a cause unless there is an obvious imperfection in its causality.[80]

There would be a reason to deny perfect causality to will-power, if there were some feature of the will-act for which will-power could not account. Now habits are usually posited to explain the agent's ability to function easily, delightfully, expeditiously, and promptly. The fourth position does not deny that habits are needed to explain such modalities. Rather it insists that all of them have to do with the suitability of the action to the power *insofar as it is a passive receiver of the action and not insofar as it is an active producer of the action*. Consequently, it concludes that the habits in question

---

[77] Scotus, *Lectura* I, d.17, p.1, q.u, nn.75–6, 79, 83, and 85–7 (Vat XVII.205–9); *Ordinatio* I, d.17, p.1, q.2, nn.32–40 (Vat V.152–6).
[78] Scotus, *Ordinatio* I, d.17, p.1, q.2, nn.79–80 (Vat V.178–9).
[79] Scotus, *Ordinatio* I, d.17, p.1, q.2, n.85 (Vat V.181).
[80] Scotus, *Ordinatio* I, d.17, p.1, q.2, n.47 (Vat V.157–8).

are passive disposing principles that make the power more receptive to its function.[81]

When all is said and done, Scotus opts for the third approach—that will-power and infused habits are efficient partial causes of the will-act of loving God above all (see section 5.5). But before he can work out the details, Scotus needs to attend to the second question: can there be formal active principles of moral goodness or merit in particular?

5.7 Habits as Active Causes of Moral Goodness or Merit?

"Yes" might seem to be the obvious answer. Aristotelian action theory dictates that an agent can do (be an efficient cause of) acts of type A only if it has within it a formal active principle of A-ing. Scotus agrees: Aristotle's *Ethics* can be read as implying that moral virtues are active principles.[82] Likewise, theological consensus dictates that the infused habit of charity is necessary for an agent and its act to be accepted by God as worthy of eternal life. Doesn't it follow that moral virtues are formal active principles of acting morally, and infused charity a formal active principle of earning merit?[83]

Technically, Scotus thinks, the answer is "no." The bottom line for Scotus is that both moral goodness and merit signify relations to norms: in the former case, conformity to right reason;[84] in the latter, to Divine statutory policies for accepting acts accompanied by infused charity as worthy of eternal life.[85] Moreover, these relations (like the relation of similarity between two white things) are internal relations, in Scotus' sense that—given the existence of the relata—they cannot but obtain.[86] Consequently, the existence of such relations does not require any further efficient causal explanation over and above what is involved in the production of their relata. Scotus concludes, we do not have to suppose that the habits are or contain formal active principles that explain the moral goodness or the merit of the acts. If heat heats, it is a formal principle of heating. If the will loves, there is a formal active principle of loving in the will. A habit of

---

[81] Scotus, *Ordinatio* I, d.17, p.1, q.2, nn.48–50, 87–91 (Vat V.158–9, 181–4).
[82] Scotus, *Ordinatio* I, d.17, p.1, q.2, nn.57–9 (Vat V.161–2).
[83] Scotus, *Ordinatio* I, d.17, p.1, q.2, nn.121–2 (Vat V.198–9).
[84] Scotus, *Ordinatio* I, d.17, p.1, q.2, nn.60–2, 94–8 (Vat V.163–4, 184–9).
[85] Scotus, *Ordinatio* I, d.17, p.1, q.2, nn.142–5 (Vat V.208–9).
[86] For an analysis of Scotus' theory of relations, see my *William Ockham*. See also Henninger, *Relations: Medieval Theories 1250–1325*, ch.5, 68–97.

charity, whether acquired or infused, may even be—as Henry, Godfrey, and the third opinion claim—a formal active principle *of loving*. What there is not, according to Scotus, is a formal active principle *of moral goodness* or a formal active principle *of meriting*.

Scotus makes two further points. First, if what right reason dictates is what it is prior to and independent of anyone's will, the statutes regarding Divine acceptance and merit are instances of positive law whose existence and contents do depend on the will of God, the ruling legislator. No creature is intrinsically—by the very nature of what it is—worthy of eternal life, because it is a finite good. Finite goods provide the Divine will with a reason to love them, but the reason is always defeasible.[87] Only infinite goodness (i.e., the Divine essence Itself) constitutes a reason for loving that cannot be trumped. That there are any statutes relating humans to eternal destinies, and that they are what they are, is a product of God's free and contingent volition.[88]

Second, Scotus observes, infused virtues are not merely ornamental; they exert efficient causal power to incline the will. Scotus holds that moral virtues[89] and infused habits[90] are highly suitable to the rational soul. Because he understands beauty to be constituted by suitability relations, Scotus compares virtues to ornaments that contribute to making the soul beautiful and furnish a reason, albeit defeasible for Divine acceptance. Nevertheless, Scotus denies that mere ornamentation is sufficient to make the soul's acts meritorious. Even souls with infused charity perform indifferent acts (e.g., willing to stroke one's beard) and commit venial sins.[91] Scotus rejects the view that infused charity is merely ornamental, insisting that it inclines the will, whether by being a formal active principle (as the third view holds) or a passive receptive principle (as the fourth view contends).[92]

With these explanations in hand, Scotus lays out his own position. Following the third view (section 5.5), Scotus maintains that will-power is the principal, while infused charity is a secondary efficient cause of the love-acts.[93] Scotus seems to limit God's efficient causal contribution to producing the quality that the love-act is, to infusing the habit and general

---

[87] Scotus, *Ordinatio* I, d.17, p.1, q.2, n.149 (Vat V.210–11).
[88] Scotus, *Ordinatio* I, d.17, p.1, q.1, n.144–5 (Vat V.208–9).
[89] Scotus, *Ordinatio* I, d.17, p.1, q.2, n.62 (Vat V.163–4).
[90] Scotus, *Ordinatio* I, d.17, p.1, q.2, n.131 (Vat V.203).
[91] Scotus, *Lectura* I, d.17, p.1, q.u, nn.58–60 (Vat XVII.201); *Ordinatio* I, d.17, p.1, q.2, n.132 (Vat. XVII.204).
[92] Scotus, *Ordinatio* I, d.17, p.1, q.2, nn.133–5 (Vat V.204–5).
[93] Scotus, *Ordinatio* I, d.17, p.1, q.2, n.151 (Vat V.211).

concurrence.[94] By contrast, *God* is the principal cause of any act's counting as meritorious, because God is the One Who lays down positive laws ordering acts and agents to eternal destinies.[95] When it comes to the criteria that God has chosen for counting an act meritorious and so ordering it to an eternal reward, both infused charity in the soul and the free exercise of will-power according to the dictates of right reason are still involved. But the priorities are reversed: where God's reasons for Divine acceptance are concerned, infused charity is the principal reason and the exercise of free choice the secondary reason.[96] Scotus emphasizes, God would not have to make infused charity a necessary condition for Divine acceptance and merit. God could have established other policies. Scripture and the sayings of the saints persuade him that this is God's actual policy, however.[97]

Thus, for Scotus, whether or not a love-act is produced, and whether or not a will acts in accord with conscience, remains, always or for the most part, within the will's power. But whether or not the soul has infused charity and whether or not any of its acts count as meritorious are not within the will's power but depend rather on free and contingent Divine policies. Scotus finds this division of labor acceptable, however, because merit and eternal destinies should, in the last analysis, be up to God.

5.8 Re-interpreting Lombard

Bonaventure and Aquinas agree: Lombard did not hold that the Holy Spirit is *the act* by which we love God and neighbor, but rather that the Holy Spirit is *the efficient cause* that acts immediately—without the cooperation of any infused habit—to produce that love-act in us. Scotus rejects their interpretation. Scotus' Lombard *does* think an infused habit is involved in the production of the love-act and of meritorious acts generally, although—Aquinas and Bonaventure are right to think—it is not an infused habit in the will. Rather, in *Sentences* I, d.37, Lombard recognizes a supernatural habit of grace, which is infused into the souls of the regenerate to make them tabernacles of the Holy Spirit. To borrow Aquinas' language, it is infused grace in the soul rather than charity in the will that is the foundation of the relation

---

[94] Scotus, *Ordinatio* I, d.17, p.1, q.2, n.191 (Vat V.229).
[95] Scotus, *Ordinatio* I, d.17, p.1, q.2, n.146 (Vat V.209).
[96] Scotus, *Ordinatio* I, d.17, p.1, q.2, nn.152–7 (Vat V.211–14).
[97] Scotus, *Ordinatio* I, d.17, p.1, q.2, nn.160 and 164 (Vat V.215 and 217).

of being indwelt of which the Holy Spirit is the term. Because grace is infused into the soul rather than the will, it can function as the root of the other virtues of faith and hope infused into the soul's powers. The latter don't ground relations of being indwelt, because—unlike grace—faith and hope involve imperfections (a lack of certainty and a lack of possession) and so will not be retained after death.[98] The disanalogy between the way the Holy Spirit produces acts of faith and hope in us on the one hand, and love-acts in us on the other, is not that the Holy Spirit acts by means of habits in producing the former but without any habit in producing the latter. Rather Scotus' Lombard does not recognize infused charity as a really distinct habit from infused grace and the soul. Accordingly, he thinks that the Holy Spirit acts together with infused grace and the soul's will-power to produce the act.[99] Scotus analyzes the position he attributes to Lombard into a sequence of instants of nature:

n1: grace or charity is infused into the soul and the Holy Spirit thereby indwells;

n2: grace infuses faith and hope (and no other habit) into the soul's powers;

n3: the Holy Spirit elicits an act of faith by means of the habit of faith and an act of hope by means of the habit of hope;

n4: by means of grace in the soul and the Holy Spirit that indwells, the will elicits an act of love.[100]

Likewise, for meritorious acts generally: the Holy Spirit sanctifies the grace-infused soul by indwelling it. And by means of infused grace and the indwelling Holy Spirit, the will elicits a meritorious act.[101]

5.9 Special Connection and Divided Trinity?

Scotus seems not to deal *ex professo* with the Special Connection and Divided Trinity Problems. It is literally in passing, in his discussion of

---

[98] Scotus, *Lectura* I, d.17, p.1, q.u, nn.32–7 (Vat XVII.194); *Ordinatio* I, d. 17, p.1, q.1, nn.167–71 (Vat V.218).
[99] Scotus, *Lectura* I, d.17, p.1, q.u, n.39 (Vat XVII.195); *Ordinatio* I, d.17, p.1, q.1, nn.169–70 (Vat V.218–19).
[100] Scotus, *Lectura* I, d.17, p.1, q.u, n.38 (Vat XVII.194–5).
[101] Scotus, *Lectura* I, d.17, p.1, q.u, n.41 (Vat XVII.196–7).

Lombard, that Scotus hints at his answers to them. Scotus explains that according to Lombard, it is "by means of grace and the indwelling of the whole Trinity, which is appropriated to the Spirit," that "the will elicits a meritorious act."[102] Evidently, Scotus is attributing to Lombard the view that, properly speaking, it is not only the Holy Spirit but the whole Trinity that indwells the grace-infused human being. Just as the whole Trinity acts in concert to infuse virtues, so, properly speaking, the whole Trinity indwells by means of the root-virtue that They infuse. It is only "by courtesy" that such indwelling as belongs to the whole is "appropriated" to the Holy Spirit, the better to accommodate the language of Scripture. Strictly speaking, there is no divided action, but the Trinity as a whole may be said to foster a special connection to some creatures and not others (in this case, to the elect and not the damned)!

6. Ockham's Revisions

6.1 Elevating Agent and Action

The Holy Spirit is given to make us holy, not only to repair our nature of any damage taken as a consequence of Adam's fall but also to elevate us and our acts, to make us worthy of eternal life. Aquinas and Henry of Ghent want to explain such elevation by appeal to infused supernatural habits. They take these habits to exceed nature twice over: we have no natural passive power to receive them, and no creature has or is active causal power to produce them. These habits, they think, give us supernatural being (*esse*), re-order us to our supernatural end, and constitute formal active causal principles that perfect our acts by making them meritorious.

Scotus and Ockham agree that special Divine action is required to elevate rational creatures to worthiness of eternal life, of beatific vision and enjoyment of God. But not even God can fit us for our supernatural end simply by infusing habits, and that for two reasons. First, Scotus thinks it is metaphysically incoherent to imagine that any power could make us receive habits which we have no natural passive power to receive. Not even God could augment the receptive power of the intellect so that it could be the subject

---

[102] Scotus, *Lectura* I, d.17, p.1, q.u, n.41 (Vat XVII.196–7).

of color![103] Second, whether or not such habits are naturally producible or receivable, they will in any event be created qualities. Creatures are only finite goods; what they essentially are constitutes at most a defeasible reason for producing them. No creature is by its very nature intrinsically worthy of Divine acceptance. Infusing finitely many finite accidents into a finite substance could not raise any rational creature to such a level of natural excellence as to make it naturally entitled to eternal life.[104]

Ockham agrees with Scotus that the meritorious act of loving God above all has to have the creature's own will for its chief formal active principle.[105] So far as Aristotelian method is concerned, Ockham also joins Scotus in contending that neither experience nor demonstrative reason would lead us to posit infused habits to explain the human acts we witness. Infused habits are not required to account for the action or its intentional direction. Unadorned will-power is itself power to love God above all and for God's own sake, and power to will what right reason dictates because right reason dictates it. Infused habits are not required to account for the intensity of the action. There is no level of intensity of will-acts that falls outside the scope of will-power as such. Nor are infused habits needed to account for the manner of an action (that it is performed promptly, delightfully, expeditiously, etc.). Acquired habits would do just as well.[106]

Where meritorious acts are concerned, Divine action is not required to be or (by infusing habits) to supply extra efficient causality for the production of the act over and above that involved in general concurrence. Rather Divine action is needed to accept the created agent and/or its act as worthy of eternal life. Divine ordinance is what sets the norms that make such created actions count as meritorious. Like Scotus, Ockham emphasizes that the criteria for Divine acceptance and merit are a product of God's free and contingent volition. God could have made free choice in accordance with right reason and/or Divine commands sufficient for worthiness of eternal life. Metaphysically, there neither is nor could be any necessary connection between the inherence of an infused habit before death and the soul's continued existence after death, much less the perpetual existence in the soul of acts of beatific vision and enjoyment. If—as the Saints say—God also

---

[103] For an extensive discussion of Scotus' insistence that the soul must have a *natural* passive power to receive any accidents that it receives and his critique of Aquinas, see Wolter, "Duns Scotus on the Natural Desire for the Supernatural."
[104] Ockham, *Scriptum in I Sent.* d.17 (*OTh* III.452-3, 455-6).
[105] Ockham, *Scriptum in I Sent.* d.17, q.1 (*OTh* III.470, 473-4).
[106] Ockham, *Quest. in III Sent.* q.9, a.1 (*OTh* VI.279-80); *Quaest.*, q.6, a.8 (*OTh* VIII.246-7).

demands infused habits in the agent, that is a function of Divine free choice and it was within Divine power to choose otherwise.[107]

6.2 Twisting Lombard's Wax Nose

Ockham notes the controversy over how to construe Lombard, when in *Sentences* I, d.17, he seems to deny infused charity, but in *Sentences* II, d.27, he appears to posit infused grace in the soul. If others try to harmonize by bringing Lombard closer to the common opinion, Ockham counters by turning Lombard into an Ockhamist. What if, when Lombard claims that the Holy Spirit is the charity that makes us love God and neighbor, he means that charity without which no one can be accepted by God or do anything meritorious—viz., God's will to accept? Taken that way, "charity" principally signifies the Divine will and connotes someone worthy of eternal life. What if "love God and neighbor" is short for "love God and neighbor meritoriously." Lombard's meaning would then be this: God's will-act of Divine acceptance is the charity that makes our will-act of loving God and neighbor meritorious. No Genuine Agency Problem arises on this interpretation, because Divine charity does not keep created wills from being efficient causes of their will-acts, but rather counts them as worthy of eternal life. Nor would Lombard have to deny the further gift of an infused habit that inclines us to the love of God. What he would be claiming is that the infused habit is not of itself what makes its possessor worthy of Divine acceptance or his/her acts meritorious, because the infused habits without the charity that the Holy Spirit *is*—viz., the Divine will to accept—will not suffice to make the agent or its acts acceptable.[108]

6.3 Special Connections, Divided Trinity?

When it comes to theological statements about the procession, the sending, and the giving of Divine persons, Ockham finds the issue more verbal than substantive. All agree that the following are to be maintained:

---

[107] Ockham, *Scriptum in I Sent.* d.17, q.1 and q.2 (*OTh* III.445, 452–5 and 471–2); *Quaest.*, q.1 (*OTh* VIII.21). For an extensive discussion of Ockham's position and his interactions with opponents such as Peter Aureol, Walter Chatton, and John Lutterell, see my *William Ockham*. See also Wood, "Ockham's Repudiation of Pelagianism."

[108] Ockham, *Scriptum in I Sent.* d.17, q.3 c (*OTh* III.476–7).

[1] each and every Divine person is an efficient and final cause of each and every creature;

[2] two Divine persons—the Son and the Holy Spirit—eternally proceed, and two Divine persons—the Father and the Son—eternally produce;

[3] each and every Divine person can cause a special gift in a rational creature—not only gifts given to those already graced, but also a gift that makes the creature graced;

[4] only the Son and no other Divine person is incarnate;

[5] each and every Divine person can be provided to do whatever a rational creature reasonably requests.[109]

His predecessors have offered different ways of accommodating wording found in the Scriptures and the sayings of the Saints to express these claims. In some cases, they have advanced philosophically unacceptable theories to explain the semantics. Ockham agrees with Bonaventure, Aquinas, and Scotus: no hypostatic union is involved in the Holy Spirit's proceeding, being sent or given to elect rational creatures; only God the Son is sent via hypostatic union into human being.[110] Nor is the Holy Spirit's proceeding, being sent or given to elect rational creatures to be accounted for in terms of any doctrine of non-mutual relations (such as Aquinas espouses), a doctrine which Ockham regards as philosophically incoherent. Ockham contends that a relation of reason's obtaining between X and Y depends upon some intellect's comparing and thus relating them, and is thus a being of reason. By contrast, that X and Y are really related pertains to X and Y prior to and independently of any activity of the intellect relating them. The Holy Spirit really proceeds, not only eternally but also temporally. The Holy Spirit is really sent and is really given. And—*pace* Aquinas—it cannot *really* proceed, be *really* sent or given because of any being of reason![111] Nevertheless, the fact that the Holy Spirit and the rational creature are really related means neither that the real relation is a thing really distinct from its relata[112] nor that the real relation must be founded on any infused habit in the creature. The Holy Spirit is really given to a creature, the way one friend offers him/herself to another to do what the other reasonably asks, to be used and enjoyed as the other wishes.

---

[109] Ockham, *Scriptum in I Sent.* d.14, q.1 (*OTh* III.425).
[110] Ockham, *Scriptum in I Sent.* d.14, q.1 (*OTh* III.425).
[111] Ockham, *Scriptum in I Sent.* d.14, q.1 and d.15, q.u. (*OTh* III.426–7 and 435). See also I, d.30, q.5 (*OTh* IV.394).
[112] Ockham makes this explicit for procession in *Scriptum in I Sent.* d.14, q.1 (*OTh* III.428).

But this can happen whether or not any other gifts, in the form of infused habits, are given to that rational creature as well.[113]

Given [5] above, however, there seems to be no metaphysical basis for saying that it is the Holy Spirit that is given as opposed to the Father and the Son. The Saints' way of speaking singles out the Holy Spirit and assigns It this function "by appropriation." In fact, the Saints say that the Holy Spirit is given when graced-making grace or charity is infused. Ockham observes, this is primarily conventional usage. They might just as well have said that the Holy Spirit is given when wisdom or faith are infused. But they did not.[114]

So far as missions are concerned, Ockham endorses the following nominal definition:

[Def 1] "Divine person X is invisibly sent to creature Y" entails "[i] Divine person X eternally proceeds from Divine person Z and [ii] some new effect H is produced in the soul of Y and [iii] H manifests the fact that X eternally proceeds from Z."

On this analysis, [i] means that only the Son and the Holy Spirit are eligible to be sent. The Father cannot be sent, because the Father does not eternally proceed from another Divine person. If the Holy Spirit or other Divine persons could be *given* to a creature apart from any other gifts, [iii] means that no Divine person is *sent* to a creature apart from the infusion of some habit that manifests the eternal mission of the Divine person in question.[115] By contrast,

[Def 2] "Divine person X is visibly sent to a creature Y" entails [iv] X is invisibly sent to Y, and [v] some visible sign accompanies the invisible sending and manifests it.[116]

Ockham notes that visible appearances occurred under the old covenant without any invisible mission, because the Holy Spirit is given only after the resurrection and ascension of Christ.[117] Moreover, the visible appearances are not always simultaneous with the invisible appearances that they manifest: e.g., the human soul of Christ was full of grace from the beginning, but the invisible mission of the Holy Spirit to him was manifested later by the

---

[113] Ockham, *Scriptum in I Sent.* d.14, q.1 (*OTh* III.431).
[114] Ockham, *Scriptum in I Sent.* d.14, q.2 (*OTh* III.431–2).
[115] Ockham, *Scriptum in I Sent.* d.15, q.u (*OTh* III.435).
[116] Ockham, *Scriptum in I Sent.* d.16, q.u (*OTh* III.437–8).
[117] Ockham, *Scriptum in I Sent.* d.16, q.u (*OTh* III.439).

descent of the dove.[118] As to the question whether the visible signs were a real dove and real fire or only dove- and fire-appearances, Ockham is sure only that it was whichever God wanted. Nevertheless, Ockham inclines to think that it was a real dove and real fire![119]

7. Surveying the Solutions

All of our authors agree: Pelagius was wrong, because—over and above creating, sustaining, and general concurrence; over and above publishing the ten commandments—God acts to make the elect holy. God makes the elect holy by "extras" that God efficiently causes and by indwelling their souls.

7.1 Genuine Agency

Bonaventure and Aquinas read Lombard as making the Divine will the total efficient cause of the created will-act of loving God above all. Bonaventure, Aquinas, and Henry of Ghent all agree: for the act of willing A to belong to X, it is not enough for X to have a formal passive principle for receiving an act of willing A. There must also exist in X a formal active principle for willing A. What human beings need to be the genuine agents of meritorious acts, is not for the Divine persons to be the total efficient cause of such acts, but for the Divine persons to endow the soul with more and better formal active principles. The "extras" produced by genuine Divine agency are supernatural habits infused into human souls. Henry of Ghent tries for balance. Genuine Divine agency is predominant because the Divine persons are the sole cause of the supernatural infused habits, and because infused charity is the only formal active principle in St. Paul's soul involved in producing the will-act of loving God above all. Nevertheless, the will-act belongs to St. Paul, because St. Paul is its receiving subject and because the formal active principle involved in producing it (the infused habit) is *in* him! Aquinas strikes a different balance, maintaining that the infused habit and St. Paul's will-power are each and both efficient partial causes of his will-act to love God above all.

---

[118] Ockham, *Scriptum in I Sent.* d.16, q.u (*OTh* III.438).
[119] Ockham, *Scriptum in I Sent.* d.16, q.u (*OTh* III.439).

Scotus' standards for genuine agency are higher. He maintains that for an act of willing A to belong to X, it is not enough for X to be the passive receiving subject of formal active principles for willing A. For an act of willing A to belong to X, the operant formal active principles must be *naturally suited* to X, either because they are included in X's nature or naturally suited to perfect it. Supernaturally infused habits—as Bonaventure, Aquinas, and Henry of Ghent conceive of them—are not naturally suited to creatures. So making X a passive receiving subject of them does not help secure genuine agency for X.

Scotus and Ockham contend that for an act of willing A to belong to X, X's own will-power must be at least an efficient partial cause of it. They also maintain human will-power is sufficient to account for any observed human will-acts, no matter what their intensity. No extra formal active principles need to be infused into X to enable X to be a genuine agent in loving God above all or in willing to do whatever right reason dictates because right reason dictates it. On the contrary, Scotus worries that supernatural infused habits might interfere with X's genuine agency by causally determining the will-act. Scotus flirts with demoting supernaturally infused habits to passive disposing conditions before he finally concedes that such habits are partial active causes of will-acts.

Scotus and Ockham agree. Human beings do not need God's help to produce will-acts to love God above all or to do whatever right reason dictates because right reason dictates it. The "extras" genuine Divine agency is needed to produce are Divine policies for counting human actions and agents worthy of Divine acceptance. The principal obstacle to human worthiness is not damage but finitude. Even supernaturally infused functional habits cannot solve this problem, because they also are finite, indeed less metaphysically excellent than the human soul itself.

7.2 Special Connection, Divided Trinity

Biblical language—that the Son and/or the Holy Spirit are sent, that the Holy Spirit is given, that one or all of the Divine persons indwell believers—can be construed in ways that are metaphysically "heavy" and in ways that are metaphysically "light." Going metaphysically "heavy" preserves the original intuition that indwelling is in itself a non-causal connection between God—whether the Trinity as a whole, or the Son or the Holy Spirit alone—and the human person. Hypostatic union of the Holy Spirit with the created will-power in itself leaves open what the Divine will may have or have not done to determine created will-acts. Likewise, Aquinas' suggestion that there are primitive relations whose foundations are infused habits and whose terms are either the Trinity as a whole or one Divine person apart from the others—could be combined either with Henry of Ghent's contention—that infused habits are the only active principles in producing the will-act of loving God above all—or with Aquinas' more modest claim—that infused habits and human will-power collaborate as partial active causes. Going metaphysically "heavy" also preserves the notion that indwelling is something more than the inherence of supernaturally infused habits.

Metaphysically "light" interpretations (such as Scotus and Ockham sponsor) come with fewer philosophical difficulties. The Trinity are specially connected to the elect, because they cause special benefits to exist in the elect: in this cradle-to-grave life, the theological virtues and many other habits to make them more godlike; in the world to come, infused habits plus permanent acts of seeing and enjoying God. To say that the Trinity or the Son or the Holy Spirit indwells, or that the Son or Holy Spirit is sent or given to St. Paul could be reduced to references to intra-deical Divine productions and to the existence of one or another infused habit in St. Paul's soul. Thus, "the Son is sent to St. Paul" would turn out to mean something like "the Father eternally begets the Son and the Trinity cause a supernatural habit of wisdom in St. Paul's soul," while "the Holy Spirit is given to St. Paul" would mean something like "the Father and the Son breathe the Holy Spirit and the Trinity cause a supernatural habit of charity to exist in St. Paul's soul." Likewise, "the Son indwells St. Paul" would mean "the Trinity cause a supernatural habit of wisdom in St. Paul's soul," while "the Holy Spirit indwells St. Paul" would mean "the Trinity cause a supernatural habit of charity in St. Paul's soul." Talk of one Divine person being given or sent without the others is explained away as "appropriation" or as a theologically conventional manner of speaking. On such reductions, "sending," "giving," and "indwelling" do turn out to be causal notions: there is the intra-deical causality by which the Father produces the Son, and the Father and Son produce the Holy Spirit; and there is the extra-deical causality by which the Trinity as a whole infuses supernatural habits into the elect. Nevertheless, on such reductions, sending, giving, and indwelling would not signal any Divine further interference in genuine human agency over and above the infusion of the supernatural habits themselves.[120]

---

[120] This chapter was first published in *Oxford Studies in Medieval Philosophy*, Vol. I, pp.23–60.

Bibliography

Compiled by Robert Merrihew Adams

References (mainly, but not exclusively, in footnotes) to passages in works of medieval philosophy are generally composed of two parts. The first part, which is always there, is the part that comes from medieval authors and their scribes. One of the main parts of references in modern publications was not a standard part of medieval references. Page numbers were not useful tools of reference before the invention of the printing press, because there was no reason to expect that even the most accurate copies of the verbal content of a document would have the same number of pages. Instead, the authors of philosophical works partitioned them into levels of nested larger and smaller units marked by numbers and letters; and these partitions were preserved pretty accurately in the best manuscripts.

But we live in a culture of mass production in which there are multiple ways of producing indefinitely many copies of exactly the same content. Such diversifying multiplicity has not gone very far with most works of medieval philosophy – though it certainly has gone so far with the *Summa Theologica* and *Summa contra Gentiles* of Thomas Aquinas that page references to those works are not very helpful. That would not have happened, of course, if Thomas had not portioned his Summas in medieval ways that still work well for modern readers. And for that reason the references in this book to those Summas will have only the first part.

However the most important works of most of the great philosophers of the thirteenth and fourteenth centuries, which originated in oral form – their lectures and quodlibets – have never been translated into English. Many, however, have been printed in Latin, in Renaissance or Early modern editions, or in modern critical editions, or both. In this book all the citations are of printed editions, and modern critical editions have been preferred, other things being equal.

If a footnote in this book contains more than one citation (each of which may mention several bits of related text), the citations as wholes are separated by semicolons, which are not used for any other purpose in the footnotes. And in most cases the citation will have two parts. The first part will partition them in the way that the medieval authors did, and the second part will be title and page references to a Renaissance or modern printed edition. The two parts of a citation will not be separated by a semicolon, but to make clear which is which, the second part will be enclosed in parentheses.

A main function of the following bibliography of primary sources is to provide information for understanding the first part and especially the second part of the footnote citations in this book.

Primary Sources

Aquinas, Thomas. *Summa Theologica*. Many editions and translations, in print and online.
Summa Contra Gentiles. Many editions and translations.
Scriptum super Sententias [*Sent.*], edited Parma 1856. Accessible online at http://www.corpusthomisticum.org/iopera.html
De Caritate in *Quaestiones Disputatae ad Fidem Optimarum Editionum* (Paris: P. Lethielleux, 1884), vol. II, pp. 357–409.
De Ente et Essentia. The Latin text, ed. with commentary in Latin and French by M.-D. Roland-Gosselin, O.P. (Paris: Vrin, 1948).
De Veritate. Quaestiones disputatae de veritate, ed. A. Dondaine (Rome: Editori di San Tommaso, 1970–1976) vols. 22.1–22.3 of the Leonine edition of Aquinas' works in Latin.
Commentary on Aristotle's De Anima, trans by Kenelm Foster, OP and Silvester Humphries, OP, with introduction by Ralph McInerny, revised edition (Notre Dame, IN: Dumb Ox Books, 1994). The now standard edition of the original Latin text of this work is vol. 45.1 of the Leonine edition of Aquinas' works: *Sentencia libri De Anima*, ed. R.-A. Gauthier, (Rome & Paris: Commissio Leonina– J. Vrin, 1984).
Quodlibet 10, edited Turin 1956. Accessible online at http://www.corpusthomisticum.org/iopera.html
Bonaventure, *Opera Omnia* [Quaracchi], in ten volumes. Ed. by the Fathers of the College of St. Bonaventure. (Quaracchi: Typographia Collegii S. Bonaventurae, 1882–1902).
Commentaria in Quatuor Libros Sententiarum Magistri Petri Lombardi [*Sent.*], in Bonaventure's *Opera Omnia*, vols. 1–4.
Disputed Questions on the Knowledge of Christ [DQX], in vol. 5 of Bonaventure's *Opera Omnia*.
Giles of Rome, *Quodlibeta* (Louvain: ed. by Hieronymus Nempaeius, 1646).
Godfrey of Fontaines, *Quodlibeta* I-XV, ed. by De Wulf, M., Pelzer, A., Hoffmans, J. and Lottin, O. as vols. II-V and XIV of *Les Philosophes Belges* (PB) (Louvain: Institut Supérieur de Philosophie de L'Université, 1904–1937).
Disputed Questions 9, 10, and 12 (*Disp. Quaest.*), ed. by John Wippel in Franciscan Studies, 1973, pp. 351–72.
Henry of Ghent, *Quodlibeta* I-XV (Leuven: Leuven University Press, 1979–), a modern critical edition, cited by Quodlibet number and question number, and volume and page numbers in the Leuven series. Articles that have not yet appeared in the Leuven series are quoted by folio numbers, recto/verso indications, and marginal letters in the Renaissance edition: Henry of Ghent, *Quodlibeta*, ed. by I. Badius Ascensius (Paris, 1518).
Summa Quaestionum Ordinarium (SQO) Articles I-LV (Leuven: Leuven University Press, 1994–), a modern critical edition, cited by article number and question number, as well as volume and page numbers in the Leuven series. Articles that have not yet appeared in the Leuven series are quoted by article

and question numbers, and by folio numbers, recto/verso indications, and marginal letters in the Renaissance edition: Henry of Ghent, *Summa Quaestionum Ordinarium*, ed. by I. Badius Ascensius (1520); reprinted in facsimile in two volumes,ed. by Eligius M. Buytaert (St. Bonaventure, N.Y. : The Franciscan Institute, 1953).

Hugh of St. Victor, *On the Sacraments of the Christian Faith (De Sacramentis)*, trans. Roy J. Deferrari (Cambridge, MA: The Mediaeval Academy of America, 1951).

Lombard, Peter. *Sententiae in IV Libris Distinctae*. Ed. by the Fathers of the College of St. Bonaventure. (Rome: Grottaferrata, 1971 & 1981).

Luther, Martin. *D. Martin Luthers Werke*. Kritische Gesamtausgabe, 73 vols., J.K.F.Knaake et al. (eds.), Weimar 1883-2009 [WA].

Luther's Works, American Edition, 79 vols. (projected), Jaroslave Pelikan et al. (eds.), St. Louis, MO/Philadelphia, PA 1955-2020 [LW].

Matthew of Aquasparta, OFM, *Quaestiones Disputatae de Cognitione*. [DQC] In *Quaestiones Disputatae de Fide et de Cognitione*, 2nd edition, ed. by PP. Collegi S. Bonaventurae (Quaracchi, Florentiae: Typographia Collegii S Bonaventurae, 1957).

Ockham, William. *Opera Theologica*. Ed. by Gál, Gedeon et al. (St. Bonaventure, NY: Franciscan Institute Publications, 1967–1986), vols. I-X.

Scriptum on the first book of the *Sentences* of Peter Lombard: an *Ordinatio* inasmuch as Ockham himself is thought responsible for the form of the text; occupies vols. I-IV of his *Opera Theologica*.

Quaestiones on books II-IV of the *Sentences*, a *Reportatio*, presumably based on short-hand notes of hearers of Ockham's lectures, occupying vols. V-VII of his *Opera Theologica*.

Quodlibeta, occupying the whole of Ockham, *Opera Theologica*, vol. IX.

Quaestiones Variae on the *Sentences*, in Ockham, *Opera Theologica*, vol. VIII.

Olivi, Fr. *Petrus Iohannis* (Peter John), *Quaestiones in Secundum Librum Sententiarum*, (*Sent.*) ed. by Bernard Jansen SJ (Florence: Quaracchi, 1924), Volume II.

Scotus, John Duns. *Opera Omnia*. There are two quite different sets of "*Opera Omnia*" of Scotus: [Wadding]: A renaissance edition by Lucas Wadding (Lyon, 1639). Reprinted (Hildesheim: Georg Olms Verlagsbuchhandlung, 1968). [Vat]: A modern critical edition led by C. Balic (Vatican City: Typis Polyglottis Vaticanis, 1950-2008). In these two *Opera Omnia* series, there are *three* somewhat different multi-volume commentaries on the *Sententiae* of Peter Lombard: In [Wadding] there is just one "sentence commentary," known as "*Opus Oxoniense*" [Op. Ox.] because it is believed to record a series of lectures delivered by Scotus in Oxford (vols. V.1-X). In [Vat] there are two sentence commentaries: In vols. XVI-XXI, a *Lectura*, or series of lectures that Scotus is believed to have delivered in Paris. And in vols. I-XI, Scotus's *Ordinatio*, so called because he himself (rather than hearers of his lectures) is historically believed to be responsible for the form of the text.

Opera Philosophica (OPH). ed. Girard J. Etzkorn et al. (Washington, DC: Catholic University Press, 1997-2006). *Quaestiones super Libros Metaphysicorum Aristotelis* (*QM*). Vols. III-IV of Scotus, *Opera Philosophica*. The discussion breaks off near the end of Book 9 of Aristotle's *Metaphysics*. *Quodlibeta*. In *Opera Omnia*

[Wadding], occupying the whole of vol. XII. A more modern Edition, in Latin, with Spanish translation, can be found in Scotus, *Cuestiones Cuodlibetales*. In *Obras del Docto Sutil, Juan Duns Escoto*, ed. Felix Alluntis (Madrid: Biblioteca de Autores Cristianos, 1963), available online. *De Primo Principio*. In *Opera Omnia* [Wadding], Vol. III, pp. 209–259.

Terreni, Guido. *Quodlibet* 2, q.13; *Quodlibet* 3, q.3; *Quodlibet* 3, q.6; and *Quodlibet* 6, q.6. Edited in Lauge O. Nielsen and Cecilia Trifogli, "Guido Terreni and His Debate with Thomas Wylton," *Documenti e studi sulla tradizione filosofica medievale* 20 (2009), 574–662.

Wodeham, Adam, *Lectura Secunda in Librum Primum Sententiarum*, ed.by Rega Wood, (St. Bonaventure, N.Y.: St. Bonaventure University, 1990).

Wylton, Thomas. *On the Intellectual Soul*, eds. Lauge O. Nielsen and Cecilia Trifogli; trans. Gail Trimble, in *Auctores Britannici Medii Aevi* XIX (Oxford: Oxford University Press/British Academy, 2010).

Secondary Sources

Adams, Marilyn McCord. *Christ and Horrors: The Coherence of Christology* (Cambridge: Cambridge University Press, 2006).

"Essential Orders and Sacramental Causality," in *John Duns Scotus, Philosopher: Proceedings of "The Quadruple Congress" on John Duns Scotus*, ed. by Mary Beth Ingham and Oleg Bychkov (St. Bonaventure, NY: Franciscan Institute Publications, 2010), 191–205.

"Eucharistic Real Presence: Some Scholastic Background to Luther's Debate with Zwingli" in Christine Helmer, ed. *The Medieval Luther* (Tübingen: Mohr Siebeck, 2020), 65–88.

"The Metaphysics of the Incarnation in Some Fourteenth Century Franciscans," in *Essays Honoring Allan B. Wolter*, Franciscan Institute Publications, 1985, 21–57.

"Relations, Subsistence, and Inherence, or Was Ockham a Nestorian in Christology?" *Nous* XVI (1982), 62–75.

Some Later Medieval Theories of the Eucharist: Thomas Aquinas, Giles of Rome, Duns Scotus, and William Ockham (Oxford: Oxford University Press, 2010).

"What's Metaphysically Special about Supposits?" *Proceedings of the Aristotelian Society* Supplementary Volume LXXIX (2005), 15–52.

William Ockham (Notre Dame, IN: University of Notre Dame Press, 1989).

Adams, Robert Merrihew. *Leibniz: Determinist, Theist, Idealist* (Oxford: Oxford University Press, 1994).

"The Pre-established Harmony and the Philosophy of Mind," in *Leibniz's 'New System'*, ed. by Roger S. Woolhouse (Florence: Olschki Editore, 1996), 1–13.

"Malebranche's Causal Concepts," in *The Divine Order, the Human Order, and the Order of Nature: Historical Perspectives*, ed. by Eric Watkins (Oxford: Oxford University Press, 2013), 67–104.

Cross, Richard. *The Metaphysics of the Incarnation: Thomas Aquinas to Duns Scotus* (Oxford: Oxford University Press, 2002).

Duns Scotus's Theory of Cognition (Oxford: Oxford University Press, 2014).

Dumont, Sephen D. "The Univocity of the Concept of Being in the Fourteenth Century: John Duns Scotus and William of Alnwick," *Medieval Studies* 49 (1) (1987), pp. 1–75.

"De Ente of Petrus Thomae," *Medieval Studies* 50 (1) (1988), 186–256.

Frank, William A., with Allan B. Wolter, *Duns Scotus, Metaphysician* (West Lafayette, Indiana: Purdue University Press, 1995).

Freddoso, Alfred J. "Medieval Aristotelianism and the Case against Secondary Causation in Nature," in *Divine and Human Action: Essays in the Metaphysics of Theism*, ed. by Thomas V. Morris (Ithaca & London: Cornell University Press, 1988), 74–118.

Garber, Daniel. "Leibniz: Physics and Philosophy," in *The Cambridge Companion to Leibniz*, ed. by Nicholas Jolley (Cambridge, UK: Cambridge University Press, 1995), 270–352.

Henninger, Mark G. *Relations: Medieval Theories 1250–1325* (Oxford: The Clarendon Press, 1989).

Johnston, Mark. "Hylomorphism," *The Journal of Philosophy*, vol. CIII (2006), 652–98.

Koslicki, Kathrin. *The Structure of Objects* (Oxford: Oxford University Press, 2008).

Leftow, Brian. "Souls Dipped in Dust," in Kevin Corcoran, ed. *Soul, Body, and Survival: Essays on the Metaphysics of Human Persons* (Ithaca & London: Cornell University Press, 2001), 120–138.

Lienhardt, Marc. *Luther: Witness of Jesus Christ*, trans. by Edwin H. Robertson (Minneapolis, MN: Augsburgh, 1982).

Macken, Raymond. "La théorie de l'illumination divine dans la philosophie d'Henri de Gand," *Recherches de Théologie Ancienne et Médiévale*, XXX, 82–112.

Marrone, Steven P., *Truth and Scientific Knowledge in the Thought of Henry of Ghent* (Cambridge, MA: The Medieval Academy of America, 1985).

"Henry of Ghent's Epistemology," in *A Companion to Henry of Ghent*, ed. by Gordon A. Wilson (Leiden/Boston: Brill, 2011), ch.ix, pp. 213–239.

McElrath, Damian, ed. *Franciscan Christology* (St. Bonaventure, NY: Franciscan Institute Publications, 1980).

Nielsen, Lauge O., and Cecilia Trifogli, "Guido Terreni and His Debate with Thomas Wylton," *Documenti e studi sulla tradizione filosofica medievale* 20 (2009), 574–662.

Osborne, Thomas M., Jr. "*Unibilitas*: The Key to Bonaventure's Understanding of Human Nature," *Journal of the History of Philosophy*, vol. 37.2 (1999), 227–250.

Paasch, J. T., *Divine Production in Late Medieval Trinitarian Theology: Henry of Ghent, Duns Scotus, and William Ockham* (Oxford: Oxford University Press, 2012).

Pasnau, Robert. "Cognition," in *The Cambridge Companion to Duns Scotus*, ed. by Thomas Williams (Cambridge: Cambridge University Press, 2003), ch.9, pp. 285–311.

Pegis, Anton, *St. Thomas and the Problem of the Soul in the Thirteenth Century* (Toronto, Canada: PIMS, 1934).

Pickavé, Martin, "Henry of Ghent and Duns Scotus on Skepticism and the Possibility of Acquired Knowledge," in Henrik Lagerlund, ed., *Rethinking the History of Sketpicism: The Missing Medieval Background* (Leiden: Brill, 2010), pp. 62–96.

Pini, Giorgio, "Scotus on Doing Metaphysics *in statu isto*," in *Archa Verbi: John Duns Scotus, Philosopher. Proceedings of "The Quadruple Congress" on John Duns Scotus*, Part I, ed. by Mary Beth Ingham and Oleg Bychkov (St. Bonaventure, NY: Franciscan Institute Publications, 2010), 29–55.
    "Scotus on Knowing and Naming Natural Kinds," *History of Philosophy Quarterly* 26 (2009), 255–272.
    "Scotus and Avicenna on What it is to be a Thing," in *The Arabic, Hebrew, and Latin Reception of Avicenna's Metaphysics*, ed. by Dag Nikolaus Hasse and Amos Bertolacci (Berlin/Boston: De Gruyter, 2011), 365–387.
    "Can God Cause My Thoughts? Scotus' Case against the Causal Account of Intentionality," *The Journal of the History of Philosophy* 49 (2011), pp. 39–63.
    "Univocity in Scotus's Quaestiones super Metaphysicam: The Solution to a Riddle," Medioevo 30 (2005), pp. 69–110, slightly updated at https://www.academia.edu/4720199/ Univocity in Scotus's Quaestiones super Metaphysicam: The Solution to a Riddle.
Rombreiro, Michael E., "Intelligible Species in the Mature Thought of Henry of Ghent," *Journal of the History of Philosophy* 49 (2011), pp. 181–220.
Steel, Carlos, "Henricus Gandavensis Platonicus," in *Henry of Ghent and the Transformation of Scholastic Thought: Studies in Memory of Jos Decorte*, ed. by Guy Guldenstops & Carlos Steel. (Leuven: Leuven University Press, 2003), pp. 17–39.
Teske, Roland. "Henry of Ghent and the Analogy of Being," *Essays on the Philosophy of Henry of Ghent* (Milwaukee, WI: Marquette University Press, 1992), ch.11, 247–263.
    "Henry's Metaphysical Argument for the Existence of God," in *Essays on the Philosophy of Henry of Ghent*, (Milwaukee, WI: Marquette University Press, 1992), ch.3, 65–91.
Ward, Thomas M., *John Duns Scotus on Parts, Wholes, and Hylomorphism* (Leiden/Boston: Brill, 2014.
Wippel, John F., *The Metaphysical Thought of Thomas Aquinas: From Finite Being to Uncreated Being* (Washington DC: The Catholic University of America Press, 2000).
    "Godfrey of Fontaines and the Act-Potency Axiom," *Journal of the History of Philosophy* (1973) 11:3, 299–317.
    The Metaphysical Thought of Godfrey of Fontaines: A Study in Late Thirteenth-Century Philosophy (Washington DC: The Catholic University Press, 1981.
Wolter, Allan B. *The Philosophical Theology of John Duns Scotus*. (Ithaca and London: Cornell University Press, 1990. Second edition ed. by Marilyn McCord Adams (St. Bonaventure, NY: Franciscan Institute Publications, 2015).
    "Duns Scotus on the Natural Desire for the Supernatural," reprinted in Wolter, *The Philosophical Theology of John Duns Scotus*, ch.6, 125–147.
    "Duns Scotus, John" originally published in *The Encyclopedia of Philosophy*, ed. by Paul Edwards (Macmillan Co., 1967); reprinted in Wolter, *The Philosophical Theology of John Duns Scotus*, 2nd ed., (St. Bonaventure, NY: Franciscan Institute Publications, 2015), ch.1, pp. 1–27.

"The Unshredded Scotus: A Response to Thomas Williams," *American Catholic Philosophical Quarterly*, vol.77, no.3, 315–356.

With William A. Frank, *Duns Scotus, Metaphysician* (West Lafayette, Indiana: Purdue University Press, 1995).

Wood, Rega. "Ockham's Repudiation of Pelagianism," in *The Cambridge Companion to Ockham*, ed. by Paul Vincent Spade (Cambridge: Cambridge University Press, 1999), 350–373.

Index

Abraham 101
actions viewed as *immanent* when their effects remain within the soul of the agent; as *trans-cendent* when the effects are not in the agent but in the patient 19–21
Alexander of Hales, (*c.* 1185-1245) 13
Aquinas, Thomas 2–9, 16, 20, 25, 45–74, 85–93, 108*n*, 146, 162–65, 175–77, 185, 189–99, 213
  "Full Factory Equipment" requirement 7–9
  infused intelligible species 8
  on the difference between potentiality and actuality, and their relation to God 45–50
  argues that soul-powers are really distinct from the human intellectual soul 45–50
  his views about the Islamic philosopher and Aristotelian scholar Averroes 85–93, 108*n*
  explains habits in terms of natural ends and norms (163–65)
  See also habits
Aristotle (384-322 BCE) 1–7, 15–17, 19–21, 33, 35–37, 43, 49, 51, 53, 59, 60*n*, 64, 68–70, 76, 82–107, 137, 162–63, 178, 204, 209
  in his *Categories*, teaches about primary and secondary substances 1–3
Augustine (354-430) 57, 75, 106, 109, 116, 123, 127, 129, 132–33, 153–57 179
  in controversy with Pelagius saw divine and human agency as in competition 179
Averroes (Ibn-Rushd) 36, 83–108, 138
  Spanish Islamic philosopher whose commentaries on Aristotle's works were highly esteemed by 13th & 14th century Latin Christian philosophers 84
  He argued there was only one possible intellectual substance that all of us humans share, each to the extent of the knowledge we have 84
  For Aquinas' Averroes, I understand what it is to be a cow when the intelligible species of bovinity is abstracted from phantasms of mine 88
  Chapter 4 ends with a summary of ways that medieval Christian philosophers dealt with Averroes' views on 'Whose thought is it?' 106–108
  See also Islamic philosophy
Avicenna [Ibn-Sina] (*c.* 970-1037) 147, 155–56, 200–201
  Islamic philosopher, and originator of the out-sourcing the subject doctrine 147
  See also Islamic philosophy

Bede, "the Venerable," (*c.* 673-735), 181
Bonaventure 13–14, 68, 110–15, 183–89, 213
  Held that human body and soul are distinct sub-stances that combine to share certain functions, including moral action and merit-winning 13–14
  Held that before death knowledge of creatable quiddities involves both Divine illumination and the activity of created natural powers 110–15
  Held that a doctrine of hypostatic union, in which he took issue with Peter Lombard, provides solutions to major problems about the doctrine of the Trinity 183–89
  See also Lombard

Chatton, Walter, a Franciscan, disagreed with Adam Wodeham about an argument of Ockham's 81–82

concurrence, Divine, 178–79
  Divine and created agencies collaborate
    God concurs with *all* created
      agents 178
    The persons of the Trinity express "one
      Action, one will *ad extra*" 179
    A special divine indwelling in the elect
      See three problems:
        Genuine Agency Problem 179
        Special Connection Problem 180
        Divided Trinity Problem 180
    See also Peter Lombard, on priority
        for the
      Special Connection
        Problem 180–83, 188
      and Bonaventure, Aquinas, and Scotus,
        who were more focused on the
        Genuine Agency Problem 181
Cross, Richard 96*n*, 140*n*, 153*n*

Divided Trinity Problem
  a tension among sacred texts as to whether
    believers are indwelt by Christ alone
    or the Holy Spirit alone 180
Dumont, Stephen D. 160*n*

Freddoso, Alfred J. 179*n*

Gabriel, the archangel 68
Garber, Daniel, 37*n*
Genuine Agency Problem
  Does God's plan of salvation leave room
    for genuine merely human
    agency? 179
Giles of Rome 20, 25–26, 35, 50–58,
    61–71, 74
  Agrees with Aquinas that souls are not
    really the same as their
    soul-powers 51
  is primarily driven by a hypothesis about
    the metaphysical structure of
    substances 53
God 9–10, 34, 37–38, 41–42, 46, 49, 52–54,
    61–63, 66–67, 73, 95–96, 102–103,
    106–126, 129–161, 165–71,
    176–200, 204–215
Godfrey of Fontaines 19, 21–24,
    201–202, 205
  Three arguments that will-power includes
    no active power to produce but

  merely passive power to receive
    volitions 22–24
  Contrariety Argument 22
  Other-Directedness of Powers
    Argument 22–3
  Part-Whole Argument 23
  Godfrey argues for views similar to those
    of Scotus (and contrary to those of
    Henry of Ghent) about our
    will-power's control over our
    actions 201–202, 205

habits 112–14, 162–77
  Aquinas explains habits in terms of natural
    ends and norms (163–65)
  Scotus, on habits, thinks more about
    material causality (165–72)
  and efficient causality (173–75)
Henry of Ghent 19, 24–28, 53–57, 63–65, 71,
    120–41, 153–58, 199–202, 213
  responds to Godfrey's three
    arguments 24–26
  response to Henry's response 26–28
  Henry's earlier account of the metaphysics
    and theology of soul powers 120–24
  his later critique of Aquinas, and concept
    of the metaphysics of
    powers 53–57, 125–29
  similarities and differences between Henry
    and Godfrey 202
  God's place in Henry's
    epistemology 153–58
  See also Lombard 180–189, and
    Scotus 202
Henninger, Mark 54*n*, 194*n*, 204*n*
hylomorphisms compared: ancient, medieval,
    and modern 14–18
hypostatic union of the trinitarian
    God (182–88)
  discussed mainly in relation to Lombard
    and Bonaventure 182–83

Islamic philosophy,
  Avicenna [Ibn-Sina] (c. 970-1037) 155–56
  Averroes [Ibn-Rushd] (1126-98) 36,
    83–108, 138

Johnston, Mark 14*n*

Koslicki, Kathrin 15*n*

Leftow, Brian 16*n*
Leibniz, Gottfried Wilhelm 19, 37, 43–44
Lienhard, Marc 95*n*
Lombard, Peter (*c.* 1096–1160) 180–192, 213
    held that the Biblical gift of the Holy Spirit "is the love of the Father and the Son by which they love one another and us" and the love by which we love (or were made to love) God and neighbor 181
    and rejected Bede's teaching, that the gift is not the Holy Spirit but a gift of grace 181
Luther, Martin 95*n*

matter, *See* Scotus
Malebranche, Nicolas (1638-1715) 36, 179*n*,
Macken, Raymond 124*n*, 126*n*, 140*n*
Marrone, Steven P. 122*n*, 145*n*
Matthew of Aquasparta 115–20
    In his *Disputed Questions on Cognition* Matthew argues that certain knowledge in this world depends on special divine action not perceived by us as such 119–20

Nielsen, Lauge O. 93*n*

Ockham, William 3–7, 10–14, 69–82, 101–105, 185–88, 208–215
    Ockham with Scotus versus Aquinas on which powers cause which, and which are essential to us 3–7
    The will alone is morally evaluated, not the body 14
    Unlike Scotus, Ockham assigns sensory function and intellectual function to two different soul forms that have causal relations with each other 10–14, 69–76
    He argues that contraries cannot exist in the same subject at once, but we often have contrary wills—for instance a will to eat something for the sake of pleasure and a will not to eat it, for the sake of health 70–76
    Ockham concedes more points to Averroes than Aquinas or Terreni do, but argues that the intellect cannot be the same, unmultiplied, in all humans 101–105

Much of Chapter 8 explores ways in which Ockham, and in similar ways Scotus, see the "housing of powers" in God mainly or even exclusively in God's infusion of supernatural habits, such as loving God—signaling no further divine interference in human agency (208–215)
Olivi, Peter John 38
Osborne, Thomas M. 13*n*

Paasch, J. T. 53*n*
Pasnau, Robert 150*n*
Pelagius *See* Augustine
Pickavé, Martin 133*n*
Pini, Giorgio 136*n*, 142*n*, 156*n*, 160*n*
Plato 1, 88, 100, 109, 115–16, 129 178

Rombreiro, Michael E. 140*n*

sacraments, as helpful causal factors 163
Scotus, John Duns 3–14, 29–44, 57–71, 74, 76–80, 130–61, 165–77, 185–87, 199–210, 213–15
    Ockham with Scotus versus Aquinas on which powers cause which, and which are essential to us 3–13
    Scotus's Generic Adequate Object Argument against Godfrey's Other-Directedness Argument 29–30
    Scotus on extent and limits of creatures' powers to improve themselves and each other 30–44
    Scotus concluded that the essences of the soul and its soul-powers are "really the same but distinct formally" 67
    Scotus and matter 166*n*
        unusually for his time, he held that it is meta-physically possible for matter to exist without any form, at least by divine power
    Scotus discusses soul powers in a distinctly theological context, which is also a critique of Aquinas and Giles 57–62
    and of views held by Henry of Ghent 63–64, 130–61, 199–201
    Scotus's views about those topics were partly similar to those of Godfrey of Fontaines 201–203

Scotus, John Duns (*cont.*)
    As to sensory powers, Scotus concludes they can be counted as really distinct from each other insofar as they are due to perfections in sense organs that are really distinct from one another 69
    Scotus, concluding that the natures of souls and bodies could not explain the changes revealed for the life to come, out-sources to free and contingent policies of God 176–77
    See also habits
    self-actuation (freely determining one's own motivation in acting) 35–44
    See also Scotus, and Ockham
Socrates 44, 68, 100, 178
Special Connection Problem 180
    God being omnipresent is present to every Creature, while biblical indwelling seems to be only for some, but not all, rational creatures 180
Steel, Carlos 121*n*, 124*n*, 126*n*, 129*n*

Terreni, Guido 93–97
    argued, against Averroes, that hypostatic union, as in the Christian holy Trinity, is the only way in which a human and a separate superior intellect could see the same thing 97
Teske, Roland 154*n*, 157*n*
Trifogli, Cecilia, 93*n*

Ward, Thomas M. 6*n*
Wilson, Gordon 130*n*
Wippel, John F. 22*n*
Wodeham, Adam (Ockham's former teaching assistant)
    "arrives at his own views about soulform(s) and soul-powers by way of a critique of Scotus." He comes up with an attractive reading of Ockham 76–82
Wolter, Allan B. 42*n*; 146; 170*n*, 209*n*
    with William A. Frank, 135*n*, 156*n*, and 153
Wood, Rega 210*n*
Wylton, Thomas 97–101, 108*n*
    On Wylton's sympathetic reading of Averroes, the intellectual soul is the form of our individual bodies, making one substance from birth to death 101